T0162483

DANCING ON THIN ICE

Dancing on Thin Ice

TRAVAILS OF A RUSSIAN DISSENTER

Arkady Polishchuk

DoppelHouse Press | Los Angeles

Dancing on Thin Ice: Travails of a Russian Dissenter
By Arkady Polishchuk
© 2018 DoppelHouse Press, Los Angeles

Photographs and documents from the archives of Arkady Polishchuk, unless otherwise noted.

COVER IMAGE: Arkady Polishchuk with background image of his clandestine publication *Why a Physician Was Tried*, written following the show trial of Dr. Mikhail Stern. Moscow, 1975.
COVER DESIGN: Kourosh Biegpour
TYPESETTING: Jody Zellen and Carrie Paterson

PUBLISHER'S CATALOGING-IN-PUBLICATION DATA
Names: Polishchuk, Arkady, author.
Title: Dancing on thin ice : travails of a Russian dissenter / Arkady Polishchuk.
Description: Includes index. | Los Angeles, CA : DoppelHouse Press, 2018.
Identifiers: ISBN 9780998777030 (Hardcover) | 9780998777078 (pbk) | 9780998777047 (ebook) | LCCN 2018937174
Subjects: LCSH Polishchuk, Arkady. | Dissenters--Soviet Union--Biography. | Journalists--Soviet Union--Biography. | Journalists--Soviet Union--Social conditions. | Soviet Union--Politics and government. | Human rights workers--Soviet Union--Biography. | Freedom of religion--Soviet Union. | BISAC BIOGRAPHY & AUTO-BIOGRAPHY / Editors, Journalists, Publishers | HISTORY / Russia & the Former Soviet Union
Classification: LCC DK510.763 .P65 2018 | DDC 070.92--dc23

DoppelHouse Press
Los Angeles, California

*Dedicated to Soviet human rights activists
Vladimir Bukovsky and Alexander (Alik) Ginsburg,
both imprisoned and exchanged —
Vladimir, for the first secretary of the Chilean communist party,
Alexander, as one of five political prisoners exchanged for five
Soviet spies*

The past is never dead. It's not even past.
William Faulkner

CONTENTS

A Prison For Hedonists

L OOK, BOYS! A JEW! were the first words I heard after two policemen opened the cell door to bring me in. The jailers smirked and left me facing my cellmates. Thirty-five pairs of eyes looked at me. I knew that my first reaction would determine my upcoming treatment.

"Oh, Yisrael, is that you?!" I cried into the dim light. "It feels so good to find a cousin among these Russian thugs!"

Raucous laughter flooded the stinky cell. A shaggy guy, outraged to the depths of his Slavic soul that I dared to call him a Jew, was climbing down from the upper berth to punish me. I turned back toward the peephole and affably waved my hand to the guards. I knew they stood there, in anticipation. To my horror, another inmate crawled out of his roomy den under the lower berth. He flicked a speck of dust from his battered jacket and, with a lazy gesture, stopped the swearing cellmate halfway to me. After that he shook my hand. The word "mama" was tattooed on his fleshy fingers. The bold exclamation mark on his thumb pointed to his strong filial attachment.

"Political?"

"Yes," I said, "but only in Russia. Name me a country where the wish to move to a warmer land is a crime."

My wiry guardian angel did not react and on the path back to his wooden platform said to his cellmate, "Crawl back into your fucking nest, Birdie."

Judging by the dignity with which he carried himself, my angel had a criminal record that inspired respect. Only he and three other men had the privilege of occupying platforms under the lower bunks. From the center of the cell, about one and a half yards from the bunks on either side, I could see their unshaven faces only when they wanted me to; mostly, I saw their dirty shoes.

It was evening, and the prisoners were resting after a working day, sitting with their legs dangling down, smoking incessantly. The population of the lower planks was not happy about seven pairs of muddy boots and filthy pants caressing their faces. After a lively exchange in persuasive language, a compromise was reached, and the men on the upper wall-to-wall rows lay on their stomachs facing the newcomer.

It was time for some explaining. I said with undue solemnity: "Thirteen Jews took part in a two day sit-in demonstration inside the Reception Room of the Chairman of the Presidium of the Supreme Soviet of the USSR. They were denied exit visas, some for many years."

A hurricane of questions rained down on me:

"Brezhnev's Reception Room?!"

"Are you Jews fuckin' kidding me?"

"What did you want?"

"Why did they bring you here? Not to The Land of No Return?"

"You're lucky!"

"Are you crazy?"

"Why is Israel using poison gas against Palestinians?" I recognized the lisping voice of the swearing bird.

"Did they clobber you?"

I said, "Two broken ribs."

I was in the midst of my narrative about the Jewish invasion of the Leader's Reception Room, when a tall cellmate attempted to reach an opening in the broken corner of the window's lower right pane. He put his right foot on the lower plank bed, placed the very tip of his left boot on an inch-wide ledge jutting out of the wall, and clung to the wall, his penis at the ready. I stopped talking, and with a sinking heart, waited for him to crash onto the floor or even worse, step on the cast-iron ribs of the heating radiator under the window, breaking it free from the rotten wall. The tragedy didn't happen. My listeners continued looking at me and smoking; the jailers simply ignored this direct violation of prison regulations.

Most of the prisoners had arrived at this lockup on the outskirts of Moscow for drunken brawls or just for being at the wrong place when they'd had a few too many. All of them were determined to get out in ten or fifteen days, in accordance with the Russian Criminal Code article on disorderly behavior called "minor hooliganism." Here, they behaved nicely. What fool would do something to turn fifteen days into a much longer term, in a camp, doing life-threatening work? In fact, they considered themselves lucky.

The inmates decided that, in all fairness, my place was next to Nikolai, a burly fellow also with two broken ribs. I quickly discovered that the worst air was here, under the ceiling, on the upmost stone-hard plank. Like acid in my eyes.

Peals of laughter deadened our groaning when I tried to squeeze myself between Nikolai and a puny boy.

"It hurts," I said, apologetically.

"My ribs are broken on the same side." Nik smiled like a five-star Hotel National manager greeting an American billionaire in Moscow.

We tried to laugh, but our ribs did not like such disrespectful shaking. Massive Nikolai at the moment enjoyed relaxing on his back. "I could sleep like this, except that the cellies don't allow me," he confided. "We all are like sardines in a can."

I was the seventh sardine.

"They hammered me more than two weeks ago," he said.

"Here?" I asked.

"No, at a police station in downtown."

"What for?"

"I hit a plainclothes chief of the station."

"So, you're a lucky devil. Just like us Jews. You could get no less than three years, maybe more."

"Yeah, but they saw I was completely plastered," he explained. "Oh boy, he and his goons beat me hard! They left me unconscious in their basement. I was recovering on the cement floor for ten days and had to pay for the food they were delivering. The men pocketed some of the money, but I didn't mind." He whispered, "I always carry it under my insole.... After a couple of days, I apologized and the major forgave me. He said, 'It's okay, we all drink too much sometimes.' He was good. After my mug looked normal, they took me to a court, and the judge sent me here."

"Yes, the major acted in accordance with his clear conscience," I said.

"Exactly!" said Nik.

"It's a pity," I said, "Your fancy coat has been ruined."

"I'm no hooligan and no drunkard, never swear in my wife's presence. I'm a serious man, feed a lot of important people, and manage the best furniture store in Moscow."

"Which means, in the country," I inserted.

He nodded. It was clear; soon this man would be telling me the secrets of his trade.

"Why did you hit him?" I asked.

"I was trying to stop a taxi or any car."

"Were you drunk out of your mind?"

"Oh yeah," he said, "I was dashing around like mad right in the middle of Gorky Street with widespread arms—a cop told me the next morning that I stopped a bus."

"You could've been killed."

"Yeah, and here, all of a sudden, this guy! It was my wife's birthday; I was late for the party. I brought a crate of vodka to treat my boys in the store, a bottle for every man; they envy me—she's a very good wife." He sighed deeply like a remorseful child who had not listened to his mother. "I hit him a couple of times with these shovels." He brought his open hands, fingers spread out, to his face. "You see, I load furniture."

Looking at his face between these thick sausages with dirt under the nails, I shook my head. "Yes, that police chief is a very good man!"

That first night, my ribs bothered me more than the rotten air, coughing, snoring, wheezing, squabbling over space, and the noisy, poisonous farting. The men did not seem to be bothered. They even made the farting into a sporting event and competed, for a cigarette, in duration and volume. By morning, the cocktail of tobacco, urine, and lethal sweat mostly faded away. At 6 a.m., the turnkeys accompanied by the national anthem on the radio woke us up, and we were rushed to the toilet—four stinky holes in the concrete ground, a long sloping cement trough for urination next to four rusty sinks. An eager line watched your every move as you squatted over that hole, commenting on your wasteful treatment of priceless newspaper —"A reader!" "Cultured!" "It's your asshole, use your fingers," "Leave some paper for others," and other snippets of wisdom to similar effect.

A policeman at the door kept encouraging us: "Hurry up! The mess hall will be closed in five minutes!"

No, I don't want to write about grievous events in that prison. I am determined to forget a vomiting young epileptic on the slippery floor of that shithouse, and an old man sitting next to me in the mess hall, who spat blood on the freshly painted red floor and said, "I'm from a sanatorium for consumptives."

The nurse—yes, we had a nurse—did not come.

"She doesn't have medication, anyway," said the skinny old man.

I want to forget the savage hatred in the eyes of a handsome guard wearing a gray apron over his zealously ironed uniform; he flopped three tablespoons of watery cement into an aluminum plate and pushed it toward me. But I remember the funny part of our brief exchange. I want to remember only the funny parts. He said, "If I were in charge, I'd deprive you of this kasha."

I was amused. "What a loss! Your cook can make kasha out of cement and candies out of shit."

"I'll report you to the lieutenant," he said. "In the punishment cell you'll dream of this shit."

But I ate it. A man has to eat. My cellmates surprised me. They had to come to the mess hall, but did not eat at all. They were up to something, but I didn't know what. They only drank the hot water called tea from overheated aluminum cups.

As for the punishment cell, I'm sure the kitchen cop made his report. And the warden was obviously not in charge either. It was the KGB headquarters that wanted to keep things nice and quiet. I was not deprived of my kasha. I had this kasha every fucking day. Much later, in my own apartment, in my nightmares, I ate it again and again, and a soup, for some enigmatic reason called fish soup, of the same dirty color and taste, only more watery. But at that time it was not their fault. It was my problem.

A few minutes later, a young jailer brought me back to the empty cell from the mess hall. It was nearly dawn. The iron-barred small window did not have the usual iron peak over it, and I enjoyed the morning charm of the outside world—the patch of leaden sky over the huge gray wall covered from bottom to top by generous layers of barbed wire. I pressed my cheek to the glass, sticky like flypaper. The beauty of a stunted, now leafless, tree struck me, and I realized why my cellmates called this suburban outpost of the old Moscow *Butyrka* prison, "Crooked Birch Tree Inn." Behind and above the tree stood a deserted watchtower with a searchlight. It was also heartwarming to view that little hole in the window, as it served as a ventilator and a chimney. Winter was at the door and free designs of urine and the yellowish hoarfrost decorated the outside of that opening. Usually the outlet was used when you knew that a policeman wouldn't take you to the toilet beyond the designated time; one could read a sign of misfortune on a framed piece of paper nailed to the dark brown door. The prison administration was right—we had a nice metal pail, half filled with water, thoughtfully placed in the cells in case of fire.

So, when at first a newcomer felt that his entire urinary infrastructure was on fire, he usually knocked at the door and yelled, "Hey! Boss! I'm about to pee all over myself!"

After that he used the pail. The second day he would prefer to ask someone to block the peep hole and go for the hole in the window. I thought of freedom of choice and its relationship to happiness. What's the difference between the pail reeking of urine and the same stink coming from the window and your own spattered pants?

Only sometimes would one jailer, the oldest of them, unlock the door and take the guy to the toilet. For his kindness he was given cigarettes.

The young turnkey soon entered the cell again, smiling amicably. "In an hour the air here will be much better."

"So, are none of the arrested Jews going to work?"

"No," he said. "The drunks and riffraff love it there. They guzzle vegetables and fruit over there; there's nothing we can do about it. It's a huge vegetable and fruit warehouse."

"What if they run away?"

"They're not stupid," he said. "A couple of years for a runaway."

"Freedom is sweet," I said.

"Then why"—he paused, searching for a neutral word, trying to avoid the word "Jews"— "... are you and your friends here?"

"It was our free choice."

"You're interesting people, probably had a nice job, cultured, educated. Why?"

I asked, "Are you allowed to talk with me like that?"

"Sure, why not."

"What if I convince you to move to Israel?"

We chuckled.

"So, are you going to search me and the cell?" I asked. My coat and pants were loaded with cigarettes, matches, and some money.

"Will you trust me more," he said, "if I tell you that we were ordered not to search you guys? All I want is your advice on how to make a better living."

"Did you get this job after military service?"

"Yes, and a place in the dormitory."

"The only way out of this corner is school."

"I'm attending an evening high school now. Can you help me with a couple of math problems?"

"We can give it a try. I am a journalist, not a math teacher."

"Interesting! I'd like to become a journalist, too."

"Any law school would be delighted to have someone with your professional background."

"Our job is difficult," he said.

"I know," I said. "Here you're kind of imprisoned, no matter which side of the door you're on."

"Do you have relatives in Israel?"

This question was dangerous. I shrugged it off. He did not insist. Maybe he was instructed to ask it, maybe not. How could this villager know that in order to apply for an exit visa, Jews were required to have invitations from Israeli relatives? After sixty years of isolation, almost nobody had relatives abroad, especially in Israel. During the war, in 1944, my parents received a letter and a photograph from America. That was how I learned that my mother had a stepsister and I had a cousin named Michael. They destroyed the letter and hid the photo of the Baybusky family in the attic of our apartment house. I said to the jailer, "My aunt emigrated soon after Russia was defeated in World War I and the tsar abdicated."

"No," he said. "Russia won all wars. Lenin overthrew the tsar. Haven't you seen the movie *Lenin in October?*"

I asked if I could take a nap after two sleepless nights. He said "no"; it was against regulations.

The prisoners returned from the warehouse in a good mood. Three of them obviously had a buzz on. The fellow nicknamed Butcher fake-punched my chest with the fist, quickly, like in boxing. "Did they peel you?" he asked.

"No, and your stuff is fully intact. Guards have an order not to search me."

"Can't believe it!" he said in a booming voice and opened his clenched fist; I was blinded by the shining beauty of two fat cloves of garlic. My new buddy Nikolai tapped him on the shoulder while I was consuming with passion this sweet heavenly treat.

"How do you manage to bring in the cigarettes?" I asked.

"The men are in business with us. We pinch apples, oranges, onions, and stuff, and kick down this loot to them. Right at the storage. Sometimes I climb over the fence, just two strings of barbed wire, the guys pass me a couple of boxes, and I drag them behind the corner and hawk stuff to passersby. We give money to the pigs; they buy cigarettes and some vodka for us and for themselves." Butcher punched the air with a fist.

"You're such a showoff, Butcher. Stop yelling." It was my seasoned defender of the last evening. "The guard is always walking by. You're not at the top of Mount Ararat," he added, hinting at Butcher's Armenian roots.

"The Turks took Ararat from us centuries ago," Butcher muttered under his breath. "The men who shake us down at the checkpoint, confiscate food and take their cut of fags."

After everybody had settled on the planks, they asked me why I wanted to leave Russia. I put out my sole condition, "Don't hesitate to ask nasty questions."

Someone instantly said, "Why do Jews put Christian blood in matzo bread?"

The question caught me off-guard and I said, "There are many fairy tales about Jews. Who has heard about Jews having horns?"

"I did," said one prisoner.

"Me too," said the frail boy, my neighbor.

"So, I'm here, try to find 'em." They all laughed. "Well, you laugh now, but when you heard it for the first time, did you laugh?"

"My kindergarten buddy told me," said the frail boy. "I was scared."

"Just four hundred years ago every European believed it."

"Interesting," he said, scratching his disheveled head fiercely.

The frail boy began to feel chatty. "Where did they get water in that desert for their matzo?"

I responded, "All I know is that for the first two thousand years— poor me!—I was unable to pour your blood into my matzo." Heat rushed to my face as if I was admitting my Jewish crime. It took effort to look them in the eyes. "Christians didn't even exist at that time. Is there anybody here who has ever read the Bible? Nobody. I myself read it only recently. You can't buy or get it from a library."

"Do you eat matzo bread?" was the next question from deep in the cell.

"I will, if you can find some for me. My mother used to buy it in April on the black market. It's when my buddy makes his Easter cake and guess what? He always puts on it this six-pointed star you've seen in caricatures against Zionist murderers. He says all the first followers of Christ were Jews..."

"It's a falsehood!"

"It's what the New Testament says. And he believes that they had been putting this Star of David on their Easter cakes. He, secretly a Christian, doesn't go to church—the priest is obliged to report every newcomer; my friend is a Party member."

"Did he give you his Bible to read?"

"He doesn't have one. I saw a handwritten copy of the New Testament in one underground church. Would you believe it? It's huge, like this!" I parted wide my thumb and the index finger. "And one more thing, I'm no less Russian than you are."

"You're not a Russian; you're a communist," giggled an inmate called Flier. His name aroused my interest in him.

"A good point—all of us are more communists than Russians. Twenty million Party members. Generation after generation we've been reading the same papers and books, watching the same movies, worshiping the same saints. And what do they tell us? 'We're good,' 'We're building Paradise,' 'They're bad'—"'They'" live in Hell.' Look at yourselves—are we any good? Aren't we in Hell already? Remember Nikita Khrushchev? He put in the Party Program the exact date of our arrival at that Paradise—four years from now. So boys, be patient, just wait a little and in 1980 they will destroy this prison and overnight put a flowerbed here instead. And all of us, when we wake up that morning, won't be drunks anymore. For the first time in years we'll brush our teeth, or what's left of them, and become gardeners taking good care of roses and drinking lemonade for the rest of our no-longer-stinky lives!"

And as had happened at the moment of my arrival, raucous laughter flooded the cell.

"Now," I concluded, "thanks to the inquisitive questions of my distinguished colleagues, you have learned why Jews want to leave this country. And on this friendly exchange, let's finish today's concert. The performer will be given seven years of hard labor in Perm camp #36."

"Amen!" said Flier.

"Are you actually a flier?" I asked.

"No, I'm an engineer, build planes," he said with some pride.

"Only one more thing," I said. "I don't want to emigrate. Who needs a Russian journalist in the West?"

"Then why did you take part in that demonstration?"

"Solidarity," I said. "Remember what's written across the top of *Pravda*?"

"Sure," Flier said, "Proletarians of the World, Unite!'"

"Proletarians of the World," Butcher solemnly exclaimed, "kiss my ass!"

"You're crazy," Nikolai said an hour later when I was laying next to him. "I don't understand this stuff, but I need your advice."

"Go ahead," I said.

"I'm a candidate-member of the Party. In half a year my candidate term will be over."

"And if they refuse to accept you as a full member of the Party, you'll lose your job and all the perks it delivers, and you'll load furniture for the rest of your life."

"You're very smart. Think of something! I'm sure the guys covered my absence in the store for a while. I always did it for them."

"Take the lead," I said. "Write a letter to your Party committee. Beat your breast. Blame it all on the love you bear for your wife. Tell them the truth, but not the whole truth. Say that you, drunk like a sailor, tried to catch a taxi in the middle of Moscow's main street. Police arrested you, you stumbled on a stair at the police office, broke two ribs, damaged your cute face and, after fifteen days in jail, you stayed at home for another two weeks, burning with shame. Until all healed. Give the honest Party word that never again shalt thou drink."

"You think it will help?"

"It might, if you have no enemies. Russia has been soft on drunks for centuries. They can extend your trial period, your candidate status. I also had a problem with my term of probation for Party membership."

"Tell me. What happened?"

"Ah, in short: I published a satire, some twenty years ago, but a member of the Party's Central Committee was offended and my piece was pronounced 'anti-Soviet.' These guys are more important than several ministers lumped together. If this big gun were to succeed, I'd be a lumberjack for the rest of my life."

"Listen," Nikolai said, his face lighting up, "could you quit whatever you do now and work for me? You'll get rich soon."

"So you're also crazy. The KGB would put you in jail in a heartbeat."

"You're right." He sighed. "But listen, if you need money, come to me, I will help. I'm serious."

"Thank you, Nik."

I thought, poor Nikolai! He still has healthy impulses.

"I know some very, very important people," he whispered. "They might help."

"Be careful," I said. "Important people are good at dumping their friends. Unless they need you."

"Did they dump you?"

"No. Thanks to important friends, I didn't go to jail for seven years, and I remained a journalist after that satire."

Finally I understood what we had in common. Naiveté.

Everybody was already asleep. Nikolai pressed his turned-up nose against my ear and whispered, "Sometimes Brezhnev buys furniture for his whores in our store."

"You've got to be kidding."

"One of his assistants always calls and asks us to deliver the same suite of furniture to a new address. He always tells me to control the delivery carefully, to go with the suite and the loaders I trust, and to be present when it's unpacked and follow the instructions of the person who's waiting for us."

"A person? A half-naked beauty?"

"No. All three times it was the same man in a custom-made dark suit. He always knew how and where to put it all."

"Did you like the apartments?"

"New houses, you know, very good apartments for a family of four—a bedroom, a nice kitchen with a window, you can even put a small table there, a decent living room with a balcony, an anteroom. Nice!"

"You should see if this guy who calls you can help."

"Yes."

"I wouldn't be surprised."

"The invoice always lists office furniture. It was his idea. It was he who encouraged me to join the Party."

"They entrusted you with a top state secret. And they wouldn't want to lose sight of you and have you become a loose cannon."

We again had something in common—I also possessed a top state secret, and the KGB for sure did not want to let me out of sight. It was a sad irony in my thinking. What was more dangerous— to know how many beds Comrade Brezhnev had given to his mistresses or the identities and assignments of a dozen Soviet spies? I did not reach a definite conclusion and asked, "Have you ever seen this man?"

"No, but he gave me his phone number, and I called him a couple of times when we were waiting too long for the next delivery from Egypt."

"From Egypt?"

"Yes. It's great furniture, better than Finnish. Lots of gold and ivory."

"For every sweetheart exactly the same reward?"

"Yes."

"This is what we call true democracy," I said. "Equal pay. Equal rights. Equal opportunity employer."

"I think," said Nikolai, "the presidents of Israel and the USA also have whores."

"Yes," I said, "but they buy them different suites of furniture, and this creates an inequality of women's rights."

Laughing quietly, Nikolai then said in all seriousness, "The main thing is to make sure that the bed won't creak."

"If it creaks, not only you, but I bet also the bureaucrat who calls you, would be sacked and expelled from the Party. The president of Egypt might also lose his job."

"It's not real gold and ivory," said Nik.

"The founder of this state promised to use gold in communist society for toilet bowls."

"Vladimir Ilyich Lenin? You're kidding," whispered Nik.

"Actually, I'm not."

On the fourth day after my arrest a newcomer shook my hand. He had heard on America's *Radio Liberty* about our demonstration—a broadcaster had mentioned me by name. Listening through heavy jamming required patience and craving for knowledge. And in this way I was introduced to the goddess of lucky chance, Miss Publicity. Quickly word spread through the mess hall and toilet, so the news arrived to Victor Elistratov, Michael Kremen, and Felix Kandel, my partners in crime locked away in other cells.

The very next day, the 25th of October, each cell had its own celebrated Jew, altogether fifteen men who had taken part in a demonstration in support of our two-day sit-in inside Brezhnev's Reception Room. On October 26th another newcomer told us that the American president named either "Garter" or "Garder" sent a telegram to Brezhnev urging our release. It was the presidential candidate Jimmy Carter.

I was in the toilet minding my own business at the trough when somebody put a hand on my shoulder. I turned around—it was a black-bearded refusenik named Isaac Elkind. "Welcome to the club," I said. I hadn't seen him since Brezhnev's Reception Room, where Isaac had been quietly petitioning for an exit visa to Israel and joined us, but was not arrested with our gang because he was sitting with timid people petitioning for their imprisoned relatives. What had he done to end up here?

"Fifty Jews marched to the Party's Central Committee," he said, "surrounded by an army of plainclothes KGB agents."

A policeman at the door began yelling at us.

"Continue peeing," I said.

"This is it," Isaac said. "I can't."

"Shake it!" I said.

"We all wore yellow Stars of David!" he said, his voice broken from the effort.

"Great!" I said. "Jews are becoming impudent."

"A bunch of Gypsies saw us, and one of them yelled, 'Look! Sheriffs!'"

"Hah—ha! Hollywood should be proud of such a great cultural success. And stop the violent shaking of your toy! You might get a headache."

EVERY EVENING my cell had a political study class. There was even a student behind a wall—a young fellow in the punishment cell. He had heard our indiscernible voices and managed to hollow out a narrow hole in that crumbling wall. Sometimes I heard him shouting "Wow!" right into that breach, enthusiastic applause, and merciless beating on the old wall. "Comrade Wow" had been transferred from our cell to the windowless punishment room before my arrival.

We met by chance, face to face, so to speak. We both had diarrhea and were fortunate that the man in uniform watching our behavior in the toilet was that old carelessly-shaven policeman whose only concern was his upcoming retirement. Maybe our quiet talking gave him a chance to daydream at the door.

Before his arrest, the young man had spent the evening with his fiancée in a restaurant of the Moscow Hotel known for its good dance orchestra. They waltzed, tangoed and hugged, danced and kissed, drank some dry wine, kissed after every sip, and were happy. When the lovebirds were leaving this monument to ponderous Stalinist architecture, a collision on a scale of an ancient Greek tragedy took place. Outside the entrance there were several immense square columns. Comrade Wow rushed between them toward a taxi, to get ahead of others and to open the door for his girl. At that particular split-second two cops were coming out from behind a column. The bridegroom knocked one of them off his feet. The whole Pantheon of Greek gods could not prevent this.

He apologized many times. His fiancée apologized many times. But the policemen brought him to a police station, and when he begged them to measure his level of alcohol intoxication, the whole station laughed. When he begged after midnight to let him go—today was his wedding day, they laughed even harder. He threatened to take them to court, and that was hilarious. In the morning the judge sent him here. He was crying, swearing, kicking the cell door and demanding to see a prosecutor until guards locked him in the solitary sweatbox.

I expressed my sympathy to the fellow, "From now on you should believe in fate. Are you an atheist?"

"Of course," he said, "I'm an engineer. And you?"

"Not anymore, but I'm afraid, in my temple there is only one parishioner. Lately I've met very religious people and have come to admire them greatly."

"Jews?"

"No, Christians."

"Difficult to believe that there are still some true believers here. Who are they?"

"Pentecostals, Baptists, other Evangelicals."

"These are terrible people! Sectarians!"

"The best people I ever met. They could be a treasure for any country, but here they're considered to be weirdos—they don't drink, don't beat their wives, don't swear, don't steal."

"How do you know all of this?"

"I'm trying to help some of them."

"Why?"

"It's tempting to answer your 'why' pompously, like, it's easy to help your own tribe—it's like helping yourself, anyway, but try to help those who aren't like you.... But even this is a shallow answer. I envy them. They are innocent like children. Their only crime is their faith."

"Faith also helped to kill millions," he said.

"True. But atheism, to a large degree is also a religion; the same goes for Communism—it also killed millions, and it isn't familiar with the word 'repentance'."

Our Argus at the latrine's door apparently returned to this sinful earth from his dreams of retirement. He began gesticulating at us and yelling, "You guys have no shame!"

When we walked to the door, I said, "I'm sure, if you see a drowning child, you'd try to help."

"Go. Go!" the guard growled. "Professor!"

"But a child can drag you to the bottom," said my interlocutor.

"Yes, it happens."

While the old jailer was fiddling with the key of my cell, the young engineer asked, "Why didn't you talk about them with your cellmates?"

"I'm here as a Jew," I said.

The prison administration was aware of my sermons and took measures to stop this disgrace. The lieutenant brought two of the stronger cellmates to his office and suggested they knock the crap out of me and write a report about my anti-Soviet propaganda. They refused, and one of them was proud of it. The other fellow was nervous, yet managed to bring me a tiny onion. Once Nikolai brought a skimpy lemon. The dirty, unripe lemon with greenish skin tasted sweet, not sour at all. There must be a medical explanation for why the lemon was sweet. On that day, I managed to pass a small onion to Anatoly Sharansky, a fellow inmate from the next cell and a future Israeli minister. He had a high fever and was sick as a dog.

Alas! I never got a second lemon.

My sumptuous feasts ended the very next day. From then on, prisoners were unable to bring anything. Their supply of cigarettes was severely cut down, and this could damage the concord between the law enforcement and the petty criminal world. The KGB had obviously uncovered shocking facts of our life of luxury.

Finally the administration found a good citizen. Soon after arrival this former navy warrant-officer, a brave boxer, called me a saboteur and promised to put me in my place if I dared to offend his patriotic feelings. Nobody paid attention to him. We continued our political study.

Birdie, who failed to punish me on the day of my arrival, now became an expert on Christianity. "Why did you kill this Jesus?" he asked.

"Do you really care?" I said. "Maybe you'd prefer to tell us why you killed sixty million Russians during the twenty-nine years of Stalin's rule?"

"I didn't kill them. It was Stalin," Birdie said.

"I didn't kill Christ either," I said. "Anyway, it was his predetermined destiny. But what an athlete this Stalin was! He alone killed more of his own people in peace-time than Hitler during the war. Could it be that our mustached God had millions of helping hands? Who were those turnkeys, and interrogators, and judges?"

"Jews," Birdie said.

"I didn't serve as a jailer or as a prosecutor, or in a shooting squad, or as an informer. Your neighbor did. He would help Stalin to send all of you to a camp—just for listening to me."

"You're crazy," he said.

"Remember how tsar Nikita Khrushchev dragged the embalmed Stalin out of Lenin's Mausoleum and put him in the garbage? Our saints aren't immortal anymore. Today Nikita himself is in the garbage and we all dearly love you-know-whom..." I did not dare to utter the name of the Leader.

The main topic seemed to be quite innocent, and I was surprised when, thirty minutes later, the warrant-officer pushed me from behind in front of the urination trough. I lost my balance and stepped with one foot in the stinking gutter.

He said, "I'll make you drink piss from the pail."

The cop at the door was glowing with delight.

"We'll see," I said while walking to a sink. I took the shoe off and rinsed it under the tap. I took a sock off, washed it and used it to clean my naked foot. I washed and wrung the sock again. The good-natured jailer said, "Hurry up."

My cellmates already knew about the threat. When we were taken back, one of them immediately blocked the peephole, two guys took hold of the patriot's hands while the fourth—my taciturn friend from the wooden platform—quickly grabbed his hair with one hand and with the other covered his nose and mouth with a dirty cloth. In seconds, they began dragging him to the pail. The rest of the cellies were swearing approvingly. The more the patriot shook his head and mumbled through the rough cloth, the more they twisted his arms; he was becoming more and more bent forward to the stinking pail.

"He's a brainwashed fool," I said, "Let him go, guys. A happy slave."

"You don't know who the warden will bring here tomorrow," my coolheaded friend knew what he was talking about. "You're in trouble if they send in two more dogs like this." For the first time he demonstrated an ability to produce sentences in correct Russian. After that he turned to slang again, "Check this out, piss-pot, next time I'll bust you up." To make his point more convincing, he hit the back of the patriotic warrant-officer's head.

That quiet evening we talked about the over-fulfillment of the State Planning Committee's five-year economic plans. To my surprise the audience found this subject easy to grasp. Flier summarized my boring delivery: "If you have to make ten screw-bolts in one day and instead you make fourteen, it means that the Socialist plan isn't truly scientific. But if it's scientific, it means that you screwed up all the bolts."

"You should teach at Moscow University," I said, "and make your students analyze the official slogan 'Perform the five-year plan in four years!' The government urges true patriots to do hack work. So, who is the saboteur? Remember Khrushchev's favorite slogan 'Catch up with and overtake America!'? In fact, this task was proclaimed during Lenin's rule, in the early twentieth century. At that time even the new Socialist names were invented—Dognat (Catch-Up) and Peregnat (Overtake)."

Butcher interrupted me. "It's not a big deal, and we can catch up with America." He checked to see that everybody was looking at him, and finished triumphantly: "But if we overtake them, all the Americans would see our bare asses."

I concealed from the audience that I knew the joke.

It seemed like ages since my fellow inmates stopped smuggling little goodies for me. The anxious men in uniform told them that if they were caught with even a rotten potato, this would be the last day of their cigarette business. My stomach struggled even with bread. Watery and gluey, it kept adhering to the teeth and gums, and only fingernails helped to unstick and push it down the gullet. Mother Nature is wise—my difficulties with our strict diet were fully compensated and balanced by unstoppable diarrhea.

One lucky day I enjoyed some rare solitude in the toilet. My bare bottom was hanging over the hole in the concrete floor. I ignored the nasty bouquet and thought about the meaning of life. My exalted thoughts were rudely disturbed by someone tickling my anus. In fear and disgust, I reached out and right away grabbed something slimy and wriggling between my fingers. At that crucial moment the only wish of my life was not to tear it apart or allow the creature or a part of it to slide back inside my intestines. What else can a human dream of?

I began slowly bringing the unlucky thing out and before my

eyes. A five inch worm was dancing in my fingers. It was in one piece! What a relief! Alive and kicking! Sadly, it preferred suicide to my diet. I threw it into the hole.

One evening I saw a happy smile on the usually gloomy face of our navy warrant-officer. He said, "I have something for you," and began unbuttoning his pants.

Someone yelled, "Hah, the boxer is an exhibitionist!"

Another one shouted, "No, I always knew this penis wrinkle was a fag!"

The warrant-officer kept struggling with his pants. He had difficulties bringing out his member. Eventually, he overcame the muddle and displayed a hidden treasure for public viewing. The prison walls were nearly shaken by the thunderous roars of laughter. A thick carrot was attached by a string to his otherwise unattractive penis. He did not allow an eager volunteer to tear away the carrot, which he gingerly untied and passed to me.

"Thank you very much," I said politely. "You've turned me around your little finger." He smiled from ear to ear. I rubbed the carrot with my coat and relished it thoroughly as I ate.

At dawn of my fifteenth, and last day in prison, I said, while shaking thirty-five hands of my cellmates, "To avoid our last plenary session, they might kick me out before you return from your paradise."

Birdie shook my hand longer than the others.

In the afternoon I had two visitors, the warden and the lieutenant. Never before had I seen the warden. The overweight lieutenant colonel came to tell me that each day of my stay in prison I had been earning a transfer to solitary confinement for fifteen more days.

"I haven't broken any prison regulations," I said.

"You tried to foment a riot," he said.

"No," I said. "We talked quietly about the meaning of life."

He shook his head and said, "You're lucky," and they departed.

An hour later the lieutenant was back. He said, "For systematic violation of regulations you are transferred to solitary confinement for seven days."

I said, "I declare a dry hunger strike."

I spoiled their game! The warden knew the meaning of the word "dry"; for him it meant a hospital after three days of not drinking any liquid, and for the KGB it meant new publicity for the Jewish emigration movement.

Two hours later I was released.

Just released from prison. November 5, 1976.

ONE

The Cliff Edge Where It All Began

M Y BUMPY DESCENT into that prison began nearly twenty years before I was locked up there.

In the fall of 1958, after my escape from the northern city of Kostroma, where I had been living since 1956, I called Markevich, department head of the *Working Woman* magazine, *Rabotnitsa*. The essay I had just completed for him on the women of the forest was already in the galley, and recently he had talked of prospects for long-term cooperation. Markevich sighed, "So, you've returned to Moscow." He sighed again. "What happened in Kostroma?"

"The First Secretary of the Regional Party Committee didn't like my piece."

"That was clear from the *Literary Gazette*'s response to the criticism for publishing your satire," said Markevich.

"Oh, so you know," I said, surprised.

"Well, that's beside the point," he said. "You've got to come in. My editor-in-chief wants to speak with you. She won't publish your work."

An hour later, as I walked into his office, Markevich asked, "Is it true—you sent us a piece already published in your Kostroma paper?"

I choked with hurt, "My editor knew that I was submitting to you the work mostly about the same timber enterprise. She called it 'great publicity for our region.'" My voice was faltering. "I didn't cheat. Your story is three times longer."

"I think you're in trouble. Tell Vavilina what really happened."

The whole country knew Valentina Vavilina. As an appointed staunch opponent of the Western warmongers, she was an ever-present member of Soviet peace delegations, of the Committee of Soviet Women, of the Committee for the Defense of Peace, and a member of the Soviet parliament—a Supreme Soviet. In addition, she was photogenic.

"Does she know about my satire?"

He nodded.

I was screwed.

"Immediately after this lampoon, they demoted me," I said, attempting to explain. "But the First Secretary wanted to keep me there until the end of the one-year trial period for my Party-candidacy. Then they could expose my political failure and moral unscrupulousness and not accept me into their ranks."

"Yes, and no publication under the sun would accept you even as a doorman."

If someone had told me that it was an incidental allusion to my distant future, I wouldn't have believed them.

Vavilina, Supreme Soviet deputy, did not give me the chance to talk, though she was as sympathetic to me as circumstances unknown-to-me could allow.

"We cannot work with you currently. How old are you?"

"Twenty-eight."

"You're young, and I hope you'll draw the right conclusion from this. By law, we'll pay you fifty percent of the fee for the galleys."

At this, the audience was over.

I returned to Markevich with the voice of an injured child. "I guess, I should see this fee as a bold manifestation of support."

"If Vavilina wanted to," he said, "she could find a reason not to pay you a kopeck."

Only one thing was clear—the Father-of-the-Kostroma-Region was able to stop even my unpublished essay. All my efforts to find work would henceforth have to be kept secret.

My parents saw our dour expressions when my wife Irina and I talked in hushed voices on the couch three yards from them. We had no other place to live.

My father spoke: "Stop whispering, children. Your secret is known to everyone. You're our family and can live in this room for as long as you wish."

"Tomorrow morning, in the line for your only restroom," I said grimly, "ask the neighbors of this communal apartment for their opinion on this hot subject."

My mother stepped into our conversation. "Aunt Fannie invited all of us to dinner," she said.

"Their son will bring a family friend who works for the TASS agency," Papa said.

But I knew that all TASS correspondents abroad were intelligence operatives. Their Human Resources would have been examining my behavior since I came into this world at the maternity hospital.

"And kids, please, don't joke about Jews on a visit to Fannie. In 1919, Ukrainian bandits..."—Mama searched for the right words—"tore this journalist's mother to pieces while he lay in plain sight in a cradle. Fannie already was in a potato sack; the Ukrainian family made a little hole in it for her to breathe, and she heard a man stomping around the bags in the dark cellar looking for her and crying out, 'Where is this skinny Jewess?!'"

"This friend must be very influential," I said. "TASS, the largest news network in the world, already has its token Jew."

"It's a widespread notion that you Jews are very good at promoting each other," Irina said.

We were having a nice dinner when the gray-haired TASS journalist said, "I've heard you are an expert on agriculture." He was quiet and confident.

With my recent experience I was cautious. "Yes, for a Muscovite I'm an expert—after two years of working in Kostroma I can tell a plow from a rake."

"Can't you be serious for a change?" My wife's voice cracked.

"Okay, I reported on various agricultural activities, about meat and dairy farms, about flax, oats, and politically illiterate corn, which, regardless of Party directives, refuses to grow in the north."

He was amused. "The political fashion!"

We left the table, and I could not help but talk about the forest and about lumberjacks freed from hard labor camps a few months before my arrival in 1956. This was three years after Stalin's death, and they still celebrated it every year, though cautiously. The TASS correspondent was not interested in the forest and asked whether I was a Party member.

"I'm a candidate," I replied.

Days later, when my new acquaintance opened a heavy door upholstered with leather, four men of commanding appearance were waiting for us in the huge office. I doubted such a procedure was routine for hiring a newcomer. Everybody shook my hand and introduced himself. The Agricultural Department's head led the conversation. He asked, "Have you ever milked a cow?"

They all laughed.

"I was brave enough," I said, "to touch the udder and even attempted to milk one unhappy creature. When she resisted, I tried to talk her into cooperation. Alas, neither party enjoyed this encounter."

My audience chuckled, and I continued to develop the story. "I also took a stab at dragging heavy cans of milk. The girls were all giggling but after that, they shared with me their concerns and worries. They still work with a kerosene lamp hanging on a hook. The mechanization and electrification of all processes is needed; otherwise, the future of Kostroma dairy farms looks grim."

"It's obvious that you take to heart the problems of our agriculture," said the Head of the Main Editorial Board, who was chairing the gathering. "I will reveal to you our little secret—our esteemed colleague was very pleased with the chance to converse with you. I don't see a reason to test your skills and knowledge; you've already provided us with compelling clippings." He smiled. "In addition, you've just shown your ability to gather the material."

I was delighted.

"There is one more thing we have to stress," said the Agricultural Department head. "I'm sure you understand the political importance of every single word produced by TASS. Our product is reprinted by hundreds of Soviet and foreign papers. Classified parts of our material go directly to the leadership of the country."

The chair concluded the meeting, "Now we can pass you into the caring hands of our Human Resources Chief."

The KGB general, I thought. As the only person making written notes during our conversation, he flashed a smile as he handed me a small piece of paper. "Call me Monday morning at this number," he said.

That big Monday morning finally arrived. I called him and only managed to say, "This is Arkady Polishchuk," before he interrupted me. This aging KGB man sounded like a young detective in a movie who caught the perpetrator in the act. "Now we know you better," he said. "You're not the person whom you claim to be."

He hung up.

I felt a sharp pain in my left temple. Only now did I understand the extent of the Kostroma Region's first secretary's influence. They called my satire a slander—but it wasn't really a crime by any stretch of imagination. Had it ruined his ambitious plans to create a branch of the Union of Soviet Writers in his patrimony? Neighboring regions already had such branches, and some boy from Moscow had dared to prevent him from acquiring his own group of nationally well-known writers. He defended the honor and dignity of the Party while I, a fool, thought that I had simply been making fun of the three literary fraudsters with Party cards in their pockets.

I DECIDED TO LOOK for help where it all began nine years ago, when instead of high school finals I had dreamed of my upcoming brilliant career in journalism. The section editor of the youth newspaper *Moscow Komsomolets* remembered me and my silly failure to understand why my first satire was slaughtered by the censor.

"I hope, old man, you wised up out there in the bucolic hinterland." The paper's old hand still bowed his head, now more grizzled, to the side and narrowed an eye as if evaluating his interlocutor.

"Not really," I said.

"Then re-educate yourself into a house manager while you're still young," he suggested cheerfully.

"I'm looking for a job and ready to be your freelancer again."

"I have a feeling that you're in trouble," he said and took me to the third floor, to "a good man at a new and rapidly growing paper."

This "good man," Yegor Yakovlev, greeted me like an old friend.

"I've read your lampoon. You whipped them nicely."

Flattered, I gave no sign of it, saying only, "I paid for this dubious honor."

"You came here right on time."

The *Lenin's Banner* was already the biggest regional newspaper in the country. Two days later I began my new work. After two weeks, I took a train to a nearby city to meet with the inventor of an antenna box that dramatically increased the range of signals that a television could receive. Now, the family of this plant worker happily, though with interruptions, watched programs from our Baltic republics and even Poland.

My article was killed when a veteran of the editorial board clasped his hands and exclaimed, "What if tomorrow this home-grown genius invents a device to watch American or West-German TV? Someone here went mad. This should be thrown out of the strip!"

"Vigilant newspaper wolf!" Yegor said, relating the story.

"Thank goodness Stalin has been in his coffin for more than five years," I said.

"Otherwise, both of us," he said, "and that inquisitive worker, would've been shot as an American and Monacan commando detachment."

I had already ranked the charming and straight-talking Yegor among my friends when I noticed a sudden change in him. After the fourth week was over, he said gloomily, "I'm sorry, old man, the editor-in-chief came to the conclusion that you haven't passed the probationary period. Look for another job."

Having gotten acquainted with my buddy Tom Kolesnichenko in *Pravda*'s restaurant, the unsuspecting Yegor Yakovlev sub-sequently advised him to avoid contact with me; I was involved in some kind of a scandal with political overtones. That was why Tom urgently suggested to me that we convene the Supreme Military Council.

And now my three university friends were sitting on our bed, my wife and I on our only two chairs, and Gena Snegiryov lying on the floor between our feet. Gena meticulously studied the small ceiling and looked like a battle-hardened commander, bent over a map. We had just rented this tiny room. My wife initiated the discussion of the crisis. "My husband finally realized that the influence of the Party extends to the entire territory of the Soviet Union."

"To hell with them," said Fred Solyanov, now a stagehand and a bard. "In my theater we need a non-drinking stagehand."

"Alik," Irina said, using my nickname. "I told you not to buy alcohol."

"Friends, I have a solution," Nahl Zlobin said.

Gena Snegiryov tugged at my pants. "Remember, I tried to persuade you to obtain a certificate from my psychiatrist?"

Nahl and Tom looked at us with great curiosity, and I had to try to explain. "This is true," I said. "It was the last year of university …"

I had to introduce Gena to his audience more thoroughly. He quit school after the fifth grade; at the age of sixteen he traveled with our Moscow University biologists and spent years dissecting animals; at the age of twenty this child tried to convince me to write my diploma paper on Buddha. Even now, with stubble on his face, Gena only barely looked like an adult. He was almost four years younger than us.

"Gena," said Tom, "my six-year-old boy loved your book about beasts and nature. We didn't know that you were such an antisocial element."

"Gena is better at socializing when at a bonfire." I was still fascinated by his memories of Tuvan hunters in sheepskin shirts below the knees over homemade leather pants.

"Yeah," Gena said thoughtfully. "At that fire Mendume had been feeding me with mutton and without him, I'd never have written my stories."

These Asian tribesmen worshiped celestial deities, and the good and evil spirits of the Altai Mountains, rivers, forests, boulders, and animals. Also, without their assistance in showing my friend Gena the way to his drug habit, he may not have needed a psychiatrist.

"Don't they have Party Committees over there?" Tom inquired acidly.

"Their Party bosses," Gena said, laughing, "also believe in spirits and ghosts."

"Lucky you, Gena!" said Fred. "You didn't waste five years of your life studying Marxist philosophy."

"I do have a solution," Nahl said again. "The entire leadership of Kostroma may not even be aware of the existence of *The Life of the Blind* magazine." He turned to Tom. "I've been its traveling correspondent for a year, and I'll go into science after they take me into the Party ranks. I'll recommend Alik as a worthy replacement. So our satirist will join the Party at *The Life of the Blind* after having stayed with the magazine for a year. After that, with the Party membership card in his pocket, he can run away wherever he damn well pleases."

"Right!" said Tom. "And then I'll smuggle you, abandoned and forgotten by all, into my estimable socio-political magazine *Asia and Africa Today*."

"I've read only one book about Africa," I said, "and it was in verses."

"You'll have a whole year to study," said Tom. "You don't want to be at the forefront of official propaganda, so you'll write about colonialism and white racism. Just never step again on the regal toes of senior Party officials."

"So convincing!" said Fred.

"And after his victory over Western colonialism," said Gena Snegiryov wistfully, "we'll appoint Alik President of the USSR, the greatest loony bin in the world, and every day you'll feed me lunch."

"And me—dinner with vodka," said Fred promptly.

I solemnly promised but warned, "On the condition you two join the Party."

"It will depend on the amount of vodka," said the principled Fred.

"Comrades, it's too much!" Tom suddenly brightened up, and then changed his tone and in feigned seriousness said, "Don't encroach on the sacred! We cannot allow a Jew to lead our great Motherland!"

"Maybe we should baptize him first?" tentatively proposed Irina.

"It won't help," Nahl said firmly.

TWO

The Life of the Blind

D URING THESE TRYING TIMES of 1959, Tom introduced me to his cronies in *The Soviet Militia*. This police magazine was held in high esteem among freelancers for its high fees. There was a certain irony in the fact that I had to use a pseudonym. The editor asked, "Why Irinin? You have a nice Ukrainian last name." I had to explain that my wife wanted me to honor her name.

Shortly after this magazine published a report by its new freelancer, Nahl Zlobin took me to the All-Russian Society for the Blind. At the flimsy door with a sign reading "Head of the Department of Culture," he said, "Pay no attention to how Natalie treats me. We're just good friends. They believe that the blind are more sensual than the sighted, and thus they have stronger sexual desires, and are better lovers."

We heard a melodious laughter from within. "I agree. Nahl, come in, darling."

We laughed, went in, and I shook her soft, outstretched hand. Her dark pupils wandered strangely, as if trying to roll up somewhere behind her upper eyelids with thick lashes. Not letting go of my hand, Natalie squeezed it gently. "I thought I already knew everything about you, but now I see that someone shattered your nerves."

"Nahl did that," I said. "Hard to hide anything from you, even behind closed doors."

"You rely too much on your eyes; we bank on other senses. That's why you folks aren't able to read by touch."

I wanted to sound business-like and asked her how the Society earns money.

"We produce a great variety of things," she said. "We make knitted gloves, cords, ropes, brushes—even for cleaning medals—as well as brooms for sweeping ship decks. Should I continue?"

"I think I get the idea," I said.

It was clear that they had difficulties in finding work suitable for the blind.

"It'll be your job," she continued, "to show our readers that we are productive members of society."

On the way to the editor-in-chief of *The Life of the Blind*, Natalie asked, "Alik, do you play chess?"

"Yes. Are we going to play chess with him now?"

"He'd love to."

The editor-in-chief Victor Andreevich came around his desk to greet us. "Get ready, Arkady, you'll be told scary stories. Who needs an armless or legless war veteran? Some are abandoned by their wives."

"There is always room for joy as long as we have a nose to sniff the flowers," I said, somewhat pompously.

"Nice talking, brother Arkady," sneered Nahl.

"I like it," said Natalie. "I have flowers at home and take good care of them."

"Among the blind," Victor Andreevich said, "there are many people who don't have even a high school education. Therefore, we want you to be as simple as Chekhov."

I promised to write like Chekhov.

Most of the year I spent on the road. The first trip was just two hours from Moscow by local train and bus. I traveled to Rusinovo to write about a unique experiment. Shortly after the war, while the European part of Russia was still in ruins, it was decided to build three exemplary cities for the blind where they would gather from all over the country. The equality of their residents would be determined by the common problems they faced. It sounded like a weird materialization of the Marxist idea, which was still smoldering in me: somewhere, away from the Party bosses, people were trying to fulfill mankind's ancient dream of creating a society of justice, equal opportunity, equal rights, and mutual aid. At least, for the blind. And I was going to witness it.

When a battered bus, rattling over potholes like a giant tambourine, stopped at the edge of the fiery autumn forest, the road dust settled and I saw a sign that read, "Caution: blind pedestrians." It was nailed directly to a red-headed tree. We drove into Rusinovo.

The city of the blind looked like the only street of a large village, though quite a long one. Getting off the bus, I glanced in both directions and did not see a soul. Across the street stood a gloomy four-story building. Over the wide black gate made out of sheet iron, hung a big sign that read: "The Training and Production Enterprise of the All-Russian Society for the Blind." The venture, half staffed with the sighted, was churning out mounting panels for a manufacturing plant which just two years ago started producing Ruby-brand black-and-white TV sets. The Society was proud of the fact that it participated in the production of such a technological marvel. That Moscow plant had some heavily guarded shops, as it did work for the military and space-exploration industry. It was rumored that "our" boards were about to fly into space. Just a year earlier, in October 1957, the first Sputnik had been successfully launched into orbit around the Earth.

Next to the factory stood an abandoned kindergarten and two unfinished five-story boxes with gaping window intended to become homes for the blind, but obviously the money had run out. This gray reality was in stark contrast to the bright roadside fall forest. A stray thought flashed through my mind—well, it's good that they don't see it.

The administrators of the plant were waiting for me, but, at first, I went to the nearby highrises, knocked on a dilapidated door on the first floor, and soon heard shuffling footsteps behind it. A person stopped, listened to my signaling cough, and continued shuffling back and forth behind the door. I said aloud, "I'm a correspondent for *The Life of the Blind;* please, open."

In the end, curiosity won out over caution and the door creaked open a crack to the length of the stop chain. I caught the unpleasant odor. An old man, cursing, slammed the door in my face. "You, crook, here again!" he shouted. "I remember you! Get out of here if you don't want to be shied away with this hammer on your head!" And he hit the fragile door with a heavy object.

I said, "Okay, calm down. I'm not a swindler and will try to talk to your neighbors."

I was almost on the second floor, when he flung open the door and shouted, "If you're so smart, you should've come with someone whom I knew!"

"You're right," I yelled.

"Come back when my wife returns from the factory!" he cried. "In an hour! She's half-sighted!"

"Thank you!" I yelled. "Maybe I will!"

On the second floor, a toothless pale woman opened the door without even asking who I was. Gray strands of hair were sticking out from under her well-worn headscarf. The appearance of a correspondent startled her. "It's so good of you to come! Please help us to get some medication," she mumbled.

The two blind sisters had lived in this studio since this house was built ten years ago. The head of the woman slightly quivered.

"We've been living in this village since childhood," she told me. "When the authorities decided to build a city of the blind with this plant, a lot of blind people already had lived and made a lot of things right here, in Rusinovo."

The sisters smiled, revealing the remains of yellowed teeth, and the one who had opened the door, continued mumbling.

"We felt grand that from now on we would have our own city where no one could be hurt," she said. "With this apartment, we no longer had to worry about firewood and water. In our basement there is a boiler, and we almost never have shortages of coal."

I began to understand her slurred speech.

"We were so grateful to the Soviet authorities!" she averred. "Only once, coal was delivered late; there was a severe frost, and the water pipes burst. We had to trek through the snow for two weeks to our old well half a mile away, near the house where Masha and I grew up."

The other sister kept smiling.

"Who's older?" I asked, "You or Masha?"

"I turned fifty last month. She's two years younger, but she's as sick as I am."

Masha kept smiling. "You see, I too lost half of my teeth," she said. "Thanks to the plant director, he's never denied us assistance. If there were no trucks, he'd always give us a horse-drawn cart to ride to Balabanovo's railway hospital. All our bad teeth were pulled out over there."

The sisters laughed. They were enjoying my presence.

"Under anesthesia?"

"Under what?" Masha asked.

"Did they freeze your gums?"

"Why freeze? It was done in summers, too, any time of the year."

"You mean they just pulled it out with tongs, so your eyes nearly popped out from pain?"

"No—no, if a tooth resisted, they pricked the gum, and after that the gum went numb."

"Good," I said.

The older sister said, "My teeth sometimes move—they move and fall out by themselves. It's because we can't afford to buy meat and vegetables. Even if we had a garden, we wouldn't have the strength to cope with it. So in the winter we buy frozen potatoes and slimy cabbage."

Masha said, "We've gotten disability pensions and for months haven't worked—I because of a stomach ulcer, my sister after a stroke. Sorry, she speaks so slowly; this is the result. Please write that we always were good workers."

Her sister said, "Often there is no money for medicines. Anyway, the drugs aren't always available."

They laughed again, displaying gratitude and a fragile hope that I might be able to help them.

I was getting frustrated. I did not want to see stripped wallpaper, cobwebs, untidy beds, worn clothes, and deformed faces any longer and left this stinking house. The multicolored forest somewhat comforted me, and I walked by a ruined church with no dome, to another five-story building. Man is such a beast, I thought spitefully; it gets used to everything, and that is why this wretched house looks a bit more inviting. Those sweet and virtuous people in Moscow would never allow me to write about this despair and hopelessness.

On the first floor, an angry bearded man almost hurt me with a crutch. "Don't humiliate me!" he shouted, "Go away!"

From a safe distance, after joining forces with his wife, I persuaded him to let me in. On his only foot he had a patched felt boot, out of season. His little son closely watched my every move. I stroked his head. The kid did not mind but still was on guard, ready to defend his parents. At first, the man turned his face to the ceiling and listened to my conversation with his wife. After several minutes, he began giving approving nods.

"We came here from faraway places, like many others," she said, "in the hope of settling in the dream city. We were very young and fell in love." She touched his knee, and his face softened. Only their six-year-old son could see my sad smile.

I asked, "How did you know that you liked each other?"

"By voice," he said, speaking up for the first time.

I said, "Interesting, I also loved the voice of my future wife."

"Is it true?" she asked.

"For a long time, the telephone was our only connection."

The man said, "We don't have telephones here. You can't call a doctor."

"Here our children were born," she said.

"Tim died," her husband said.

She patted his knee again. "Stepan is a true hero," she said. "He didn't complain much about his diabetes, about the deep wounds on both legs. They were aching and aching. And smelling. That's why they cut off his right foot."

The boy climbed up on a chair, stood on tiptoe, and opened a narrow window.

"Forgive me," the wife went on slowly, "you might not like it, but since then I have kept praying about his left leg every day. And he was joking—he said, since here in the Soviet Union God had no means of subsistence, he lived abroad. Please don't write about that."

I promised. Now they looked relaxed.

Stepan patted her hand, still on his knee. "It wasn't just her voice. Nastya also hit me."

The youngster giggled. "She hit me hard, with a piece of furniture," his father said, grinning.

Now came my turn to laugh loudly, and Stepan continued:

"There had been small workshop here, and we made furniture before the factory was set up. She got scared, apologized, and hugged me. That was it."

Nastya said, "That's how we got better acquainted." She giggled, and her son burst out laughing like only the young can do.

I said, "It's good that you didn't work with bricks."

We all laughed again. The boy could not stop.

I said, "My wife also hugged me first."

Stepan continued, "We worked on the presses when she damaged her arm, cleaning the wires. Now I can't work, but Nastya still goes there. Maybe I should try to make quilted blankets, like she did in her hometown."

There was a knock on the door.

"Come in, Petrovich!" Nastya called, raising her voice, "We have a guest—the correspondent of the blind magazine."

In the doorway stood a broad-shouldered man in a faded soldier's field shirt carelessly tucked into his pants. "Yes, truly an eyeless magazine," he said. "They just write about how our plans are being over-fulfilled and what songs we sing."

"Maybe I'll write about how your friends raise their children," I said.

"Stop looking at my hand!" He shook his tousled hair. "I was holding a machine gun when a German shot off all my fingers except the thumb. As you see, a dozen fragments landed on my mug too. Oh boy, I was a good-looking youth! Big eyes. The girls couldn't keep from looking at me."

"Petrovich is a good man, quiet," said Nastya. "Only, like today, we're at times tipsy."

"Because money jingles in my pocket, especially on Victory and October Revolution Days. I put my orders and medals on this tunic and walk, begging from car to car on the Moscow-bound train." He turned his face covered with small scars toward his hostess. "Who brings candies from Moscow for your child every time?"

"You do," said the little fellow.

"Have you ever been to Moscow?" I asked him.

The boy looked at his mother.

"I want to take him there," said the soldier, "but she's afraid that I'll get drunk there and Gypsies will steal the boy."

The mother's voice faltered. "Have you seen many Muscovites who help the blind to cross the street?"

The soldier said, "The war has made us all cruel."

And Comrade Stalin has made us kindhearted, I thought bitterly, but said, "The war ended almost fourteen years ago."

"No," Petrovich said firmly. "We're still at war. I listen to the radio every day."

The woman said, "Petrovich knows everything about politics."

Petrovich turned to her. "How can we not speak about this damned war? America and Germany are about to attack us. The border is long, and we have enemies on all sides. That's why all of our money is spent on defense."

The host put his arm around his wife. "That's why your military pension is so small?"

He sounded ironic.

"Stalin made a big mistake, that he didn't take the whole of Germany," Petrovich said, completing his review of the international situation.

As I was departing, the kid asked, "Why did you come to us?"

"I wanted to get acquainted with your parents; they are true heroes."

"I know," he said.

"And they love you very much."

"I know," he said.

"Learn well."

"I know," he said. "I'm learning how to read. I will read books for them."

Climbing to the next floor, I started panicking. Nahl had played a dirty trick. I was in a leper colony. There was nothing I could write about them. I was frantically looking for a way to say at least half-truths about their everyday concerns instead of reporting on the contribution of the blind to our common cause of building socialism.

I kept climbing the smelly stairs, up and up, and realized it only when I was already on the top, on the fifth floor. I leaned my damp forehead against a wall of indeterminate color and spoke to myself, "It's easier to break this wall with this stupid head than to find a way out of this impasse. If we glorify the wounded and dying soldiers, why couldn't I sing of the disabled's daily fight for the right to stay alive? This fight blows up human flesh just like the war."

A cheerful fellow of my age opened the door. "I heard you talking with someone about the war," he said. "Looking for some war veteran?"

"What a relief!" I said. "Probably, I was looking for you."

His unseeing eyes were focused directly at me. He was healthy and recently married, and his heavily pregnant wife was at the factory and threatened to deliver the baby right on the shop floor.

"Did you choose your wife for her voice?" I asked brazenly.

"I touched her."

"And you could not stop touching anymore?"

"Uh—huh. I touched her . . . breast."

"And she?"

"She said that I wasn't shy."

"And you?"

"I said, 'If I were not bashful, my hand wouldn't have moved from your body as quickly as if it hit a burner.'"

"And she?"

"She laughed."

"And you?"

"I said, "My fingers are still burning ..."" He furrowed his brow.

"Are you going to write about this?"

"I'd love to, but a prudish censor would ban it."

"Do we have censors?"

"Yes. They guard our state secrets. Our enemies shouldn't know that Russian women have breasts. What do you do for fun?"

"Sing in a choir. Together. I hope it's not a state secret."

"Let's ask a censor."

We two authentic men enjoyed each other's company.

"Why are so many blind people ill?" was my last question.

"From poverty," was his lightning-fast response.

On the way home, I muttered angrily under my breath, "They have nothing. No guide dogs, which are busy guarding our borders. A city of the blind in the country of the eyeless. Fred was right— get a stagehand position and, in the midst of this painted plywood universe, forget about the real world."

ABOUT THREE MONTHS LATER, on my way toward an assignment in the huge Siberian city of Novosibirsk, I felt lucky. This time my job seemed easier for a change and even entertaining—to cover preparations for a nationwide show of blind amateurs. I kept looking from my sleeper carriage at the forests and on the third day clearly realized why I was so pleased that the trees had already dropped their leaves. The lush fall in the drab "city of the blind" was still on my mind. But Rusinovo was quickly forgotten when I stepped on the concrete railroad platform of Novosibirsk. In a minute I felt like one of Napoleon's soldiers dying in a Russian snowdrift. I had left my felt winter boots, my *valenki*, at home, and my toes quickly informed me why this third most populous city in the Russian Federation was the capital of Siberia. My leather boots with warm lining, a gift of my parents for work in the fields and forests of Kostroma, had served me faithfully for two years of my extensive travels. But even with woolen socks, they were not able to withstand the murderous Siberian frost.

Someone had to meet me on the platform, but the damn someone was late, and to save my life from negative-forty-degree temperatures, I decided I'd run inside an unheated station building and within a couple of minutes jump back onto the platform. In the station, a girl in a downy shawl which covered her eyebrows and the mouth, came up to me from behind and said, "Forgive me for being late, Comrade Polishchuk!"

"How did you manage to recognize me from the back?" I asked.

She said, "You are the only person in this town with no *valenki.*"

Life at the club was in full swing. The city was home to a large community of the blind, with its own amateur theater. Everyone was convinced that the Moscow correspondent would glorify creative Novosibirsk across the country and that my assessment would affect the selection of participants for the nationwide show of the amateur blind. After the play rehearsal, all were eager to hear my opinion. I was determined to hide it. As in any theater, in the struggle for better roles all means were acceptable—from intrigue to attempts to make a drunkard out of the unstable artistic director. One girl whispered in my ear, "It's high time for this old cow to stop playing Juliet, and to play her grandmother instead."

After that we listened to poets, singers and musicians, among them two good accordionists. It was late, and the whimsical frosty patterns were no longer visible on the blackened windows. The cold was gathering force, and all but the tipsy artistic director hurried home.

"Want to see the seventh wonder of the world?" came a voice

behind me, hoarse from the cold air.

I turned around. A man in his forties and a boy, both in sheepskin coats, stood next to me. The kid looked not so much at me as at my shiny boots. On his father's right shoulder hung an instrument in a wide black case which could be an accordion or its close relative, the Russian *bayan*. The empty left sleeve of his coat was tucked in his pocket.

"Sure," I said, and glanced with concern at the director sitting next to me, already dozing off.

"Quick, my boy! Prepare the stage!" ordered the father.

They dropped their gloves, coats, and winter caps with earflaps on a bench behind us and headed to the stage. The man was wearing an untucked Russian shirt of ancient style with a collar that fastened at the side. It was red, with embroidery on the edge of the flap, and belted with a narrow Circassian strap.

I shouted, "Wow!" and the musician waved to me and yelled, "My wife sewed it from a Soviet flag!"

I expressed my amazement again.

The boy helped his dad climb the stairs to the stage and walked him behind the curtain. A minute later the son appeared again, apparently in anticipation of a command from his father.

Finally a loud order "Open up!" was given, and the curtain began to move slowly apart. First, I heard a heavy rhythmic stamping of felt boots, which meant dance. By that time the director's chin had firmly come to rest on his chest. Then a merry raucous singing started which soon was joined by the heartbreaking sounds of a *bayan*. After the audience was electrified, the curtain fully opened, and I saw the glorious performer. At first glance, his instrument looked like a hybrid of a large manual harmonica and a push-button accordion popular in the Russian countryside. However, the left keyboard was not there. Instead, there was just a smooth surface. All the vertical rows of bass buttons had been moved to the right side of the instrument, where both keyboards were somehow lumped together. The musician used his left stump only to stretch the *bayan* as wide as the bellows would allow, even a bit wider. In response it roared like a wounded Siberian bear. He sang, or perhaps I should say shouted, two folk songs and not very funny limericks. When he went from raucous baritone to effeminate squealing, the artistic director was already sleeping serenely.

It was all the same to me how well or poorly this strong-willed man played and sang. It was amazing!

After coming down from the stage, he said, "The secret of the *bayan* is that the listeners cannot weep. You can only have fun, dance and sing bawdy ditties with it."

His wise observation has been supported by Russian drug addicts of this century who call the syringe used for injecting drugs, the "*bayan*".

I asked why he called himself only the seventh wonder of the world, not, at least, the third one. His upper eyelids dropped and he said, "From modesty. People don't know, but there is also an eighth wonder of the world."

I asked, "Who? Comrade Stalin?"

He said firmly, "No. In Vologda."

"I was in that city and didn't find anything special," I said.

"Now, now. There is another war veteran over there, a one-armed *bayan* virtuoso. Like me."

The man certainly did not know a thing about the seven remarkable structures of classical antiquity.

We were leaving the club, treading carefully on the plank floor so as not to wake the snoring artistic director. The musician noticed, "Good music will never wake a drunken man, but steps, even cautious ones, can."

"Dad," his kid said on the threshold of the club, "we need the same general's boots as this friend has. They can stomp louder."

In the frozen bus on the way to the hotel, I looked at my knee-high boots and recalled the one-armed cobbler who sewed them. When I was fifteen, I saw him for the first time through the iron bars covering two window wells. The shoemaker raised a hammer to his mouth, disengaged the index finger and the thumb to take one of the tiny nails gripped between his lips, pressed it with the stump right to a graceful heel, and with one stroke drove the baby into it up to the very head. Meanwhile his stump cleverly held the shoe to a metal stand turning it around in all directions. I watched as he pressed to his chest dummies of different forms with leather and carved out of it a future shoe.

I walked past those windows barely protruding above ground quite often, and he looked up and smiled at the sight of me, with silvery nail-heads sticking out of his clenched lips. The shoemaker did not know that he also was one of the wonders of this Russian post-war world.

In my report I did not mention the wonders of the world but wrote about the kids of the blind who grew up caring for their parents.

WITHIN ONE YEAR, I had traveled extensively, and my reports appeared in every issue of the magazine. My offers to use pseudonyms were rejected. In the summer of 1959, my last assignment brought me to Chelyabinsk, the city on the mountainous border of Europe and Asia. On the warm July day of my arrival, the Chelyabinsk Hotel's manageress in a lacy blouse confided to me some state secrets. Two of them had been known to the whole country since the war. The natives called their Southern Ural city *Tankograd*, the City of Tanks; it also could be called the *Katyusha*-Town, after the truck-mounted missile launchers.

The third secret still was not known to the one million of its residents. The chatty manageress solemnly warned that I would have to leave as soon as a classified message came from Moscow about the upcoming arrival of a foreign dignitary. I was the lucky last traveler allowed to stay in this freshly painted hotel, surrounded by a fragrant circle of brand-new asphalt. The four stories above us had been already sealed and guarded for several days.

I said, "It's probably the American vice-president, Richard Nixon, with a huge entourage. They say he offended Khrushchev on July 24, at the opening of the American National Exhibition in Moscow."

She was impressed by my knowledge of state secrets and asked, "Did he call Nikita Sergeevich some bad names?"

I reassured her that Khrushchev knew far more bad words than the completely out of touch U.S. vice-president.

"Why did Nikita Sergeevich go to such a foolish exhibition? America is capable of employing any provocation," she said.

"To promote world peace," I said. "The whole of Moscow was trying to get there. People stood in line for hours to have a look at it all. Indeed, this had never happened before."

The stunning news of Nixon's upcoming arrival to Chelyabinsk was known only to the Party apparatus, to the KGB personnel, and, thanks to me, from now on, to the manageress of the best local hotel, and to her employees, friends and acquaintances. She wanted to show me the luxury accommodations with new Finnish furniture "brought from Moscow" for the picky overseas visitors and said to a guard in a black suit, "Let the Moscow correspondent have a look at the paintings of our artists in this corridor."

He looked at me keenly. "No one should go near the pictures."

This smart-ass required my favorite shtick, and I used it. "One doesn't need to look at these local paintings to know what's depicted there."

He screwed up one eye. "What?"

To prolong the suspense, I said, "The foreign bastards couldn't swipe them from their rooms, even if they wanted to."

When a nervous expectation lit up his face, I said, "Khrushchev's portrait; happy steelmakers around an open hearth furnace; beautiful collective farmers in long skirts and sturdy high boots, maybe with red carnations in their hair; Chelyabinsk's famous tractors with red flags; a military parade in Red Square, and the Ural Mountains in different seasons, all painted with photographic precision."

The manageress was impressed again.

"It's not entirely accurate," said the guardian of art, and he wouldn't let us in the hallway.

She said, "Don't worry, we don't have bad paintings here. All of them were selected by the Regional Party Committee."

In the morning she knocked on my door and whispered, "He isn't coming."

I asked, "Could I move upstairs? Fresh asphalt smells a bit."

"No. It will take some time to remove the new furniture, crystal vases, carpets, silver, and all that from all four floors."

"And the paintings?"

"Yes, how do you know? You're so sharp. They ordered me not to touch them."

"The KGB art collectors will do this sophisticated job themselves."

"Yes."

"Sorry, I've got to run," I said. "Could we have a rendezvous tonight at your restaurant?"

"What a romantic French word!"

"Which one?" I asked.

She laughed, raising her shoulders and pressing her elbows to her sides and her palms to her thighs like a child who was all of a sudden tickled. "I'll tell you why we shouldn't have invited this warmonger, what's his name, Nixon."

The workshop on the edge of the town looked from a distance

like a long stable inappropriately set amid village houses. On the way from the bus stop, the half-blind chairman of the regional branch of the All-Russian Society for the Blind was carefully checking with his lofty stick the downhill cobblestone road that had long yearned for repair.

"This shed is probably much older than me," he said to maintain a conversation.

"The first rope was produced by monkeys," I said, endorsing his point of view. "It was called liana."

He tactfully corrected me: "Yes, manufacturing of ropes is likely older than the production of wheels."

I also corrected my faux pas. "It'll be necessary for centuries to come."

"Yes, we've made the right choice," observed my companion.

The door and small windows of the low structure were wide open. On a bench near the door two blind workers smoked cigarettes rolled from newspaper. I hadn't seen such do-it-yourself cigarettes since my childhood during the war. Large dust particles stuck to their hair, shoulders, and unshaven faces.

I stepped inside and saw the particles of dried hemp dancing in the air. A gray string of slouching workers was slowly walking inside this translucent shroud, from one end of the barn to the other and back again. They held onto a faint rope along which they moved and looked like convicts on a chain gang. Soon the top of my throat began tickling, and my eyes started to get used to the countless particles wavering in the air that were produced when the workers curled together a new thread at the end of the barn.

I walked through the blurred veil to the end of the shed and saw the plant fiber passing through a primitive breaker resembling a wooden comb. This ancient device was removing dirt and making myriad particles fly. They were sticking out of nostrils, ears, sockets of blinking blind eyes, and from lips.

I was in the fifteenth century and so overwhelmed that I could not understand how these straight, long, loose strands were twisting and braiding together to form a rope. These gloomy workers had descended from the paintings of Brueghel the Elder right into socialist Russia. My eyes began hurting. Through the gleefully dancing dust, I looked at the reels placed on a rotating wooden disk twisting individual fiber strands. Yarns, spun from these strands, were twisting in directions opposite to each other. There was a blatant contradiction between the slow monotonous movement of the blind and the rapid irrepressible twitching of all that surrounded them—the twists of the yarns and the counter-twists of the strands and the twists of the ropes stretched along the length of the barn.

I panicked—what if the braided strands somehow got into someone's hair or clothes? What questions could I ask them? I didn't want to be there anymore and didn't talk to anyone. Why should I remain in this hell if nobody allowed me to write about it?

"Well, did you like it?" asked my guide on the way back to the bus stop.

"It's a health hazard."

He stopped, "Do you realize that these people are happy that we have provided them with secure jobs?"

"I do," I said. "I just don't know what to write."

He said, "I understand."

In the evening I met with the hotel manager again. She had grown up near Moscow, and she missed cultured people. I impressed her with my manners. Maybe here, at the restaurant, she just wanted to talk about something intelligent and sublime, because her redneck husband did not understand this woman's follies.

Soon I learned that he, a military man, told her to stay in Chelyabinsk while he would be involved in cleaning up large areas of nuclear contamination. Never before had I heard that the people of Chelyabinsk Region had suffered two nuclear disasters, the last one just two years before I was there. She was unable to grasp the reasons for allowing Nixon to visit the city when people were dying from nuclear radiation in its hospitals.

"We came here in 1951, after radioactive waste had been dumped for six years into the river, the only source of water for dozens of villages," she explained. "He worked in a closed city called Beria ..."

I interrupted. "Beria? After the head of the secret police who was shot after Stalin's death in 1953?"[1]

"Yes. He refused to say how far it was from here."

"Do you understand the meaning of it?"

"Yes."

"The entire military-nuclear industry here was built on the bones of prisoners," I said.

"Yes."

"What a perversion!" I burst out, "Stalin rewarded Beria with glory, even when the very existence of these cities was a top secret."

"They began working there on the first Soviet plutonium production complex half a year after the war. Now this city is called Sorokovka."

"Sorokovka?! The City of the Forties?"

"Yes."

---

1 Under Lavrentiy Pavlovich Beria (1899–1953), the secret police agency was called NKVD, the People's Commissariat of Internal Affairs, which in 1943 was renamed MVD (Ministry of Internal Affairs). In 1954 it became the KGB while Beria, as a powerful member of the Politburo, continued to lead the entire ramified punitive machine of the country. Beria was also in control of Soviet efforts to develop nuclear weapons. After Stalin's death, Beria was accused by his colleagues in the Politburo of spying for numerous Western countries. Ten months later he was shot to death after a trial behind closed doors. The members of the Politburo were afraid that Beria would seize power in the country and kill his competitors. Of course, the name of the city Beria was changed, not to mention for the fact he was a known sexual predator, rapist, and murderer.

I exclaimed, "A veiled memorial to the dead!"

Who would have guessed that my journey from the fifteenth to the twentieth century could be so short!

"A couple of years ago a great misfortune happened again, elsewhere near Chelyabinsk, and," —she squeezed my hand on the table—"my husband got nauseated and completely lost interest in me. Even before, he rarely smiled, and now he has stopped smiling. Completely." She sighed. "They sent him to some military hospital for treatment, he said, and he wasn't allowed to give me the address. Do you think he lied? During the last two months I haven't heard from him."

"If something really bad happened, you would be informed."

She said, "We have no children."

Only when the waiter brought our food did she remove her moist hand from mine.

I asked, "Who were all those criminals?"

She did not understand my question.

I explained, "Those who built all these nuclear sites."

"I don't know," she shrugged. "Criminals."

The third nuclear disaster in the Chelyabinsk Region happened in 1967. Having been a center for the production of weapons-grade plutonium, the territory is now one of the most contaminated areas on the globe. The details became known only in post-Soviet times. The Russians had truly held a nuclear bomb suspended on a medieval rope.

After one year of work in *The Life of the Blind*, I was admitted to the Communist Party. My buddy Tom Kolesnichenko, the managing editor of the *Asia and Africa Today,* gleefully congratulated me. "Now, with this mighty red pass to the bright future in your pocket, we'll try to move you, forgotten by your almighty enemies, from the blind to the blinded."

THREE

How to Become an Expert on Africa

M Y WORK AT *Asia and Africa Today* started in 1960 under pitiful circumstances. A drunk Nikolai Nikolayevich Polyakov, its deputy editor-in-chief, pleaded to find a public restroom quickly. He begged us to stop the car and clutched at the steering wheel, but Tom tore his hand away, and we continued our perilous travel through the center of Moscow. Every two minutes, my friend kept solicitously asking the desperate man twice his age, "Have you not crapped yet, Nikolai Nikolayevich?"

It sounded like a cheerful refrain to a bawdy high school song.

Sitting in the back seat, I also begged Tom to let Polyakov out at any gateway.

Tom was adamant. "I just don't want a former senior functionary of our great Party being arrested, drunk and shitted, violating the laws of our socialist society."

Nikolai Nikolayevich Polyakov—behind his back everybody called him Nik-Nik—moaned like a haggard bull, "W-we s-a-a-id, we t-take him."

This "him" was I, now drawn into this ridiculous scrape.

Earlier, in the morning, when I was editing a poem of a blind poet in the office of *The Life of the Blind*, Nik-Nik had doubted my suitability to work in his magazine. "Why do we need this reporter from some second-rate magazine for people with disabilities?" he persisted.

"Yesterday you praised his article in *International Affairs*," responded Tom, who had actually written that boring piece about the struggle of the African peoples for a brighter future.

"Why didn't he sign it with his own name?"

"Because he adores his wife Irina."

My friend had kept in mind my recent troubles and had signed the article with the name A. Irinin. Nik-Nik, as Tom put it, still could not forget the glorious days when he would decide whom to send to a concentration camp and whom to prison.

At noon Tom had placed a bottle of good Armenian brandy on Nik-Nik's desk and half an hour later gently tried the door of his office—the deputy editor had locked it from the inside. He phoned me, "Nik-Nik should see you taking good care of him. Invent a reason to abandon the blind for a couple of hours, and we'll take the old swine home."

Polyakov lived at 26 Kutuzov Avenue, the address of the highest ranks of the Party. The police would not let me in, and Tom planned to drop me off at the entrance gate and pick me up on his way out of the heavily guarded compound. "We cannot repeat this grave political mistake," he said.

"What mistake?"

"One time I let him out, and he went straight to the sacred entrance designed exclusively for Politburo members Brezhnev and Andropov. The guards luckily put him in the right elevator."

"Lucky for him! So for two years you were the right hand of this boozer?"

"Yes—yes, to get this friend of mine Arkady Polishchuk out of shit, I'm trying to send Nik-Nik to hell ahead of time. High blood pressure."

A portrait of Bobojon Ghafurov (1908–1977) and his book *Tojikon* (*The History of Tajik People*) on a fifty somoni bill issued in 1999 by the National Bank of Tajikistan in honor of the 90th anniversary of Ghafurov's birth. (National Bank of Tajikistan)

In 1956 Khrushchev had arranged his modest purge of some of "Stalin's falcons," and both of my future bosses, Polyakov and Ghafurov, were sent to live out their days in honorable and well paid internal exile. Three years after Stalin's death, shared fate brought them together. Bobojon Ghafurovich Ghafurov, former first secretary of Tajikistan's Communist Party, became director of the Institute of Asia and Africa and editor-in-chief of its publication *Asia and Africa Today*. His once-a-month duty was to sign the next issue of the magazine that he had never read—"Bobo" was busy with more serious matters. (We called him Bobo, but only behind his back.)

For twenty years, the very name of this lame runt shook the mountains on the border between the Soviet Union, China and Afghanistan. Now it made tremble just the Institute, which had only six hundred Party members. The Party still needed Ghafurov's ethnicity, instincts, and expertise for the implementation of the Russian policy in the East: born in a mountain Tajik village, an author of several books on the history of Tajikistan, and a full member of the Academy of Sciences—not every senior Party worker could boast of such a biography. Nevertheless, none of these achievements could've helped him to preserve his main instrument of power if he had not also been a protégée of the leader of the USSR, Nikita Khrushchev. For this reason only, he remained a member of the Central Committee. This new position also made him the informal Moscow representative of the first secretaries of all the Central Asian republics.

When Tom brought me to his office lined with Persian rugs, Bobo said in his quiet manner that the magazine needed good journalists capable of editing clumsy scholarly writings. Then he apologized for being very busy and listlessly shook my hand goodbye. When we returned to the huge hall, Tom said, "Did you understand our Sultan? You were given a job that includes writing his books and articles."

"He speaks in broken Russian."

"All his books have been written in Russian and after that translated into Tajik. He's a Tajik, not a Jew, and he doesn't need to be able to speak, much less, to write in any language."

"How did Ghafurov and Polyakov react to your upcoming move to *Pravda*?"

"Nik-Nik almost shed tears when he saw my first tiny piece in *Pravda*. As soon as you, Alik, begin writing for *Pravda*, for The Truth," Tom solemnly raised his finger to the sky and then pointed it toward my chest, "you'll begin receiving love letters from the Supreme Ruler who kicked you out of his Kostroma principality."

"Fred Solyanov was right," I said. "As a stagehand in his theater, I'd have greater self-respect."

"Are you joking? You're born a journalist and would've died of boredom and misery in that theater. Don't you know—all of our theaters, inscriptions on the walls, songs and textbooks for first-graders—are part of the same propaganda machine? You better keep in mind, Nik-Nik will constantly check whether you've read the latest issue of *Pravda*. This is his favorite morning exercise. It gives him undeniable authority."

By the time *Pravda* published my first freelance article not long after this conversation, Tom and Irina declared me a bummer and laughed it off when I named all the blacklisted writers who did not produce anything for years, or like our friend Gena Snegiryov, turned to writing for children. Talking with them about the regime was pointless. It was our world, our universe, beyond which was eternal emptiness.

A couple of years later, in 1962, I pulled a dirty trick. When Tom handed me an honorary certificate on the occasion of the sixtieth anniversary of *Pravda*, I placed on his desk a satire about a celebration of this Soviet Press Day in a Congolese village. A made-up *Pravda* correspondent described the event in detail. Drunk out of his mind, the correspondent did not cut out of his report one sentence that revealed none of the villagers actually knew of the existence of the Soviet Union. The head of *Pravda*'s foreign department saw it as just a bug which, in order to avoid political disaster, needed to be fixed. He did, and the report was published.

Tom was resolutely tearing my gem into small pieces when Yevgeny Primakov, my new *Pravda* friend, entered the room, "My congratulations to our awardee!"

"Alik continues to misbehave," said my buddy.

"Don't be so cruel," roared Primakov with a charming Georgian accent. "Let me read it."

"No," I said, "Tom is right. I behave like a schoolgirl in a brothel; she wants to make some money, but is determined to remain a virgin."

DESPITE MY IMPROPER ATTITUDE, my career advancement continued. It was helped along in 1963 by the political error of our managing editor at *Asia and Africa Today*, Simon Verbitsky, who got the position after Tom had moved to *Pravda*. Simon had edited an article written by Professor Boris Sapozhnikov on an innocent subject about the tribes of the tiny mountain kingdom of Bhutan, which unfortunately had a common border with China. In our special repository for foreign publications and the TASS reports not intended for the general public, the professor found an appropriate sketch of Bhutan's boundaries. The chart, copied with tracing paper, went to our censor and eventually was published with Sapozhnikov's article. This is where a censor of higher rank initiated a huge scandal. He phoned Nik-Nik and ordered him to destroy all copies of this issue. The watchful censor was able to see on the faded image almost invisible dotted lines indicating China's territorial claims to the Russian boundaries. Such was a brazen display of the new imperial attitude of Chairman Mao Zedong, whose timidity had disappeared after Stalin's death.

Ghafurov immediately summoned all guilty parties. An hour later, Simon told me about the melodrama that had played out on the expensive Persian rug: "Congratulations! You and I are interchangeable," he said to me. "Thou shalt become managing editor while I go back to supervise your information department."

But I was expecting even worse for Simon, given what was happening on the border. It was the period of Beijing's "cartographic aggression." Chinese maps, atlases and textbooks kept including areas under the jurisdiction of the USSR as being part of China. The "aggression" began with an uninhabited area in the Pamir plateau and several small areas in the Far East, including two uninhabited river islands near Khabarovsk City. These borders had been drawn more than a hundred years ago by the expanding Russian Empire, and now Mao wanted to demonstrate his contempt for Khrushchev's weakness and unscrupulousness toward the West. In the corridors of our Institute, normally reserved experts on China discussed which Russian territories Mao might tomorrow declare as his own. Universal opinion fully coincided with the opinion in the corridors of the Central Committee—we should dress them down harder.

Right at Ghafurov's door, Polyakov had said that Simon should be fired and the question of his Party membership must be immediately addressed.

"No need to rush," Bobo had retorted—Simon mimicked the favorite soothing gesture of Ghafurov when resolving difficult situations—"I'll talk to the comrades in the Central Committee. Only a man with a magnifying glass in his hand could make out this map."

Then Ghafurov had revealed what we did not know about the author of the article in question. "Tell me, Comrade Sapozhnikov, how could you, a former deputy head of the Special Propaganda Department of the Red Army, make this mistake?"

Sapozhnikov had stuttered that he knew that border inside out and had been crawling on those moors and hills on his belly long before the battle with the Japanese at Lake Khasan. Ghafurov returned a smile. "For that fighting in 1938 you got an order, and your chief Vasyli Blukher was shot several months later. I think the Institute's Party Committee should discuss this map incident and take appropriate action."

It meant that Sapozhnikov's case had been soft-pedaled and most likely even closed. Fortunately for the participants of this melodrama, it was still a number of months before Mao's inflammatory statement that Russia had stripped China of vast territories. Playful fate saved the professor and Simon from brutal punishment.

The following ten years, until my rebellion in 1973, I worked at *Asia and Africa Today* as the managing editor.

Soon I saw firsthand how important a place Ghafurov occupied in the impressionable hearts of the powerful first secretaries of the Asian republics, who were all members of the Central Committee. Our magazine was gaining strength and in addition to being an organ of the Academy of Sciences, became an organ of the Committee for Friendship with the Peoples of Asia and Africa. Thus, our editorial team found itself in the front ranks of fighters for world peace, but this political success had no effect on the circulation of the monthly, and Ghafurov decided to send me on a promotional mission to Dushanbe, the capital of his former fiefdom, Tajikistan. The importance of this visit to a small republic was not clear to me. However, Michael Kurgantsev, the head of the magazine's culture department and Ghafurov's leading ghostwriter, understood and instructed me: "Bobojon Ghafurovich asks you to stay away from local political games, even if your hosts try to draw you into them. Everyone will think that you're his envoy, so you should strongly deny this."

"What if they don't believe me?" I said.

"Don't drink with them, don't mess with their women and do not take bribes."

"You doom me to complete stagnation."

Upon returning home, I spoke at an editorial briefing about my presentations, first of all, at the republican Central Committee. Nik-Nik immediately asked if Comrade Rasulov had attended the meeting.

"The Second Secretary introduced me," I said, "and mentioned that the pride of the Tajik people and the greatest scientist of the USSR, Bobojon Gahfurovich Ghafurov, had sent me to Dushanbe to brief the republican leadership on the current international situation."

"Did you sit next to him?" jeered Vlad S., the head of the book review department and secretary of our Party cell. He obviously had spent his lunch hour well, but we were holding this little secret sacred; after all, no one so far returned from lunch on all fours.

Our team of fifteen men and women had no informers, except for Polyakov himself, of course, who couldn't publicly imagine any deviation from the Party norms of decency under his leadership.

"Yep," I said. "I even addressed my words directly to him."

"You did the right thing," Polyakov said, complimenting me.

"My greatest achievement was my sixty-minute solo presentation on Tajik television."

All of them gasped. "Sixty minutes!?"

"One short call from the republican Central Committee did it," explained Polyakov to this band of naifs.

"Rightly noted," I said. "The charming TV presenter just informed the viewers that instead of some worthless movie they would admire me."

"Was she really pretty?" Vlad S. asked sternly.

"I don't know," was my almost sincere response. "I looked at my thousands-strong audience."

"Lucky you, you didn't hear their remarks," he said.

"Did they like your lecture at the KGB headquarters?" asked Nik-Nik.

"Very much so, Nikolai Nikolayevich. Otherwise, I wouldn't be here now."

He ignored my stupid joke. "Where else did you speak?"

"At a gathering of local journalists and at a huge collective farm."

"Cotton growers?"

"Yes, sir."

"What did you tell them?" asked Vlad S.

"Exactly what I told the KGB."

It was the gospel truth. The KGB and party officials have always believed that what Moscow lecturers were telling them was classified stuff intended only for the initiated. They would call it nonsense if some informant told them that farmers, workers, students, local lecturers and journalists were getting the same "inside story" about the moves and habits of some African and Arab politicians. That's why I preferred lectures to closely controlled writing. In the lectures you could avoid some official lies and have more fun.

"Tell us whether the cotton growers speak Russian or not?" asked our Party secretary.

"No idea," I said. "What's the difference?"

"Soviet cotton farmers are our national pride!" Nik-Nik said, and repeated another well-known slogan from *Pravda*, "Cotton is the white gold of the Soviet Union!"

I reminded my audience of our childhood heroine Mamlakat, an eleven-year-old girl, whom Stalin had awarded the Order of Lenin after she learned to pick cotton with both hands. I had seen two pregnant women in the field who worked with both hands and could hardly resist the temptation to ask Polyakov if all the other women and children were unaware of the very existence of their second hands.

Fortunately, he asked, "Did you read *Pravda* there every day?" but suddenly hurried somewhere without waiting for my answer. Everybody knew where he went: this apparatchik went to Ghafurov to report immediately of our success in Tajikistan. And I said to the door which slammed shut behind him, "No, Nicholai Nikolayevich, I read the newspaper *Pravda* Tajikistana in the Tajik language."

Vlad, choking with laughter, began to slide under his desk.

I revealed details intended just for Ghafurov only when Vlad, Simon, and Ghafurov's ghostwriter, Michael Kurgantsev, remained in the room: in the evening, while having tea on the hotel's veranda, I was approached by the son of Tursun Uldzhabaev who was seated on the vacant throne of the first secretary of the Party now that Bobo had been sent to Moscow. The son, in prosecutor's uniform, nervously looked around, pitifully stared in my eye and half-whispered, "My father—a true communist—a disciple of Bobojon

Ghafurovich; he didn't do anything wrong. Dishonest people framed him."

His daddy had been expelled from the Party two years before, and since then he had been a chairman of a cotton-growing farm. I told the young prosecutor that I didn't know a thing about Tajikistan, never before had visited a cotton collective farm, and could not do anything for him.

"Oh no! You can help! You're a very intelligent and tactful person. That's why you talk about cotton. Please tell Bobojon Ghafurovich," he had pleaded, "that my father physically cannot live without the Party."

The explanation came after the Soviet Union's collapse, in declassified documents of the 1961 Central Committee's Plenary Session. The senior Uldzhabaev was guilty of "systematic falsification of accounting documents. The sale of cotton reported by him was fully falsified; these plans were never fulfilled."

A quarter-century after he was framed, Uldzhabaev was reinstated in the Party, most probably, with the blessings of liberal Michael Gorbachev, the last ruler of the USSR. Nobody could have foreseen the poor timing. Soon it became more fashionable for leaders of the Party to turn overnight into true Muslims and Orthodox Christians.

SHORTLY I WAS IN Central Asia again. My wife and I arrived in Tashkent armed to the teeth—in my briefcase lay Ghafurov's sealed letter to Sharaf Rashidov, the first secretary of the Uzbekistan's Communist Party. All I knew was that it contained a personal request to help in the dissemination of our magazine in the republic with the third largest population in the country.

I had never met a more beautiful and gentle man. He said in a soft voice, "Please tell Bobojon Ghafurovich that I appreciate his work and we'll do everything in our power to promote your esteemed journal. My assistant"—he nodded toward the smiling man standing at the door—"will do all that's necessary."

The impeccably polite assistant had already wished Irina, who was waiting for me in the reception area, a good time in Tashkent while her husband was busy with manly chores. My wife told him that she was struck by the faded bunches of grapes at the local farmers' market. The grapes, stored in flat wooden boxes and richly covered with sawdust, survived for many months, until the spring. We could only dream of grapes in still-snowy Moscow.

After that small talk, Irina dealt him a blow below the belt by suggesting that his Uzbek language was probably perfect. He spread his hands, "Alas, there was no time to learn."

She continued her provocation by suggesting that he probably read all novels written by Comrade Rashidov.

"Of course, I did," the assistant said. "In Russian. He's a prolific novelist and a winner of multiple literary state prizes."

Irina wondered how such a hard working statesman could find time for writing.

"He's a genius," said the assistant.

This meant to me that Rashidov had more ghostwriters than Ghafurov.

Typically, in all fifteen Soviet republics and their major cities, the first secretaries represented the main local ethnic group. Ethnic Russians had always been the second secretaries, their right hands. Not so in Tashkent. Here this Russian first secretary with his sleeves rolled up showing his powerful hairy forearms, was a God and a sultan. After I had expressed a desire to meet with the local intelligentsia, he summoned one of his aides. "Bring the lists of our intelligentsia," said the secretary without using the word "please."

I could not help asking, "The lists? In the fourth largest Soviet city?"

"Yes, we keep a hand on the pulse," the secretary graciously smiled. "Who do you prefer—engineering, humanitarian, or creative intelligentsia?"

I preferred our readers and those who were interested in the problems of the Third World.

"Will do," the secretary said resolutely.

"Realistically," I asked, "when will it be possible to meet with our audience?"

He looked at me kindly. "Realistically," he said, savoring the word, "they can be rounded up quickly."

Soon three weighty folders were there before the secretary, one on top of the other. He laid both hands on the folders and asked the question that made me shudder. Party leaders and secret police officials had been asking this question over the many years of Stalin's rule. They did it throughout the country, upon receiving Moscow's quotas for catching spies, saboteurs, and traitors.

He said, "Whom should we take?"

For an average citizen this question had only one meaning, "Whom should we arrest?"

In the evening, in the hotel, I still wondered how many times in the past Tashkent's first secretary had asked this perennial question. Irina preferred to talk about beautifully coiffed pyramids made of small, smooth stones in our corridor restroom. A day later, there appeared a bucket of water, where these stones had to be thrown upon the conclusion of the procedure. With a cry "Historical progress! Glory to the Party!" Irina ran into our room with a question, "Why don't they cut neat squares of your favorite newspaper?"

"Do you want the citizens to wipe their bottoms with their leaders' portraits right here, in a public place?" was my counter-question. "A list of these assholes would end up on the desktop of the First Secretary."

As far as I remember, toilet paper appeared in the Soviet Union about the same year that two Americans walked on the Moon.

I had long been in the West when the whole country saw the portrait of First Secretary Rashidov of Uzbekistan in a mourning frame and read of the sudden death from a heart attack of this "prominent leader of the Party and the Soviet state." Half a year later, in the summer of 1984, his cotton scam was exposed. A plenary session of the Uzbek Communist Party was held. All speakers, including secretary of the USSR's Communist Party, Yegor Ligachev, exposed Rashidov as a corrupt despot who created a land of servility, sycophancy, and cronyism. The session unanimously decided to exhume his remains from a memorial erected in the center of Tashkent and rebury them in his village cemetery.

Uldzhabaev's offense in small Tajikistan looked like a childish prank compared to Rashidov's armed robbery of the gold reserves of the country. Every year Tashkent reported to Moscow a cotton harvest of three million tons. In reality it was a million and a half at best. In political circles everyone believed that the former head of the KGB, Yuri Andropov, at that time secretary general, "advised" Rashidov to commit suicide.

FOUR

What to Do If You Know Many Russian Spies

B EFORE ENTERING our large editorial room, the fellow knocked at the door. He looked like a soldier who recently completed his service.

"I am Evgeni Biryukov," he said and ceremoniously shook hands with his new colleagues.

No one expressed the slightest surprise. The mousetrap has slammed shut, I thought; you'll never get out of it. Nik-Nik had already informed us that from now on *Asia and Africa Today* would have a network of foreign correspondents and our duty was to help them. He did not mention their true boss—the KGB. Our editorial staff was happy—with such colleagues no one would dare close our magazine.

"This desk is yours," I said, pointing to a stack of our magazine's issues. "Start reading. If you have any questions, ask."

Evgeni Biryukov did it diligently all day long, wrote something in his notebook, and did not ask a single question. I had no doubt, he had read it all before at the KGB headquarters.

The next day Biryukov, our first correspondent to Tanzania, watched with interest as our art director and I put together the layout of a future issue. At the same time, I gently tried to find out what he knew about the country of his destination and whether he could for starters send us a photo essay about Dar es Salaam, the capital of the young republic. After all, he was trained to take pictures of military facilities.

"Do you have a good camera?" I asked.

He hesitated, apparently assuming that I was meddling in affairs that were none of my damn business. Then he understood the ridiculousness of the situation and said, "Of course." Every Soviet child who read Soviet books and watched Soviet movies knew that spies had excellent cameras.

Biryukov clearly believed that a photo essay did not require the ability to write.

"Just don't take pictures of savage rites," I explained. "Personally, I'm not against them, but the sensitive censors won't approve of it."

"What kind of rituals?"

"Like the cutting or removal of external female genitalia with broken glass," I said, trying to throw him off-balance.

He winced.

"It would be even better to write about the socialist ideas of President Nyerere." I did not smile. "Interview him and ask which rural cooperatives he would suggest you visit. He'd love such a question."

To my delight, Biryukov knew something about Nyerere's form of African socialism based on cooperative agriculture. I asked if he had ever visited Russian collective farms. He said, "I was born on one."

It seemed to me that Biryukov regretted having said that, either because he betrayed a state secret, or because he lied. I smirked inappropriately. "Maybe Julius Nyerere should have to first get to know our collective farms' instructive experience. This might lead to some amendments to his socialist ideas."

Nothing changed in our correspondent's face. I needed to learn from him how to do that.

When he asked if we could help him with his article, I was delighted with his frankness and explained that the main thing for him was to write something that we were unable to see or hear. I promised to edit his stuff so that even he wouldn't believe what a great writer he was. Biryukov was happy.

Over three years he wrote a half-dozen stories, for which my schoolteacher would have given him a failing grade. But we made them readable. After all, they were signed by our correspondent in East Africa, and this made us look much better.

The word was that before Evgeni Biryukov disappeared back into his underworld, he was awarded a military decoration for his work in Tanzania.

Western secret services could not have ignored the fact that our not-very-important publication with its scrawny budget all of a sudden decided to have expensive foreign correspondents. But nevertheless, the KGB was careful. Our correspondents' KGB bosses never came into direct contact with us. Yet, when their handlers were displeased with deathly silence of their boys, somebody from the Central Committee called with the same request: "Help your colleague." Once or two times a year, they would stay in our editorial room for a week. The new colleagues had nothing to do at the office, but they stayed with us instead of vacationing somewhere at a Black Sea resort. It was part of their game.

So, it became a routine—someone from the International Department of the Party Central Committee would notify the editor-in-chief or his deputy, or me on the phone, "Tomorrow a correspondent in such-and-such country will join your staff. Please help him." After correcting grammatical mistakes, we would publish their trash. No one twisted our arms. But for some of their writings I wanted to kill them—there would have been a lesser threat to our heroic scouts from James Bond.

Constantine Geyvandov was our second correspondent and quite logically worked on the other side of the continent, in Nigeria, its most populous country. Unlike the others, he was a journalist and a likeable guy. We had common friends, and during his vacation he expertly baked legs of lamb for some of us: Tom, now a *Pravda* correspondent in Western Africa; Primakov, when he wasn't in the Arab world working for *Pravda*; and for me.

Constantine would have taken part in our New Year's Eve party in 1966, but he was in Nigeria. At the table were three *Pravda* reporters—my bosom buddy Tom Kolesnichenko; Yevgeny Primakov; Vitaly Zhurkin, correspondent in India; and Victor Kudryavtsev, Moscow Radio correspondent in Egypt—all of them rising stars in their mid-thirties. Primakov also brought with him the top radio commentator Valentin Zorin, known for his tireless bashing of American imperialism.

At first, we celebrated this most popular holiday in full compliance with the long-established tradition. We saw off the old year, were having a good time, drinking wine and watching the best performers of the country. Five minutes before midnight, we listened to General Secretary Brezhnev, who, keeping in mind the apolitical nature of the event, only briefly mentioned in his televised address the many achievements of our country, the shining example for the entire world.

Immediately after that, Kremlin Spasskaya Tower with its gleaming red star appeared on the screen, and holding up another glass of wine, we counted down with the deep strikes of its clock. With the last one it was every Russian's duty to instantly empty his or her glass.

The unexpected happened after this ritual. Valentin Zorin assumed a solemn air and proposed a toast to the health and leadership of Leonid Ilyich Brezhnev. Tom kicked me right away under the table and eagerly expressed his compassion, "Did you hurt yourself?"

I produced a noisy "Ouch!" and "Yes, you..."

In fact, I was entertained. Everybody else stood up with their glasses in hand and looked our direction expecting more inappropriate jokes, except Zorin, who did not belong to our little gang and looked at me with suspicion. Tom, with awfully strenuous effort, helped me to rise, and everybody drank to Brezhnev's health. My hand was trembling from "pain," and a good part of my liquor went into a nearby crystal vase with flowers.

Primakov rumbled leisurely, "Alik, you didn't need to stand up."

I said, "None of us needs to stand up—Comrade Brezhnev wouldn't feel offended; to my great regret, he isn't at this table."

Primakov's wife Laura let out a giggle.

I peered at the New Year fir tree in the corner of the room and mused, "It looks so shamefully apolitical with its toys, garlands of bulbs, candles, ornaments, and candies." Then I whispered to Laura, "Next time, let's hang all Politburo members, I mean, their photos, on the tree."

She giggled again.

After moving to a sofa, I asked her husband, in a low voice, "Why did he go on like that?"

"To help advance his career," was the answer.

"But who would inform the KGB or Brezhnev of such sincere affection?"

"Zorin believes all of us have good connections."

"Am I also a suspect? Doesn't he know that you guys are pushing this Jew up this shaky ladder?"

"For him it might mean that you have the most powerful connections," Primakov said, chuckling. "Otherwise you wouldn't be present at this party, wouldn't be published in *Pravda* and the *Izvestia*, and wouldn't be able to appear on Central TV."

"But the guy is half-Jewish himself!"

"The more you talk about Jews, the more suspicious Zorin will become."

"Zhenya," I said, using Primakov's nickname, "do you suspect me of being a Zionist sympathizer?"

"I just want you to be more objective," he said. "You do know, I criticize you only in our narrow circle of friends. That's a sort of a preventive measure. Stop being so emotional, I will always fight against both—anti-Semitism and Zionism."

Tom joined us on the couch and put his arm around me.

"Zhenya," I prodded, chuckling, "what if the Zionists became our best friends?"

He burst into laughter. "I thought you were smarter."

"Do you remember who brought Israel into existence?" I asked.

"I certainly do."

"Do you remember how Stalin and more than a dozen countries who loved him dearly, unanimously voted in the UN for the establishment of the Jewish state in 1948?"

"So what?" Primakov asked.

"Do you remember why we were so supportive of Zionists?"

"Sure. Stalin wanted to make Israel a communist outpost in the Middle East."

"If his dream had come true, you would've reported today from Jerusalem about the righteous struggle of our ideological brothers in Israel for the liberation of the ancestral Israeli territories to the east of the very Jewish Jordan River."

Now Tom burst out laughing at this scenario.

Primakov shook his head. "Such jokes, if overheard by unfriendly ears, can be misinterpreted," he said. "I don't know why my Georgian wife likes you so much. Anyway, why are you so aggressive tonight?"

"Georgians are smart," I stated.

left: Yevgeny Primakov when he was Director of the Russian Central Intelligence Service. December 1991. (Russian International News Agency). *right:* Valentin Zorin receiving the Order of Alexander Nevsky from Vladimir Putin for his many years of service to Russia as a journalist and "Americanist." May 21, 2015. (Kremlin)

A little irritated, he continued, smiling through his teeth, "Can't we talk of something more romantic on this beautiful New Year's night?"

"Sure," I said. "Thanks to Zorin, I ruined the roses in that vase."

"The hell with the roses," said Tom. "You wasted a good Italian wine, and we're well aware that you've done it on behalf of the Elders of Zion."

At that time only Tom knew that I was thinking of ending my career. One time he said to me, "Don't forget, you know more than a dozen spies working abroad. A dozen! If you make a stupid move, you might just drown in the Moscow River, or die in a car accident."

"Don't worry," I said, laughing it off, "I hate swimming and don't have a car."

I would've fallen off the couch with a roar if someone at

that party had foretold the future of our friend and *Pravda* correspondent Yevgeny Primakov: in a quarter of a century—the first deputy director of the KGB; after the collapse of the Soviet Union—the head of the Russian spy agency; and later, in 1998—the prime minister of new Russia.[2]

---

2 The latest news about Primakov came to me in early February 2018: "In Moscow, a monument to the former Minister of Foreign Affairs and the Chairman of the Government of Russia, Yevgeny Primakov, will be installed. This decision was unanimously adopted by the Moscow City Duma Commission for monumental art," reports Interfax. "The monument will be installed in the Smolenskaya-Sennaya square in the center of the city, opposite the Foreign Ministry building."

FIVE

My Good Friends in the KGB

M Y MEMORY ONLY ALLOWS me to mention by name three KGB correspondents who benefited the magazine more than others—the charming Constantine Geyvandov, the brilliant Vladimir Savelyev, and Cyril Karpovich who became our Nigerian correspondent after Constantine turned into a *Pravda* correspondent, first in Lebanon and later, in Canada.

Following the awarding of the Nobel Prize to Alexander Solzhenitsyn, the author of *The Gulag Archipelago*, the outraged Cyril Karpovich said, "I would've hung up this enemy with my own hands!"

Everyone in our editorial room understood how dangerous Karpovich was, so we said nothing. Once, Polyakov, our deputy editor, asked him if he has seen a *Pravda* article about Americans spying in Nigeria. Karpovich glanced at a *Pravda* copy in Polyakov's hand, "Yes, I read the original piece in a Nigerian newspaper. The country is full of American spies."

"Are you familiar with the author?" I asked.

"Yes, he's a Marxist," he said. "We met in Lagos." I asked Karpovich to book this Nigerian for a larger article on the same topic of American espionage in Africa. It was obvious that the author would not be able to elaborate on the subject, but Polyakov swallowed the bait and said, "Yes, Cyril, that would be very useful

Asia and Africa Today as guests of Monino Military Academy near Moscow. 1963. This institution was always particularly important. The future commanders from two dozen communist and Arab countries studied in it, and the Academy worked in close contact with the nearby Star City, where the future Russian cosmonauts were trained.

left to right: Constantine Geyvandov, our KGB correspondent in Nigeria; Simon Verbitsky, the head of the information department; Vlad "S.," the head of our book reviews department, and me.

to return to this subject again with a more detailed article."

In the room also sat our freelancer, an Arabist by training and a seasoned journalist. During our conversation a smile wandered over his face. After the deputy editor left the room, he said, "Arkady, let's go to the canteen for a cup of tea. I want to discuss with you some problems in my troublesome life."

Cyril smiled understandingly. A minute later the Arabist and I were sitting alone at a table.

"What's up?" I asked.

"I wrote that article," he said, "and didn't want to say it in Cyril's presence, since his father is the head of the APN's personnel department."

The bloody war in Angola. My buddy and *Pravda* correspondent in Africa, Tom Kolesnichenko, posing as a tired Communist rebel next to the real one. What a good joke for his friends in Moscow!

"The Novosti Press Agency should be proud of you," I said solemnly.

"The son of this KGB general could decide that I was divulging state secrets."

In accordance with its charter, the news agency APN intended to "spread abroad the truth." Sixty newspapers and magazines were doing this difficult job in forty-five languages in more than one hundred and twenty countries. That is why, after many failures, the KGB's successor, the post-Soviet Federal Security Service (FSB), allowed the Russian Wikipedia to make this delicate understatement: "In Soviet times, using the status of a journalist, intelligence officers sometimes worked at this news agency." That was unique openness. Such candor can be compared only with that shown in one of the post-Soviet interviews with Yevgeny Primakov. The nostalgic Yevgeny allowed himself to share with humanity a touching fact of his younger life—that he and our buddy Constantine Geyvandov drank cheap wine as students at the Institute of Oriental Studies. This bold revelation reminded me of the gigantic bottle of whiskey, nearly impossible to lift from the floor, that Primakov brought home from a long foreign assignment. To see such a vessel for the first time was a discovery of immense proportions equal to seeing a genie in a bottle.

Detractors suspected Primakov of trying to cover up his Jewish origins with Georgian hospitality and a heavy Georgian accent. They ignored the simple fact that he had grown up in Georgia. I knew his Jewish mother. He never knew his father, but, judging by the very fact that in 1949, the year of virulent official anti-Semitism, this nineteen-year-old youth was accepted by the Institute of Oriental Studies, it must have been that the most important line of his internal passport (Line #5) identified him as an ethnic Russian. Had he been born twenty years later, it would not have protected his career from being ruined and he might still be living in Tbilisi speaking with a Georgian accent. Destiny plays with mortals. When a quarter of a century after Hitler's suicide in his bunker, Primakov's son Sasha (Alexander) was taking the entrance exams at the Institute of International Relations, the applicants had to fill out a form indicating the ethnic backgrounds of both parents. Fortunately, Primakov's wife Laura was a Georgian in good standing.

OUR CORRESPONDENT in East Africa, Vladimir Savelyev and I liked to walk together in the long hallway of our historic building. When I told him about Karpovich's burning desire to hang the author of *The Gulag Archipelago*, he frowned, but did not say a word.

"In some institutions," I said, "Stalin is still the idol of the crowd."

"Somehow it helps to build a career. But after Khrushchev's speech in 1956 about the 'cult of personality' some Stalinists lost their jobs."

"They can be counted on the fingers of one hand," I said. "I know three such beauties; two of them you know as well. It's our Ghafurov and Polyakov."

"Interesting. And the third?"

"A former KGB lieutenant-general. He was in command of hard labor camps throughout the Far East and North East. His son told me that when his dad rode a white thoroughbred by a column of prisoners, they had to go down on their knees—in the mud and snow."

"What's his name?"

"Sorry, it's not a secret, but I don't feel comfortable giving it to you without his son's permission. We were eighth graders and goofed around together, and then all of a sudden he was gone. Many years later when he entered Tom Kolesnichenko's office at *Pravda*, we instantly recognized each other."

"You are a loyal friend," Vladimir said.

"What else do we have in this life?"

"What do you think of Kolesnichenko?"

"I love him."

He repeated, "You are a loyal friend."

The corridors of the Institute of the Peoples of Asia were a very special place. There could be seen Turks, among them, the great poet Nazim Hikmet; Egyptians, Syrians, Iraqis, numerous

Palestinians, and Kurds. One of them, a charming and cultivated man who wrote well in Russian, told me that he had recently been elected president of the Kurdish Academy of Sciences in exile and was going to live closer to home, in Baku, the capital of Azerbaijan.

"What country do you consider as yours?" I asked.

"We're like the Jews," he said. "Our country was taken from us and divided among our neighbors. We are therefore hated by everyone who took our land. My family fled to Europe from Iraq, and I got my education in Holland and France."

"Then you are a French communist."

"And a Kurdish nationalist."

I told Vladimir Savelyev about this conversation and asked him not to share it with his colleagues.

"This is what we call a national liberation movement," he said. "Sometimes our agendas differ with these communists from the Middle East."

"I simply cannot imagine this decent person manipulated by anyone," I said.

After reading a couple of my book reviews in Foreign Literature, he asked why I wrote so seldom.

"There's less politics in those African novels," I said.

"It's good that Karpovich did not hear your answer," he said with a smirk.

During another one of our corridor walks, I nodded at an unusually broad-shouldered man with the sad eyes of an intelligent saint.

"It's an Iranian general," I said, "one of the officers—conspirators who escaped execution by the Shah. They're all communists from the Tudeh party."

"I marvel," Vladimir said, "what these Marxist-Leninists think now of the Soviet Union."

At that moment a carefully dressed man quickly walked past us.

"This one I love the most," I said.

"Azerbaijani?" asked Vladimir.

"And a very religious one. He has just made a pilgrimage to Mecca. I didn't know that a Soviet citizen could perform the Hajj."

"Quite young," said Vladimir thoughtfully.

"He visited Mecca with a fake beard," I said, chuckling. "Let's go to the canteen, we might see him consuming his favorite food."

When we entered the canteen, our Hajji was wolfing down a pork chop.

"Poor man," I said, chuckling, "he missed it badly in Mecca."

"He has a very important job," Vladimir said. "Just imagine that someday some Muslim dictator will make an atomic bomb."

He was surprised that I had a Russian-language Koran and wanted to read it. It was published by our publishing house, and my copy had its limited edition number. The Party's Central Committee allowed it to be translated, but before publishing the revelations of Allah to Muhammad, it approved a list of highly qualified recipients of divine truth; no Muslims were on that list, only some Party officials, scholars, and journalists. In strict accordance with this roll call, the exact number of copies was issued. I was among the chosen.

Vladimir liked my remark. "That was a bold decision of our Party," he said. "I hope that soon they decide to publish the Bible."

One time I returned from Polyakov's office and Nickolas Laane, another correspondent with whom I had friendly relations, asked, "Are you okay? You look sick."

"I've just been asked to participate in writing the denunciation of an innocent fool," I said.

"Big deal!" said our slightly tipsy Party Secretary Vlad S. "This is still a popular literary genre. People make a good career. Just do it."

"I managed to avoid this disaster."

"How?" asked Nickolas.

"I don't want to draw our chaste correspondents into our dirty affairs," I said.

"Well, really, tell me!" pleaded Nickolas Laane. "I won't sell you out."

I gave it up. "Polyakov wanted to accuse someone of bourgeois nationalism and I, without batting an eye, told the jerk that it would be dangerous because the Tatar was to take a job at the Party's Central Committee."

To my delight, our correspondent laughed until he started hiccupping.

What happened was that I had speared an article by this Tatar, and to entertain my colleagues, was reading aloud a couple of illiterate sentences from it when Polyakov entered the room. He learned who the author was, and with his fierce face expressing delight, he took the manuscript and told me to drop by. In an hour he said, "We are obliged to inform the Party about this ideologically harmful article written by a spiteful nationalist."

The episode seemed to have awakened Polyakov's sweet memories of his power in the fight against nationalism in the Soviet republics. He told me that when Latvia joined the USSR, the Party had appointed him chief editor of the Latvian republican newspaper and that its managing editor, a Jew, helped him expose Latvian nationalists in every single issue of the paper. And here I was—another Jew, another managing editor. But Polyakov was more secretive than even our foreign correspondents. Not wanting to upset this naturally taciturn man, I did not even ask my boss whether his exposés occurred during the short period of Soviet occupation before the war or immediately afterward. Most certainly the next step after exposing nationalists was arresting and sending them to the Gulag.

"Perhaps it was dangerous," I suggested. "After all, you could've been killed in the street."

"Times were hard, but we did a good job," he confessed. "To tell you the truth, between us, I was given a pistol."

After the collapse of the Soviet Union, I found Polyakov's name in the documents and articles about the plans to deport all Soviet Jews to the Far East. According to these materials, he had been the executive secretary of the committee created by Stalin to prepare this deportation. The very existence of such committee has been disputed. An anonymous author even claimed that he interviewed N.N. Polyakov about these plans shortly before his death. It was hard to believe that such an interview had indeed taken place. The former senior staff member of the Central Committee N.N. Polyakov who I knew was not capable of remorse and lived in complete harmony with his conscience.

I keep asking myself questions to which I have no clear answers. Did he think that his "openness" could help to cover up his participation in Stalin's plan to kill all of us? A dozen years later, did he want to show that he had had friends among Jews? And again, I vividly recall that late night of October 1952 and my father's trembling hand pushing away a plate of untouched food. He told us about the eviction of one hundred Jewish families from suburban Davidkovo where Stalin's favorite villa was located. He had just visited his friends there. His voice broke, "It could be merely a trial balloon."

At that time the police stopped many Jews in the streets, but they never stopped me. If Stalin had not died on March 5, 1953, in Davidkovo, I would have definitely been a good deal better informed of my fate.

SIX

The Struggle for Purity in the Party Ranks

T OM WAS STAYING overnight at my place when the phone woke us up. My wife had recently left me for another man, but occasionally she still called me. Our conversation was short, and I did not mention her name but Tom immediately said, "That was her."

"Yes," I said. "Good night."

"What did she want?"

"Nothing. Just asked if I had matches."

"In the middle of the night? From the other end of Moscow?"

I said, "Good night!"

"Was she drunk?"

"Good night. It sounded like it."

"Did she want to come here?"

"How would I know? I wouldn't allow it anyway. I think."

After a few minutes of silence, he said, "I know how to get back at her."

"Go to hell!" I said.

"It's good that I helped you obtain the rare privilege of traveling to West Africa. Your return home serves as direct proof of your loyalty to your Motherland."

"Stepmother-land."

"We'll make you deputy managing editor of *Pravda*. You'll have money, status, and an editorial dacha in Silver Wood."

"She doesn't need your shitty cottage. Her father already has his own."

But it was impossible to stop him, "It's a damn hard and thankless position. No good reporter of our paper would want it, but I'll try to convince the top brass that we need one exemplary Jew. In the West they call us an anti-Semitic paper."

"I agree with the West," I said. "I don't want this job and don't want to go abroad with a KGB escort anymore."

"You idiot, the Fatherland needs you! I always hoped that such a trip could make you a chosen Jew. You'll be plowing for three or four years like a mule, night and day, and in return you'll be sent as a correspondent to a vacation in Africa for the rest of your life. Then you could write your children's books about Tuaregs and their camels."

"What if I escape to the West?"

"You wouldn't do that to your parents and me."

"Don't criticize Irina," I said. "I divide people into two categories—those that I understand and women. About them I know only one thing for sure—they pee sitting down."

I had long forgotten about that conversation when Tom called me. "Vadim is interested," he said. "You should come over here. Otherwise, not only I, but also Primakov and your boyhood chum Zhukov, will look like a bunch of fools."

Herculean efforts to rescue me from myself were continuing.

Vadim Nekrasov was *Pravda*'s deputy editor-in-chief for international affairs. He asked if I had ever worked on a newspaper and why I had stopped writing for *Pravda*; he did not say a word about my marital status, which could only mean that Tom had already briefed him in detail and that Nekrasov was a tactful man. At the end he asked, "How did you get that footage for your TV-presentation on Angola?"

Front pages of *Pravda* from the 1960s. (Russian International News Agency).

The film had been shot by Americans, and we cut twenty minutes of tape out of it so that no one looking to interrupt our aims would be able to try us for a copyright violation in a foreign court.

"I was surprised to see you," said Nekrasov, "not him, with these unique shots."

"Tom recommended me for this job."

I promised Nekrasov to show to my next TV audience a photo of Tom with some cool Angolan rebel, both with Soviet sub-machine guns and in Soviet military uniforms. He knew the picture and laughed. "It should be shown all over the world," he said. "I'll recommend you, but be patient. It's a long process."

OUR MEETING TOOK PLACE in mid-May, 1967. On May 27, Egyptian

President Gamal Abdel Nasser declared, "Our objective will be the destruction of Israel. The Arab people want to fight."

On June 5, Israel pre-empted her three Arab neighbors and attacked their armies concentrated on her borders. Thus Israeli aggressors insidiously destroyed the strategic plan of Tom Kolesnichenko for my intrusion into the ranks of the ruling nomenclature with its variety of benefits. He called me from his office, "Are you rejoicing, scoundrel?"

"I'm delighted," I said. The Soviet leadership felt humiliated. Moscow was intensely preparing its friends for this war and hoped that it would put an end to the very existence of the Jewish state. Within six days, Israelis took control of the Gaza Strip and the Sinai Peninsula from Egypt, the West Bank and East Jerusalem from Jordan, and the Golan Heights from Syria.

"Your new friend," Tom said, "has informed me that our drinking party has been postponed indefinitely. His royal family sobered up, and you won't be allowed to their feast within firing range."

"During the wake?" I said. "Give them my condolences."

A year later, the defense of the joint postdoctoral thesis about the Six-Day War by two *Pravda* correspondents, Yevgeny Primakov and Igor Belyaev, was held behind closed doors. By declining to attend this defense, I deprived myself of a unique opportunity to learn at least some truth about the events that had been the subject of misinformation unprecedented even for the Russians.

I was examining a cover of a Syrian magazine with a depiction of a hook-nosed Jew writhing on the bayonet of a swell Syrian soldier, when a surprised Polyakov poked his head into the room, "Why didn't you go listen to your buddies?"

The old man was not stiff-faced anymore; he was pathetic. I took pity on him and lied. "Somebody forgot to include you and me on the list of invitees."

He approached my desk and looked at the soldier dumping the last Jew into the sea.

"From the special repository?" he asked.

I nodded.

He put down his heavy hand. "Don't leave it on the desk."

I ALREADY WAS very selective in my writing, but still tried not to disappear from the public eye. The Soviet-led invasion of Czechoslovakia in August 1968 delivered the final blow to my fading desire to write. Many ordinary citizens were disappointed. Some of them wrote carefully worded letters to the Central Committee with a polite request to withdraw from the fraternal country. In response, the Party took a step which had successfully worked throughout all years of its rule. Mighty waves of meetings swept Russia. All who had hands raised them in a unanimous vote on the resolutions in defense of the brotherly country from American imperialism and its Czech accomplices.

My university friend Fred Solyanov did not raise his hand. Recently he had found a new job at the Theater Museum and abandoned his old one as a stagehand. He hoped that no political shocks could threaten the world of great actors' worn costumes, dusty great masters' set designs, tattered playbills, and theater programs yellowed with age. But the day came when, at a general meeting, all the staff of the museum approved a resolution in support of the action in Czechoslovakia. Everybody raised their hands. Except for Fred Solyanov. Colleagues tried to convince him, "What are you? Crazy? Just raise it! You can't fight a cannon with a peashooter!"

But he did not raise his hand. And was promptly fired.

In my magazine, instead of voting, Simon and I pretended to be very busy preparing the latest issue.

"We can't pull this off—such a cheap trick," said Tom.

Politburo ordered many correspondents to be sent to Czechoslovakia on short assignments, one after another. Tom and my classmate Vladimir Zhukov, now an expert on the USA, were also sent to Prague.

Vladimir lived in a heavy building near Mayakovski Square with his parents. After Stalin's demise, his father, a KGB lieutenant general, was expelled from the Party, kicked out of the KGB, and stripped of his rank, but the huge apartment was not taken from him. Then he, the former ruler of Dalstroy, a conglomerate of hard labor camps at the farthest northeastern part of Russia, was generously given the job of director of a large hotel on the edge of Moscow.

I had a rare opportunity of observing him only when his icy eyes showed interest in the young women in our company. Georgy S. Zhukov would tap with his foot on Vladimir's door and, without waiting for an answer, with the words "Gifts from Georgia!" bring inside a basket with bottles of rare Georgian wine, strong homemade grape vodka called chacha, young cheese, and fruit one couldn't buy in Moscow.

The former two-star-general embarrassed our ladies with his French. Once I brazenly asked him, "Where did you learn your French?"

He beamed. "In Paris! I had an unforgettable teacher. Oh yes, it certainly was a she."

When it was time for me to go home, Vladimir whispered at the door, "My father and his Georgian friends remember their adventures as you and I remember our school antics."

"When we were kicked out of the classroom by our teachers into the empty hallway?"

"Is that a hint?" Vladimir said.

I whispered, "He's a mystery to me."

"To me, too," said Vladimir.

I was always sure that all forced labor camps were parts of the Gulag system. Only years later, when I was living in Washington DC and attempting to find some information on Vladimir's father, did I discover that Dalstroy (an abbreviation for Remote Construction Sites) with its more than five hundred camps, divisions, and subdivisions, was not connected to the Gulag at all. It was spread over the entire uninhabited Kolyma Territory rich in gold, tin, cobalt, uranium, and other strategic minerals. This area, about the size of France, was reachable only by sea from the inhospitable northern Pacific shores.

Now I questioned the tale of the white thoroughbred that the general rode at the camps. An enormous part of Kolyma lies within the Arctic Circle with its permafrost and tundra. On the permafrost even rats die.

Our paths had diverged long ago, so I was surprised when a drunk Vladimir suddenly called me. He was supposed to start working as the *Pravda* correspondent in New York, but all of a sudden had an unpleasant assignment and needed an advice from his old buddy. From his unintelligible mutter I understood that some twenty-year-old idiot named Natasha wanted to go blind after reading his article about a blind Chairman of the USA Communist Party. With the blessings of romantically inclined local Party officials, she proclaimed to all mankind, including Leonid Brezhnev and *Pravda*, that she was offering her eyes to Comrade Henry Winston. She was convinced that the Soviet medicine could work miracles. The Central Committee of the Party supported this ambitious local initiative. To interview her, Vladimir had to fly to Novosibirsk where he had lived with his parents years ago.

Vladimir's father said to his son, "If you want to dance, you have to pay the piper."

The white prancing thoroughbred immediately came back into existence.

Now it was my turn to give Vladimir some qualified advice. I said, "Make your father convince his former buddy in Novosibirsk to cancel the entire affair for the sake of common sense."

"They drank a lot of Georgian chacha with the former first secretary. Now the man lives at some Black Sea resort."

Vladimir suddenly hung up. In the end, I thought, transplanting eyes is a simple procedure in comparison with the construction of a paradise on this planet.

A week later, Tom told me that Zhukov and the paper's photographer continued drinking during the flight and were not sober when Natasha got their call from a Novosibirsk hotel. They invited the girl to the hotel, expressed their admiration, interviewed her, drank more, now with her, took pictures of her and with her in various positions, winking to each other, hugged her, drank again, laughed for no reason, kissed and caressed her again until she broke free from their hugs and, frustrated, ran away, perhaps in tears.

The next day the indignant first secretary of the Novosibirsk Region rang Moscow. The two culprits were expelled from the newspaper. But not from the Party. Both received reprimands with a serious warning of expulsion from it. After that, someone's mighty hand arranged for them to work at the Novosti Press Agency (APN) and they had a serious conversation with its head of personnel—the KGB general Karpovich, who happened to be the father of our man of principle in Nigeria, Cyril Karpovich.

Before long I found out which crimes the Party could not forgive.

Usually it took only a couple of days for our Party secretary to collect the monthly dues of our editorial Party cell. Once an enraged member of the Institute's Party Committee entered our editorial room and yelled at Vlad, "How many times we must ask you to bring the dues immediately, just a hundred yards down the corridor?!"

Our colleague blushed and muttered that he had again forgotten at home the key to the safe where the money was kept.

"We're going to refer this matter to the District Party Committee!" barked the activist as he slammed the door behind himself.

Fortunately, in the room were only Simon Verbitsky and I.

"Speak!" I said.

Vlad muttered, "You know."

"Drank away the money?"

He nodded. The blush never left his face.

"Better if you killed someone," I said dejectedly.

"I know," he said.

Simon threw up his hands, "Why didn't you tell us before, damn you?"

"We would've collected this shitty money," I said, staring out the window.

Five minutes later Simon and I stood before that very Committee member with a promise to put our colleague at once into a clinic for alcoholics.

"It's too late," he pronounced. "You chose an irresponsible drunk as your Secretary."

Vlad already owed three months' money, and the District Committee had been informed.

"You're right," I said. "We are all responsible for this."

"The Party Charter doesn't provide for collective responsibility for failure to pay dues," said the jerk.

When we came back, Polyakov had been already in the room

and was chastising Vlad, "You encroached on the sacred by stealing the Party's money!"

I said, "We should warn him about being expelled from the Party like they did recently to Vladimir Zhukov in *Pravda*."

"It won't work," said the experienced Polyakov and turned to Vlad, "You're fired."

"Nikolai Nikolayevich," I begged, "he has three children to support. Maybe in order not to wash our soiled linen in public, it could be written in his work report that he left of his own will?"

"No. The expulsion from the Party is a dangerous thing to hide," Polyakov said.

SEVEN

On the Horns of a Dilemma

WITH EVERY PASSING DAY, I was increasingly moving away from the magazine's affairs. Nobody complained—the editorial machine worked almost without my participation. Only our pedantic office manager and both literary editors had long been unhappy with me. The ladies kept asking, "What happened? You've changed beyond recognition."

What could I say to them? That I despised our constant lies? They knew it, but pretended that they did not. Did I need to remind them about that desperate Crimean Tatar who entered this editorial room and put on the desk closest to the door a battered school notebook? It happened three years ago, but I still remembered the scrawled handwriting on its cover and his husky voice, "Please publish this protest against the persecution of my people." He quickly left our room. We knew that Tatars were expelled from Crimea by Stalin when we were little kids. Fifteen years after Stalin's death, we did not open that notebook. We were still afraid. Our office manager, a mild-mannered widow, passed this bomb to the Institute's Party Committee. We all felt relieved and never talked about the man dressed like a beggar and probably out of his mind.

If I spoke about him out loud, my colleagues would start to fear each other. They would think who among them could report our conversation to the KGB. Stalin instilled fear in our genes, a mighty, conquering fear. Victorious socialism defeated us all.

It took years for me to turn into a true escapist. I stopped reading our materials and was just putting my initials in the corner. To my surprise, Tom treated this revelation calmly. "For years I haven't read the pages of *Pravda* devoted to the achievements of this great country," he told me. "I'm only interested in what goes on outside our borders."

"Do you want to be duped just on foreign policy issues?" I said. "Don't be choosy. Sorry, Tom, but I don't even read your articles anymore."

Tom snorted.

BY CHANCE, I found a graceful way to confront my frustration. Freezing October rain was falling from the sky, when I saw two cheerful high school girls with figure skates proudly sticking out of their bags.

"Getting ready for winter?" I joked and told them that before they were born, I played hockey for the Moscow University. They invited me to come to their ice skating rink. Long before the winter? In the open air? I was impressed.

The next day I went to the Sokolniki Park's artificial rink and watched the amateur dancers from the stands. Soon I bought figure skates and joined the group. Several months later, in early springtime, when we sunbathed while training, a skillful twenty-year-old girl said, "Arkady, you keep a nice edge and have a stronger push and a longer step than some young boys. I will teach you sequences and patterns, and you'll make a good partner."

I was happy.

In three weeks the ice began melting. We had a long summer break, and my cheerfulness disappeared. In the fall, we were back, and again I danced away my worries, sometimes even in the light drizzle while ignoring the dangers of shallow puddles. But my dark mood returned during our fifteen-minute walks to the subway and, unable to hide my bitterness, I subjected to my anti-Soviet tirades a married couple I had met on the ice.

The young husband said once, "Arkady, you don't know us."

"I trust you, Alexei," I said.

"Aren't you afraid that you might go to jail for this sort of talk?" his wife asked me.

"Hard-working KGB men, snitches, and Party workers don't do ice dancing."

I was wrong. In the spring of 1971, when the sun began melting our ice again, Alexei invited me to a perfect rink. He had been helping to expand a miniscule group of Soviet elite ice-dancing lovers who were training at the only enclosed figure-skating rink in the largest city of Europe, off-limits to us. Coached by a European ice dancing champion, mostly women, led by an overweight deputy chairman of the USSR's Council of Ministers, they needed men. Professionals, who under the guise of amateurs took part in the Olympics, used that rink all year round. I was ready to sacrifice my convictions and asked Alexei not to tell this deputy chairman that in the last elections I managed to slip into my pocket the ballot with the name of his boss, Premier Kosygin. Under the watchful eye of plainclothes patriots, I put a blank piece of paper into the ballot box.

"What did you do with the stolen ballot?" asked his wife.

"Presented it to someone."

"Do you have children?"

"No," I said.

"Do you have parents? Friends? Aren't you a bit old for this mischief?"

"I want to embellish my boring life. It's sickening to know that if I play by the rules, I'm destined for success."

"Arkady, you're playing with fire," she said.

"All of these are childish pranks," I said. "What else is there to do? Blow up Lenin's Mausoleum?"

"Some Jews have begun emigrating," Alexei sighed. "Maybe you too should go."

"I'm forty one, have the wrong occupation, don't know any other languages, and my only sister and her husband are much older," I said. "The KGB will never allow me to go. They might imprison me—I know a few of their secrets. I don't want to lose my friends. My mother will cry her heart out for as long as she's alive. Shall I go on?"

I shared this encounter with a gloomy Tom Kolesnichenko. "You don't even know what you want," he said. "To quit your job? It's crazy. To emigrate? It's even worse. The KGB will never let you go. The simple truth is that the whole world is mired in shit. Any state is a cage; you escape one only to find yourself in another. Here is shit, and there is shit. A good place to be is the only one where we've never traveled."

I was not convinced, so he became more specific. "If I were the KGB, I would let you go to the West," he said. "You'd be an outsider; nobody needs you there. You couldn't survive a day without the Moscow chatter, and you'd be dumb and silent. You'd die of longing for me."

"Now you've convinced me," I said. "I will stay in this cage and join the dissidents."

"They're either plain crazy or suicidal. You're making me upset." Tom babbled some nonsense: "I will secretly feed this unemployable derelict for the rest of my life. ... Let's find you a bride with ties to the Politburo."

The rest of my friends also expressed their strong opinions.

"If I were a Jew," said Gena Snegiryov, "I'd leave today. On foot. It's unfair—why don't they allow ethnic Russians to emigrate?"

"You, in your sweet sixteen, sailed in the Pacific with ichthyologists to Chukotka," I snapped, angry for no particular reason. "Why didn't you jump ship on an ice floe, sailing to Alaska? Today the Jews are clambering up it."

"I was too young!" Gena said condescendingly, and before starting his usual search for any kind of pain medication in my apartment, he said wistfully, "Send me a pair of jeans from America."

I promised.

Fred Solyanov, a stagehand again, said, "It's madness to be so open with people you just met."

"Look who's talking?" I shot back. "Wasn't it you who in 1968 shared his not so humble opinion with the entire staff of the Theater Museum?"

"I didn't have as heavy a stone hanging around my neck as your correspondents. Be ready for a long incarceration."

Another university friend, Nahl Zlobin said only: "When you suddenly started to dance on ice, I knew that the whole show was coming to an end."

ONLY ABOUT TWO YEARS later did I finally decide to talk to my sister and her husband. Maria's dreams were fixed on the future of her daughter and on having the right contacts in food and clothing stores. Her husband Simon's life was devoted to a new phenomenon in Russian life—his vegetable garden. He tolerated useless flowers only near the gate. This land, allocated for factories to fight food shortages, was the most visible part of Khrushchev's economic reforms after Stalin's death. Workers were happy to get these smallish plots, usually far away from their homes and workplaces; the green light was given even for building summer cottages there. With the permanent housing crisis, the regime feared that allowing construction of heated houses in these suburbs would lead to the plundering of building materials across the country. To prevent this explosion of antisocial behavior, small summer kitchens were permitted to be built only at a considerable distance from dwellings. This wise solution was explained as a measure to prevent fires. Thus, the citizens were forced to steal and cheat less in their attempts to provide for better living conditions in their summer nests.

There was no phone in their community, three miles from the nearest village Odintsovo and its railroad station, and the road was sometimes impassable even for pedestrians in high rubber boots, except for my brother-in-law Simon with his high spirit. My sister hated this garden. The piercing smell of the stolen chicken manure lovingly spread over their plot pursued Maria even to her Moscow communal apartment. Lucky Simon bought this treasure for a song on a neighboring collective farm.

Maria's first question to me was not rhetorical: "Are you crazy?"

"Would you go if it weren't dangerous?" I asked.

While she pondered the answer, Simon said, "We might."

"You have to emigrate for the sake of your future grandchildren," I said.

"Tanya will soon marry a nice Russian boy," my sister said, perking up a bit.

"Mazel tov!" I said, trying not to sound ironic. "Will you try to squeeze him into this birdhouse?"

She shrugged. Explaining anything was useless. Our worlds were far apart, but I had to introduce to them my world with its choice between imprisonment or maltreatment and an attempt to emigrate. I promised to apply for an exit visa on one sole condition— if they would also apply. For their sake, I thought, I'll keep quiet as a mouse in anticipation of the official answer. Probably, they'll get the visa. No doubt, I'll be denied it.

"Because you've been published in *Pravda*?" asked Simon.

I burst out laughing. "No, because your daughter was born in the Ural Mountains," I said. "Does she know how you, as a Jew, were kicked out of your Moscow plant a couple of years before Stalin's death, and forced to accept a similar position in Kamensk Uralsky?"

"It wasn't easy to get back here from the Ural Mountains even after his death," he said. "That's why I'm an ordinary engineer now."

They had a good chance to get visas. Nothing but state abuse and humiliation threatened them if they applied for it: they were old, and Tanya's future occupation as a high school geography teacher was laughable as far as the KGB was concerned. In Russia, there were few schools with this position. "Simon," I said, "When they unanimously expel you from the Party, scream that as soon as the plane lands in Tel Aviv, you'll join it again. Blame it all on me."

I did not want to cause a heart attack, but I had to dot the i's and cross the t's. "I know one state secret," I said, "and the KGB knows that I know it."

Fear froze their faces. They did not dare ask me what it was. Both were dejectedly silent. I myself was not so sure that my chance to survive this was by balancing on a tightrope—keeping silent on this sensitive subject, but making a lot of noise about the regime's human rights abuses. I made it clear to Maria and Simon that I would start hectoring the KGB as soon as their plane took off.

They could not bear to think about the ordeal that I brought to their table, but, as always, I was deliciously fed. My sister looked at me the way people look at a corpse. After dinner, I tried to broaden their horizons. They were unaware that in their Ural city, they lived with the descendants of Russian slaves who, ninety years before, had been permanently assigned to factories. As I spoke, their tired, empty eyes made me stop the history lesson.

"Why do you think we'd be allowed to go?" Simon asked.

"They would benefit from isolating me from my family," I said.

"And, in the worst-case scenario, even from the parcels of black crackers that my sis would be allowed to send me twice a year," I added, delicately hinting at imprisonment regulations.

"Give us some time," Simon said.

"Okay. Just remember, my silence will be working against me."

"I don't understand this," Maria whined. "You make twice as much money as we two together. You have a lovely apartment. Papa was proud of you."

A few days later Simon called. "We agree," he said, his voice cracking.

"Don't discuss it with Mama," I said. "I'll do it myself."

"And you, please, don't talk about it with our daughter."

I kept my word and went for the first time to the only synagogue in Moscow. My heart was pounding. Outside there was a crowd of Jews who had applied for exit visas or who had talked about applying for years. Many spoke in whispers, inquisitively looking at each other, and, warily, at the police and the passersby. I felt like a full member of a global Jewish conspiracy.

My first step was to get acquainted with a man whose name I never bothered to find out. On the street outside the synagogue I passed him a piece of paper with the names and addresses of the new five-member Zionist cell, including my mother who never learned of her participation in this global cabal. He often looked around and during those moments fell silent.

"This invitation," the man said, "is a mere formality, but without it no official will talk to you. Some diplomats and tourists bring them."

He obviously knew about some mysterious relatives who would be delighted to invite us to live in Israel, though they wouldn't be frustrated if we ended up somewhere else. I asked him if he ever entered the doors of this synagogue.

"Why?" he said. "To listen to that KGB man in a yarmulke? There are enough of his colleagues right around here. What's your occupation?"

"Journalism," I shyly admitted.

"Don't waste your time. Master a more respectable profession."

"Like what?"

"Anything. Car mechanic. Doorman. Electrician, plumber."

"How will I get the invitations?"

"Come here. Get acquainted with refuseniks. They will help. All the others are very passive—they want to sail quickly and that's that."

"The KGB could easily block this flow of invitations," I said. "There must be a reason why they don't do that."

"I never thought of that," the man said.

I thought, what if he was going to deliver our names right to the KGB?

Soon I entered this strange world. In the morning, as usual, I went to work. And in the evening, instead of ice-dancing, I was making friends with people who just yesterday had been of little interest to me. Many of them had been ostracized for years, thrown out of society and driven from their jobs in disgrace. The Soviet citizen lived from paycheck to paycheck. Somehow the refuseniks continued to exist. People took up any job. Massive Russian corruption helped many to survive. A foreman and a plant manager enrolled his wife/mistress/niece to the post which was held by engineer Katz expelled yesterday in disgrace. The work was still done by Katz, and everybody was happy. A relative/mistress/friend received a salary and honestly gave half of it to the grateful Katz. There were many other win-win options. My friend Victor Elistratov the engineer became a stoker, doctors washed floors in hospitals, teachers gave private lessons, and a surgical nurse continued to work in the operating room with a salary of a cleaning lady.

A large group of refuseniks preferred going to the synagogue to having any contact with people suspected of political activities—only "hooligans," people close to my heart, sought such acquaintances. Some refuseniks were sincere in saying, "We don't intend to change this country. All we want is to get out of here." Some were hoping that such a "neutral" stand would protect them from more serious trouble.

Yet all these groups were not isolated from each other by a stone wall, and those who yesterday took part in scientific and cultural workshops, sometimes out of desperation joined the "hooligans" and participated in various protests, including demonstrations, hunger strikes, refusal to serve in the army, and sending abroad collective letters addressed to the Soviet authorities. Nevertheless, there was a group who lived in complete isolation, avoiding any contacts outside their immediate families, and hoping that good behavior would be eventually rewarded with visas.

Rather than exposing a new Jewish conspiracy and sentencing to death a few conspirators and spies, the authorities cracked open the steel gate, and thousands of Jews, humiliated and robbed by the state, were allowed to leave the country. Just a few hundred of them were punished severely. It seemed that the Party, by slightly opening the society, which could operate only in complete isolation, had gone mad and lost its sense of self-preservation.

EIGHT

The Unpredictable World of Dissent

WITH RESPECT TO the security apparatus, the refuseniks lived out their segregation under a transparent dome, and yet I was surprised to be detained while heading with innocent intentions to the Korenfelds, a hospitable family of refuseniks who often hosted an extremely motley crowd.

We were all arrested in different parts of the neighborhood—in the street and at the streetcar stop, at their apartment building entrance, and next to the elevator. Had the KGB waited to arrest us all at the door of this family, it would have needed only a fraction of the agents involved in the sting operation that was intended to prevent a demonstration which, as it turned out, was not planned by anyone. Maybe the top brass sought to demonstrate to higher command the scope of the operation foretold to be a complete success. In this respect the KGB was no different from other ministries, whether it was the Ministry of Culture, Defense, Health, Foreign Affairs, or Agriculture. Part and parcel of everyday life, this kind of bureaucratic cheating was embodied in Newspeak by one simple word known to every citizen—"*pripiski.*" At least six words are needed to translate it into English: "gross exaggerations of achieved results and fake reports." They—*pripiski*—were used not only in Uzbek cotton production and the Kostroma milk yield, but also in building up the military power, in running elections, and in reporting on the progress in the struggle for world peace.

I worried. What would happen to me at work after the KGB notified everyone that the executive editor was actually a rabid Zionist? Our editorial Jews and half-Jews and quarter-Jews would shit their pants on the spot. I had hoped that my first chance to try out my strategy would not come until after I had sent my Party card to the District Party Committee and my sister had applied for exit visas. Now suddenly, I was exposed fluttering and then pinned to the wall like a butterfly. This could definitely spoil my game, and so, desperate, I decided to challenge the two KGB officers, to show that I didn't fear them, didn't give a damn, and wasn't about to be intimidated with such a trifle as the first arrest.

They ignored my challenge and more than that, the blond who handled us acted like a normal human. This KGB man was unusually frank. He had just returned from a business trip in Mordovia (everybody knew that this forested republic had more prisoners than local citizens); we were detained for our own good, and he warned us against attempting to join the next day's demonstration timed to coincide with the arrival of Henry Kissinger. He hinted at the Mordovia option. In the past Blondie had worked as an instructor of a District Party Committee. He even shared with us a much more serious secret—the following day he was expecting there to be a lot of work if it were necessary to arrest and bring to court another fifteen people.

To maintain my mental health, my subconscious likely ordered me to forget the details of this first encounter which earned me a place on the KGB's list of public enemies. This memory lapse tells me how deeply this first apprehension disturbed me. Fortunately, among us was an architect, Gary Berkovich. Thanks to a passion for recording significant events in his life, Gary's 2006 memoir *Guinea Pigs*[3] revived in my memory many details of that encounter.

---

3 Подопытные (Moscow: Sergei Dubov Foundation). Abbreviated when translated into English as *Watching Communism Fail: A Memoir of Life in the Soviet Union* (McFarland, 2008).

According to Gary, when the officer said that he was writing a thesis, I asked, "On the use of force against detainees?"

The Jews at the police station were shocked by my senseless impudence. Blondie replied in a good, cultured manner, "No, my dissertation is on the role of grassroots Party units in the fire departments."

I will never believe that Gary, even with his sardonic grin, could invent such a gem about the Party heroically battling these apolitical forest fires on both sides of the barbed wire while thousands of prisoners were felling trees inside. So, my good friend must have also certainly quoted me correctly.

Probably, after a hard fight with my facial muscles, I was able to ask innocently, "In Mordovia? On logging projects?"

At that moment Blondie's boss came into the room and asked, "What are you talking about?"

I blurted out, "Chicks, what else?"

He ignored my vulgarity. When the man said that he had also written a thesis, I lost all concern for self-preservation. "About defending the interests of an individual in a democratic society?" I asked.

The boss abandoned his scholarly manners and put a stop to my innuendo. "Don't get smart with me, Polishchuk," he snapped. "The interests of a person are subordinate to the interests of the state."

At this point my sense of humor forever abandoned me, and I became hysterical, "Don't you know that people hate you and your state?"

"This took my breath away," wrote Berkovich. He magnanimously explained my behavior by my long experience as a desperate refusenik whose tough life had shattered his nerves. In fact, like Gary, I still worked and had not received an invitation from Israeli "relatives."

I never behaved so stupidly again.

Those two PhD impersonators with poker faces obviously shared the popular belief that all Jews were smart and educated so, to find a common language with us, they talked about their theses. To strengthen Jewish respect for them, their jackets were decorated with the commemorative badges of Moscow University graduates. They certainly could not imagine that shortly after graduating from that University, I presented my diamond-shaped badge to a neighbor's boy who paraded it around the neighborhood sandbox.

So we were arrested only to be quickly released to help prevent the upcoming demonstration. Our captors' wise superiors understood that we would immediately begin warning everyone about the impending arrests. At midnight I woke up the veteran refusenik Vladimir Slepak. He forgave me. The "hooligans" hadn't planned such a demonstration in the first place.

The next morning at the editorial office I felt like a tiny fish in the KGB's glass bowl. By the end of the day I told Simon Verbitsky about my arrest and suggested, "Begin your speech at a Party meeting like this, 'I always suspected Polishchuk of political disloyalty and duplicity. On the front line, we shot such traitors on the spot.'"

Simon stared at me sadly.

Nothing exciting happened the next day, either, except that as I approached the police cordon near the synagogue, my heart was pounding again. I already knew a few people and was amazed when my new young friend, Anatoly Sharansky said, "I don't want to miss the service."

"Do you miss this KGB-hand of a rabbi?" I asked. "Haven't you read his anti-Zionist spell in the newspapers?"

"I'm going to the temple, not for him," Sharansky said calmly.

A year earlier, this rabbi, Yaakov Fishman and I had stayed in the same hospital. He made a strong impression on me by his ignorance and animosity towards those who wanted to emigrate. He apparently believed that we both belonged to the chosen, which, for him, meant people chosen by the Party.

"Wait!" I said to Sharansky, "'Fishman told me, 'It's unfair, I am preparing cadres and they get an education and get away!' That was his word—cadres, just like a Party official. Can't I convince you? As soon as his yeshiva boys were graduating, they applied for emigration, but he asked the Ministry of Internal Affairs to deny them exit visas.'"

"So what?"

Unlike me, this twenty-five-year-old lad with chubby childish lips easily separated the wheat from the chaff. The temple and tradition made the aggressively atheistic police state and its marionette Fishman of no importance.

A QUIET STILL reigned at work; the KGB clearly was not in a hurry to push me toward further antics. After a week this began to bother me. In the evenings I warily eyed passersby and looked around whenever I heard footsteps behind me.

After a couple of months of living in limbo, Vladimir Slepak handed me the invitations to immigrate to Israel, one for my mother, one for me, and one for my sister's family.

"They've arrived," I told my brother-in-law on the phone. "I'll bring them tomorrow night."

"Come over," he said, his voice cracking, and he hung up. At night I wrote three short statements: one, of resignation, to Ghafurov; one to the Party district committee, to withdraw from the Party; and one to the Visa Office to ask for an exit visa. The rest of the night I was thinking about my relatives who failed to understand the sacrifice I was making in applying for it. I thought of the KGB only in the morning, while passing its headquarters on my way to work. What irony! They would feel more confident if I had joined their main enemy—human rights activists. They would prefer to have me inside the country, within their reach; this would guarantee that I would remain silent about their phony correspondents. The death penalty for high treason had not been scratched out of the Criminal Code.

At nine o'clock I asked Ghafurov's assistant to pass my sealed envelope to his boss. After that, I went to our secretariat and explained what kind of a letter I had just left on the second floor. Fear lit up their eyes at this horror, but all three women hugged me without asking a single question.

I rushed to the District Party Committee. The woman behind the tiny window could not understand me. "There's no such thing as returning a Party membership card," she said. "We cannot take it. This is simply impossible. I need to speak with the Second Secretary."

With my red card in her hand, she left me at her window, no less distressed than I was. I watched her walk down the hallway as if she was holding a grenade, the cotter pin already pulled. Cold sweat filled my armpits. I wanted to run away, but remained by the loophole: the Visa Office would not accept my application without written proof that my Party card had been surrendered. After five long minutes she returned with the second secretary.

He was cold. "You cannot leave the Party whenever you wish," he said. "You can be expelled only when the Party deems it necessary."

"I understand," I said.

"The question about your expulsion should be addressed by your grassroots Party organization. We cannot do that here."

"I've already resigned from my job and have no grassroots organization."

"Then the question has to be considered by the Party cell in the place of your residence. Please, take back your membership card and bring it to a meeting of the Party committee in your neighborhood."

"Could you write a note that you are in the process of expelling me from the Party?" I asked.

He did not even raise his voice after such a ridiculous proposition. He asked only, "Why such a rush? You're the first one to bring his Party card here himself. Usually we see only the relevant resolutions of the grassroots Party units."

"I wanted to avoid the bureaucratic red tape."

"You act as if you realize that Israel won't last long," he said caustically.

Instead of throwing my red grenade through their embrasure and running away, I put it in my pocket.

An hour later I posted the Party card by registered mail. I was not going to volunteer for a beating at the grassroots unit. It was now clear, the Visa Office would refuse to talk to me, much less accept my application, without going through all kinds of required bureaucratic humiliation. So, to apply for a visa in person was out of question; a registered letter could do it. And I wrote: "Please issue me a visa to immigrate to the State of Israel. I never had access to any state secrets. Enclosed is the invitation of my Israeli relatives."

To prevent them from throwing this insolent application into a dustbin and to make sure that it would be passed along to the KGB, I added: "The very existence of such exit visas contradicts the UN Charter. The requirement to provide references from the Party, trade unions, place of work, house managers, all other kinds of institutions and persons I never knew, the unanimous resolutions of meetings, the written consent of relatives and even former spouses—all of this is contrary to international law. I am not going to break it."

I imagined the outrage at the KGB and dropped my second stink bomb at the same post office.

Yes, humans are weird and inconsistent creatures! Only days earlier I had told the two PhDs of KGB Science almost everything I had been thinking about them. Today, I was shaking with fear in the Party district committee. And finally, after that I challenged the dreaded Visa Office by the outrageous mail.

I rushed to my sister's. She and her husband sat in their tiny room like two frightened statues. I laid their invitation on top of their minuscule table. "I did my part," I said. "Now it's your turn."

Simon gave a sob, his voice trembling. "I'm so sorry, but we are so afraid!"

I was devastated, I despised them. "Do you understand that I applied for emigration exclusively for your sake? Why did I go through all this humiliation?" I nodded to the invitation. "Throw it into your communal toilet. Late at night."

"Wait!" My sister came to life and extracted from the refrigerator the usual bag with homemade food in jars ready to go. To be angry with them was pointless. In this country fear was bred into everyone's DNA.

After all, they did not exactly ruin my plans. I had already done everything to ensure that a visa would be denied to me. Yes, now I'd become another refusenik, not another human rights activist. Maybe it wasn't so bad after all.

A FEW DAYS LATER, a spiteful old man demanded on the phone that I come to deal with, as he put it, "your personal case."

"I won't come," I said, and hung up. My phone rang endlessly. Senior citizens clearly had nothing else to keep themselves busy.

The very next day, in my mailbox there turned up a summons to a meeting of the neighborhood Party committee. I tore it to pieces. During the following days there were new summonses and new calls. One day an angry old man in a heavy black coat with fur collar and a mink hat stopped me near my entrance with the words, "Are you Polishchuk?"

I recognized the voice and suburban accent of that bastard and barked, "No!"

He began to shout, "You must come to the meeting of the Party committee! Too bad you didn't get in my hands in the Far East! We would've quickly taught you to respect the government!"

"What are you?!" I asked. "A former executioner, or just out for a curative walk, to ventilate your brainless chump?"

He did not expect such insolence. He flushed and panted. But I could not stop. "How many people does one need to kill, to earn an apartment in Moscow? I've got unpleasant news for you—Stalin died twenty years ago."

He swung at me.

I pushed him away and said, "Don't break down, you old fool!"

We were both furious. I opened the front door, hissing as politely as I could, "Would you like to see me to the elevator?"

He spat at the door.

In the elevator, I wondered whether his upcoming denunciation would lead to an investigation of my anti-Soviet activities.

The next phone call was from his Party secretary. She did not mention the previous day's confrontation, saying only, "I hope that by now you realize that the proceedings are inevitable, and you'll have to come to our meeting to put an end to this needless stress for all of us."

"And this humanitarian who regretted that I wasn't in his hard labor camp?" I asked. "Will he also participate in the meeting?"

"He had a very stressful job," she said.

"Me too," I said.

She promised that day he would get an urgent Party assignment. "Our committee," she stressed, "is composed of quite serious people—a professor of Marxism, a retired KGB colonel, a retired general of the Interior Ministry, and a political writer. I'm a professor of chemistry."

All they wanted was to grind me into dust. Judging by his relatively younger age, a retired military man began speaking with a ridiculous Jewish accent borrowed from anti-Semitic jokes. I did not expect this and was in shock. I mumbled something unintelligible, and, perplexed, looked at the presiding secretary with her slightly confused face and gray hair tied in a knot at her nape.

I started to come around only when he asked, "How far away from military action did your family live during the war? Somewhere in Uzbekistan?"

My voice cracked when I said, "Yes, of course."

My father had actually volunteered for the war; he was five years older than the enlistment age.

"There was nothing offensive about this question," someone said.

"For many years you've worked as a journalist," someone else said. "In Israel you'll be paid for slandering Russia."

"Yes, of course," I said.

"Judging by your answers, you don't feel any shame," someone said.

"Yes, of course," I said.

The least offensive stab was that "this country" gave me free education, free medical care and a well-paid job. (They did not mention the cheap housing; my co-op was worth a fortune.) They spoke in fiery language about the dangers of Zionism and the need to eradicate it in the Soviet Union. Time and again, they branded me a traitor, betrayer, turncoat. I tried not to listen. It lasted infinitely. The orators continued repeating what had already been said numerous times, until the secretary tactfully denied them a new opportunity to express their outrage. In the end, Arkady Abramovich Polishchuk was unanimously expelled from the Communist Party.

On the way home, I gave them a crushing, beautiful rebuff. In my head. They did not hear how I said to the happy face of that retired military-hater, "With your imitation skills you should perform as a clown for the guards of Nazi death camps."

I imagined his stomping and yelling, and then said, "I was wrong. You would've made a better career as a guard." He stomped and yelled again and I said, "In Uzbekistan we had beautiful villas with vineyards and used the blood of Christian babies in our matzos."

After that I slammed the door. What a shame, it was the door of my own apartment and my own expensive parquet was powdered with my plaster. A frightened neighbor rushed to the stairwell and knocked on my door. "What happened?" he asked.

I opened the door and said, "I've just been expelled from the Party."

"For what?" asked my neighbor, who was the Party secretary of the Soviet Composer publishing house

"For an attempt to leave the Party," I enunciated.

He returned to his apartment without another word.

In the following days I realized that my beautiful rebuffs were not so beautiful after all, and for years I regretted that I had mentally descended into that bloodbath.

SOON I WAS PARTICIPATING in my first demonstration. Many refuse-niks were detained on the way to the steps outside the Lenin Library subway station. Nonetheless half a dozen of us managed to make it to the stairs. We were not given time to deploy our modest "let us go" type banners as we were overpowered by plainclothes patriots and quickly delivered into the hands of the police, emerging in numbers from the depths of the subway. The patriots were surely placed on the steps in advance—to demonstrate to citizens the popular anger against the traitors. At the police station, after protocols of detention for disorderly conduct were filed, to my surprise, no one was prosecuted. The KGB were experimenting with democracy.

I continued testing the limits and joined this demonstration without waiting for a response from the Visa Office. Some thoughtful psychologist in uniform probably paid attention to my inadequate behavior. The following day, a woman's voice on the phone rattled off to me, "I like you very much and want to see you tonight at six o'clock at ticket booth number three, at the train station near the house of your ex-wife."

Only Tom Kolesnichenko, who also lived near the Kiev Railway Station, could know Irina's address.

It has begun, I thought.

A crowd with suitcases, bags, and the Ukrainian accent was raging by the ticket office number three. Tom and I stood in line.

"Well, where are we going?" he asked sadly.

"To Israel," I said.

A squat woman in front of us shuddered and looked fearfully at us.

"By train?" asked Tom while smiling fondly at the auntie.

"We'll see when we get to the point of departure; maybe in a freight car with bars on the windows," I said.

"If you give up your undertaking, you'll be forgiven. That's precisely what I was told. The punishment would be limited to expulsion from the Party and demotion."

"What incredible charity!" I said and asked the squat woman cordially, "Are you hearing well?"

She turned away in embarrassment and we continued our secret conversation.

"Why did they task you to undertake this noble mission?"

"Because you wouldn't believe them," Tom said.

"Would you?"

"The devil knows!"

"Did you tell them that we haven't seen each other for over a year and have nothing in common?"

"Yes."

"Perhaps you came up with it all by yourself, once again trying to rescue me."

"No. They need to protect their..."—he whispered—"correspondents."

"For that they have a variety of options," I said.

"That's what troubles me," he said.

"Why did you involve that damsel in this patriotic initiative?"

"For a laugh. To amuse you and myself. She's our secretary"—he turned to whisper again—"from *Pravda*."

"And what will you say to them?"

"What a fool you are. I will also say that thou wilt never deliver your friends."

"They will understand only because betrayal is part of their job description."

"You're oversimplifying the problem, as always."

"Said Stalin to Khrushchev after they starved to death ten million of her ..."—I nodded at the woman—"Ukrainian relatives."

The woman, who had long been lost in our conversation, clearly understood something, nodded approvingly, and looked around meticulously inspecting our neighbors, who were preoccupied with guarding their belongings.

Tom glanced at his watch; we said goodbye to the woman—she enjoyed that—and we walked toward his new home, where not so long ago I used to escort him in secret, so that he could see his lover, Svetlana. Now they were married and lived happily ever after, in her apartment. We stopped halfway. I kept glancing around, though today not for his former wife.

"A relatively new habit, this," I said.

"Too bad you weren't at our wedding," said Tom.

When we hugged, he cleverly tucked into my inner pocket an envelope and murmured: "This is for you on the grub."

I was about to leave when he asked, "What are your plans for the near future?"

"I'll try to attend the trials of Jews."

"I hope you won't be allowed to enter the courtroom," he said. "I didn't know that you were such a reckless fool."

"Neither did I."

"Don't beg for trouble."

"Don't worry; at a crucial moment I'll tell them that if something happens to me, the list of KGB correspondents would be delivered to the West."

After that I lied to my friend, for the first time in my life. "It's already in a couple of safe places. Feed this fact to them."

"They will crush you."

"This is the only guarantee for my safety."

We embraced again, and I went away thinking that it wouldn't be easy to find people who'd agree to keep such a list, let alone pass it to the West.

A month later I was invited, as I was told on the phone, for a chat in the KGB Reception Room. Tireless Sharansky volunteered to wait for me in a nearby grocery shop from where he could see its entrance so that if I did not reappear, he could inform foreign correspondents. At the threshold of that small pre-revolutionary house, a lean young man with his arm outstretched for a handshake approached me right away. The fellow acted like a movie orphan who had finally found his mother. "I recognized you immediately,

Arkady Abramovich!" he said.

I thought, what a stupid way to intimidate!

In a little office another psychologist of the same brand also shook my hand. It took a half an hour for them to explain what Tom said in few seconds. It was not too late to change my mind before I made reckless moves. I would be allowed to return to my editorial team as an ordinary employee, and my future would depend entirely on the success of my labor.

I wondered if they knew why they were ordered to treat me with such a generous proposal and said to myself, "Have no fear, Polishchuk! Otherwise the next step could be an attempt to make you an informant."

What followed was exciting for both parties of this heart-to-heart encounter. For a long time my educators explained what, too, could be summed up in ten seconds: We protect the Jews from the people's wrath. The more experienced man said, "Just imagine what would happen if we stopped protecting you."

Under threat and heavy stress I often first react, then think. Here this bad habit surfaced again. I had been reading some historians and writers of tsarist Russia in preparation for traveling out to the anti-Semitic trials, and now I decided to share my new knowledge with my well-wishers: "I know some very Russian people that would disagree with you."

"You're talking about a handful of Moscow intellectuals, divorced from the people. They're living in their own little world," said the senior in age and rank.

"In a sense, you're right," I said, and they nodded heartily.

"We keep our finger on the pulse of the country," spoke the man of junior rank.

"Yeah, no one knew the Russian people as well as Leo Tolstoy," I drawled thoughtfully.

"Yes, *War and Peace* is a very wise book," observed the chief.

"I couldn't agree with you more," I pronounced. "Do you know what Tolstoy wrote about the Jews at the end of his life?"

"What?" asked his assistant.

And then I threw a knockout: "These heinous rulers can at any time, if they wish, cause pogroms. It is within their own power to stop them."

They did not react. I signed a paper stating that I had been warned about the possible consequences of my anti-social behavior. Five minutes later, in English, Sharansky told a Reuters correspondent from a nearby phone booth about this official warning. This bloodless news was probably not even suitable for that reporter's waste bin.

NINE

The First Trial, December 1974

THE REFUSENIK VLADIMIR LASARIS and I did not feel much sympathy for each other, but we had a common cause and a common destiny for the foreseeable future. Our train was moving toward the Ukrainian city of Vinnitsa where the trial of a fifty-seven-year-old physician was about to begin. Dr. Mikhail Stern had been arrested after giving his twenty-nine-year-old son a written permission that was required to immigrate to Israel. The outraged local officials trumped up a charge of bribery. The physician had been in prison for nearly seven months, and his wife, his elderly mother, and both sons were denied access to him.

A day before our departure, Lasaris and I, along with another refusenik, Alexander Goldfarb, distributed among our Moscow acquaintances a statement of our intention to attend the trial. If we were arrested before we got there, it would confirm that the trial was only a guise for the guiltless doctor's ongoing persecution.

Lasaris and I stood by a car window and in a low voice discussed what could happen if we were detained on the way to Vinnitsa. A Ukrainian with bright blue eyes and shining teeth came by several times to speak with us; the short man could pass for forty, if not for the bulging vein in his neck and the thick gray hair that belied his true age. His rustic manners lent some charm to his benevolence and curiosity.

After talking to us once again about the usual trifles of journeying by train, he walked away to the next window and, believing that the noise of the moving train would not let us hear, said to a sergeant, "Oh boy, I shot a lot of them during the war!"

The soldier looked at us and smiled at the man who continued calmly, "They all want to move to Israel, afraid that in the end, we'll finish the job." He jerked his massive shoulders and squashed an imaginary insect between the nails of his thumbs.

We pretended as though we had seen or heard nothing. What else could we do? Spit in his face? Complain to other passengers? Kill him? It was our baptism by fire on the eve of a long trial.

"A neighbor hung my grandmother," I said, "when the Germans came to Kiev."

"And the others?" asked Lasaris.

"You know where they are," I said.

"Babi Yar?"

"Yes, in the mass grave."

We arrived without incident in Vinnitsa and easily reached the Sterns' rickety house, no different from the others.

We sat at the dinner table in a room where the walls had been ripped open, the furniture broken. The doctor's wife Ida said, "I'm sorry we have no decent spoons and forks. The prosecutor Krachenko picked them straight from this table as evidence of our riches, frustrated after a futile two-day search for Jewish gold and diamonds." She waved her left hand. "Even the penny watch from my wrist."

The prosecutor sincerely believed in the hidden wealth of the popular endocrinologist and had dispatched requests to dozens of cities, even in Siberia, to find out whether Stern kept his money in local non-interest bearing savings banks. Later in court Mikhail Stern tried to explain "whence came the myth of Jewish wealth," but the judge forbade him to speak academically on the subject.

We came to the courthouse an hour before the start of the trial. At the entrance six policemen and some sturdy fellows in civilian clothes were already counting the clock. Under their feet squelched cold mud, and snowflakes were falling on their black patent-leather visors. A first lieutenant, resolutely blocking the narrow door, stopped Stern's older son Victor and asked: "Your summons?"

"What summons? I'm his son."

"We have orders to let in people only pursuant to a summons."

"Is it a closed trial?" asked his younger brother August. Their mother and four sisters of Mikhail Stern began yelling at the police.

"Your last name?" the three brash Muscovites—Lasaris, Goldfarb and I—shouted at the first lieutenant. The local police had not yet seen such impudence. The first lieutenant stammered, "Adamenko."

Men in civilian clothes shoved us away from the door, and another lieutenant spoke, "We let inside only those on the approved list! All seats are already taken!"

All of a sudden, somewhere from the side, not from the courthouse, a big shot—a lieutenant colonel, without his coat—crashed into us. He was swinging his heavy hands and shouting, "If you disturb order, we'll put all of you in prison for fifteen days!"

The crowd around us was quickly growing. Some made a fuss, but the majority of the horde silently watched the unusual spectacle. A shabbily dressed onlooker was explaining to Ida Stern, "We have Soviet laws. If it is possible to admit relatives in, then you would be allowed, and if not—then you cannot."

I got a grip on myself and said softly, "Let the sons in. We aren't violating anything."

The lieutenant colonel barked, "For them, he's their father. For us, a criminal!"

We also demanded that he give us his name. The lieutenant

colonel was not used to Muscovite rudeness. The question extracted the sound of a racing motorcycle from his terrific set of lungs, a roar from a state of shock, as if we were telling the Vinnitsa policemen to take off their pants.

So passed an endless half hour. And suddenly, someone very important, who will remain unnamed, saw our unpunished insolence amid the crowd of law-abiding citizens. Perhaps he wondered what the corrupt capitalist press obedient to the Zionists would say about the trial. A head stuck out of the courthouse and whispered in the first lieutenant's ear. And the world turned upside down.

"Please come this way," said Lt. Adamenko ceremoniously.

In seconds the crowd, bristling with elbows, dragged us along the narrow stairs to the fourth floor.

When Stern entered the room, guarded by six soldiers with rifles and dressed as if for parade, I recalled the show trial at the railroad club in the Kostroma Region. The killer was guarded by two bored policemen with side arms.

We knew that Stern had spent a long time in a damp basement cell. He was ill. Imagine my surprise when he, with a quick and firm step, straight as a stick, walked between the rows, blew a kiss to his wife, and took his place behind his lawyer and the soldiers. A tidy rectangle of his gray beard emphasized the blackness of his hair. You would have thought that he dyed it, but we knew that the gray beard was the stigma of prison.

When the formalities began, Stern answered the judge's questions loudly, as if reciting poetry. Everything said during the trial that I reproduce here is verbatim, since I jotted it all down in the courtroom, in front of the judge and surrounded by KGB onlookers.

On the question of his ethnic origin Stern replied, "As long as the world will have at least one anti-Semite, I will speak loudly—I'm a Jew."

A middle-aged Jewish onlooker in a dense crowd at the open door suddenly became distinctly pale. The next two questions of the Judge Vasily Orlovsky were also close to my heart: "Were you a member of the Communist Party?" and "When were you expelled from the Party?"

A loyal Soviet patriot, Stern said, "For forty years I have been an active member of the Young Communist League and the Communist Party."

Orlovsky repeatedly prohibited him to speak on topics that were not related to the court proceedings, but the defendant believed that they had a direct bearing on the case. For example, he still managed to say, "My criminal case was fabricated according to the recipe of the notorious Doctors' Plot in 1952. At that time, eminent figures of medicine were accused of poisoning their patients and attempting to murder Stalin and other leaders."

"Defendant Stern," said the judge, stopping him, "we know the history better than you do. The Party long ago corrected the errors that occurred. All of this is irrelevant to the case."

"Relevant," Stern said. "The witnesses for the prosecution were told: the Jewish doctor is a spy who was paid for poisoning the Soviet people."

Prosecutor Krivoruchko jumped up, his hands outstretched to Orlovsky: "I demand..."

"Defendant," the judge said, "speak on the substance of your petition. Otherwise I will have to..."

Stern said, "The witnesses were intimidated."

Prosecutor: "The question of the witnesses for the defense can be resolved at the end of the judicial investigation."

Counsel David Axelbant: "No, it should be resolved right now. Some of the forty witnesses on our list may be present in this room, and the court is entitled to reject them for that reason. Many of our witnesses live far away in the villages, and it will take time for them to arrive at the court."

"The question of the witnesses for the defense we'll resolve in the future," the judge said.

Many days later Orlovsky agreed to hear four of the forty witnesses for the defense.

The judge turned to the reading of the indictment, and he did so with fervor. The twenty-seven pages of text narrated that Mikhail Stern tenaciously grabbed the sick, the disabled and even the dying by their pocket and shamelessly dumped out of it all he could—from fifty rubles to two-dozen eggs.

"By extortion," the document stated, "Stern forced the sick, for the sake of their health and to save their lives, to give him bribes. From twenty-one patients he extorted 775 rubles, two geese and three buckets of apples and thus committed a crime pursuant to Article 168.2 of the Criminal Code of the Ukrainian Socialist Republic."

This article carried a punishment for bribery ranging from eight to fifteen years. The document also referred to Stern's second offense: "Nineteen cases of fraud... to aid in the acquisition of foreign drugs" that he said "only he had." So, "he also received money in the amount of 754 rubles and 3 kopecks, and got a rooster and seventy eggs."

During the first break, I pushed through the crowded corridors. People were staring at me. Several former patients of Stern discussed the indictment.

"Filth!" said a man with a gray wooden crutch sticking out of his pants instead of a leg. "He annoyed some authorities, so now they tell lies about him."

"Well, how can you say that? You've heard how many witnesses!"

"We have not heard witnesses yet," countered the man. "Did he take money or an egg from you? No. From me, no. And from her he didn't take a kopeck."

"But then the doctors do take money; one cannot make a single step in a polyclinic without money," objected his interlocutor with a scarf thrown over her shoulders.

"You don't know him," insisted the cripple. "He would give his own to others."

"So, why don't you offer yourself as a witness?"

"Didn't I go? I walked right into the judge's office. I have nobody to fear. And he said" —here the man pursed his lips portraying Orlovsky, shook his head awkwardly as if his neck was made of wood, and choked out—"Stern isn't charged with extorting money from you."

I did not speak to that handicapped man, fearing possible complications for him. He had come to the court many times and always tried to put his head between the escort soldiers to greet Stern.

A woman with her hair folded into a bun probably came here like me, from the overcrowded courtroom; she counted Stern's income for those who were not able to hear: "Well, what is it? One and a half thousand rubles in ten years? This means—150 in a year, right? So... and then in a month... twelve rubles, isn't it right? Well, well, well! The saleswoman in a grocery store steals more in one day by cheating buyers!"

During the breaks, rushing out into the hallway, onto the stairs and even out into the street, became a routine activity for all of us, the three Muscovites and two sons of Stern. The local refuseniks and their children were waiting to pick up our notes. I had a more difficult time than the others because my notes were more bulky and the men sitting next to me always tried to follow me.

UPON MY RETURN to the courtroom, a new man, this time of athletic build, turned aside his knees to let me pass. I thanked him. He smiled wryly and glanced at the notebook, already in my hand. The court embarked on hearing the testimony of Hanna Overchuk, one of the two main prosecution witnesses.

A year after her last visit to the doctor, her husband and she realized that Stern had taken possession of their hard-earned money. On May 14, 1974, Hanna handed this statement to the investigator Krachenko: "Due to the fact that Stern fraudulently, under the guise of treating my son, took 65 rubles from me, please take steps to recover the said amount in my favor."

She told the court a story that we repeatedly heard from other prosecution witnesses in the following days. A military-medical commission of a district found a prospective soldier unfit for service and sent this fifteen-year-old villager to Vinnitsa for treatment in the endocrinology clinic. Thus the Overchuks appeared in Stern's office.

"Why did you put 25 rubles on the doctor's desk?" asked the prosecutor Gregory Krivoruchko.

"For a drug. He said the pharmacies didn't have it, but he would get it," said Hanna.

"Who else was at that moment at the office?"

"My son had already left it."

"Did the doctor examine your son?"

"Yes, like all others."

"And what did he say?"

"That the boy's genitals had not developed normally."

"How much money did you and your husband give to the defendant?"

"65 rubles."

"How many shots did the doctor administer to your son? How often did he travel to see this doctor?"

"I don't know."

"Were you surprised that the doctor asked him to undress in your presence?" asked Stern's defense counsel David Axelbant.

"No. He's a doctor."

The indictment repeatedly emphasized that Stern, to extort money effectively, constantly bared boys' genitals in front of their mothers. The expression "he showed her his penis" ran through many pages of the prosecutorial work. The prosecutor working in a region known for endemic diseases of the thyroid gland and the genitals, apparently decided that this method looked particularly suspect.

"Did you tell your husband that you gave money to Stern?" continued Axelbant.

"I don't remember," Hanna said.

Two days later, her husband, farmer Ivan Overchuk sheepishly replied to this question, "No, she didn't."

Axelbant then asked, "Did your wife tell you that on the first visit to the doctor, he gave your son a shot?"

"No, he didn't do it. Nobody had the medication, neither the pharmacies, nor the doctor."

"But the record indicates that in your claim of May 14 you said that Stern gave an injection to your son, and your wife in gratitude gave the doctor 10 rubles," Axelbant said.

"I don't know... We all are thankful..."

The counsel turned to Hanna, "Did Stern's treatment help your son?"

"So far no complaints."

"It seems, in fact," said the counsel, "that as a result of this treatment he grew six inches."

"Maybe as a result, or maybe, he just grew up," said the boy's mother.

"Is Victor healthy now?"

"So far he is."

"Then why did you write in your May 14 statement, even after the military medical commission recognized that the boy was now in perfect health, 'I lately had a suspicion that the doctor was treating my son improperly, so I decided to contact the prosecutor'?"

"I only had a suspicion that maybe Victor didn't need that treatment at all."

Stern interrupted. "Who taught you to say at the face-to-face confrontation that I was a spy, that someone was paying me money for the wrong treatment of youth?"

In response, Hanna murmured something unintelligible. Stern, instead of trying to get a clear answer from the witness, asked another question, "Why did you go to the prosecutor's office so late, a year later, on May 14?"

Stern continued his testimony to refute all counts of the charges. "I helped tens of thousands of people," he said, "and cannot remember how many shots of hormones I gave this boy. When the youth Victor Overchuk came to our clinic more than two years ago, on October 18, 1972, another doctor, not me, diagnosed hypogenitalism with growth retardation. The fifteen-year-old boy's sexual development was at the level of a six-year-old child. His height was four feet, six inches, and his weight was seventy-two pounds."

Throughout the year, continued Stern, other doctors were trying to treat Victor to no avail, and finally "they referred him to me." During the trial the doctor never belittled his talent, even likening himself to a medieval philosopher and astrologer Giordano Bruno, who was tried for heresy.

"Who's this Bruno?" I asked the athlete sitting next to me.

He shrugged.

I said, "He was burnt on the stake."

He shrugged again.

"I prescribed the boy hormones in my modification," continued Stern. "The pharmacy didn't have these drugs. But every day mattered, and I injected him at least eight times, as confirmed by the father and the son in the preliminary investigation and here. The boy was coming to me without his parents, once or twice a week. And he paid nothing. Most certainly my combination of hormones was worth 65 rubles! Four months later—please see his chart—we got a phenomenal result, the boy grew three inches and gained more than fifteen pounds. It seems that his parents should be happy. I saved their son." He looked at Hanna sitting in the first row. "What matters is that this honest and decent woman came to her senses. She herself was a victim of outside influence."

Answering the prosecutor, her husband suddenly became adamant—Stern was given only 50 rubles, not 65, and it was he who did it, not Hanna.

"When?" The prosecutor and the judge were trying to find out.

"I don't remember. Two years have passed," said Ivan.

Stern asked Ivan's son, "Did the treatment help?"

The high school senior Victor Overchuk swelled with pride. "I grew six inches!"

This is a story that happened to a family from a village with an ironic name Chary (Enchantment). The story was typical, except for the "espionage" and for the amount of rubles that was larger than those "given" by the rest of ninety-two witnesses and victims. All boys had one thing in common. They had been healed by Doctor Stern.

Now before the court stood Mikhail Sushko, another witness for the prosecution. The tall peasant stood at attention, petrified, like a soldier being reviewed. However, this numbness and the clumsy words that he spoke did not prevent him from standing his ground: Yes, the draft board. Yes, I brought the lad. Yes, the medicine wasn't in the pharmacies, and the doctor gave us the medicine. What kind? Like tiny buttons. No—no, he never asked for money. "I'd ask him 'how much?' and he'd say, 'See for yourself, it's written on the bottle.'"

Public prosecutor Krivoruchko spoke: "Something isn't quite clear here. During the preliminary investigation, you said to prosecutor Krachenko, 'I asked, how much is this medicine?' Stern said "Ten rubles." 'I gave him ten rubles.'"

A smile flitted across the prosecutor's face. "So, you did give the defendant ten rubles."

"What defendant?"

"Stern."

The farmer switched into his native Ukrainian tongue. "He was so good to me and to my lad," he said, "so I gave him ten rubles."

"For medication?"

"No—no! No. On the bottle it was written—30 kopecks."

"So why did you give him the money?"

"For this medicine."

The prosecutor was smiling again, "Ten rubles?"

"No, thirty kopecks."

"So why did you give him ten rubles?"

"We got along nicely, and we liked the doctor very much."

Time and again the prosecutor asked in essence the same questions. The face of Sushko became wet. The judge asked, "Do you understand why the prosecutor has been asking you so many questions?"

"No," said the farmer.

"What did you say to the interrogator?"

"Thirty kopecks."

The prosecutor jumped up, took from the judge the preliminary interrogation protocol he just quoted, and angrily approached Sushko, "Your son would be better at answering my questions!

Read your testimony!"

Silent Sushko stared at the spot where the prosecutor's finger stuck.

"Why aren't you reading?" the prosecutor asked.

"I'm reading," Sushko said.

I was beginning to suspect the peasant of bullying the Soviet court.

The prosecutor switched to shouting, "Read aloud!"

Sushko hesitated, stumbled on the letters like on rocks, but slowly, syllable by syllable, confused in word stress like a fish in a seine, gradually, he got to the fateful ten rubles. The prosecutor and the judge were delighted. The slow pace made it easier for me to record new details of the indictment. It said that Stern had sold Sushko a vial of "foreign" thyroiodine for 10 rubles, which actually cost 30 kopecks and had been produced in Soviet Belarus. Thus Stern fraudulently amassed 9 rubles 70 kopecks.

I whispered to my neighbor, "And thus he earned three half-liter bottles of cheap vodka." The neighbor, to my surprise, nodded. How could I know that he was from the KGB?

Eventually the peasant read, with a shaky voice, the last sentence written by the prosecution investigator: "When inspecting the bottle presented by citizen Sushko, it was found that the cost was erased from the bottle."

Now Judge Orlovsky considerably calmed down and almost lovingly, addressed Sushko like a terrified child, "Well, now you do remember what Stern told you, don't you?"

The victim's voice drooped, "Yes."

"What precisely did he say?" the judge asked.

Then came an eerie silence. Before us was a broken man. The hall was frozen in anticipation.

"And then. What did he say?" the judge repeated kindly.

The farmer's voice was barely audible; "Thirty kopecks."

It started all over again. Prosecutor Krivoruchko licked his lips, his handsome face twisted, he almost screamed, "Who spoke to you before the trial?"

"They came...," the victim said reluctantly. He did not look at the prosecutor, but was staring straight ahead, over the judge's head.

"Who?!"

"The prosecutor."

There was a new dramatic pause. Time seemed to stop. Nodules twitched on Sushko's skinny cheekbones, "Kra... Kra... Maybe Kravchuk?" The judge looked at our enemy regiment with disgust and found a path out of the impasse, "So then why did you give ten rubles to Stern, if he didn't demand it?"

The farmer was again agonizing in silence. I continued scribbling in my notebook, when Orlovsky asked me, "You continue writing? Earning a livelihood?"

I raised my head. Our eyes met.

The hard evidence of the bottle, of course, was produced in court. The judge examined the hapless little thing. Two silent lay judges thoughtfully twisted it between their fingers.

"The price is erased," Orlovsky confirmed on behalf of all three of them.

"Maybe it's still in sight...," mumbled the dumbfounded Sushko, while gently taking the dark bottle from the hands of the prosecutor. He held it between his thick thumb and index finger and looked through it against the light barely glimmering in the gray December window.

Later, counsel Axelbant would say in the oral argument, "The most surprising and revelatory finding for the investigating officer Krachenko is that Sushko said—there was the price. 30 kopecks. Who erased it? We must ask the investigator about this."

Stern expressed his outrage at the pressure applied to Sushko and demanded to find out who came to the peasant's home before the trial. The judge calmly interjected, "The court is going to cause Sushko to testify again and to establish who visited him."

However, this wasn't done.

After two weeks of the trial, we finally learned why the KGB, the judge, and the police had demonstrated such a high level of tolerance toward us, traitors present in the courtroom. Reports about this ordinary trial of the most common fraud and money-grubbing were published in some papers in the West. They were written by my invisible antithesis, a correspondent of the Novosty News Agency, Boris Antonov, a colleague of my former buddy Vladimir Zhukov.

All the time Orlovsky kept in mind the external enemies.

"Don't appeal to the public! Speak to the court!" These words of the judge we heard on the very first day of the trial. The following day, December 12, this phrase had become sacramental. All day, the judge constantly interrupted Stern, literally muzzled him. At the close of that day, he let Stern read his statement. But as soon as the defendant uttered the first words of protest against the interrogation techniques of prosecutor Krivoruchko, the judge's resentment boiled over, "Hush! You talk so loud!" He winced and turned to the audience, "For what purpose is this done?" The situation was novel to the experienced judge who became tongue-tied and stammered, "The man knows who they are, and we know who wrote... Nobody has the right to record the process!"

Under the accompaniment of his tirade, I frantically continued writing down almost every word in my notebook, and the judge, looking at me in disgust, continued, "The defendant is apparently aware that his words are being recorded. That sort of thing... It's known...," the judge turned to the defendant, "Do you want me to raise this man from his chair?"

I gripped my notebook in hand and braced to get up. My neighbor pricked up his ears.

Stern was confused. "I don't understand..."

"I think it's..." the judge said. At this point, while giving me another withering look, he unintentionally reassured me. "The court proceedings were recorded yesterday on tape."

In fact the "man" was not me, but Victor Stern, who was sitting beside his mother. The battered tape recorder was actually in his pocket. The judge, known for his rigidity, displayed indecision, did not make "this man" rise from his chair and did not take away our secret weapon. Those who revealed to him our secret even allowed the tape recording to continue for the time being. Even though, at one time, there was suddenly music emanating throughout the room that had been equipped according to strict canons of judicial interior—in the depths of his own pocket Victor accidentally pressed the wrong button.

"What is this? Who's playing music?" asked the startled Orlovsky.

"It's from the street," said one of the relatives.

I turned to a new personality, this time, a grim middle-aged woman sitting beside me and whispered, "Shall we dance?"

How delightful is impunity!

Dozens of women from collective farms wearing short, slinky plush coats had already appeared before us. From them Josepha Bayda was distinguished only by a slim figure and a melodious voice. Now this pretty woman of about forty, stood in the center of the stuffy room, behind the bend of a flimsy wooden barrier.

She had never been to Vinnitsa. Always a lot to do in the village. Stephan traveled with his father to the doctor with a black beard. She glanced at the whitened beard of Stern, blushed, and continued.

At home the son, as the doctor ordered, took a lot of powders. The doctor did the injections himself. Stephan traveled to him for a long time. The doctor, a good man, took her husband to the pharmacy; we—country folk, are lost in such a large city.

"How much money did your husband pay at the pharmacy?" Orlovsky asked.

"Fifty rubles."

"To whom did he give the money there?"

"The pharmacist."

"Not the doctor?"

"No. Why to the doctor?"

"And what did you say to the investigator?"

"The pharmacist."

"There are discrepancies in your testimony," said the prosecutor. "In the record of the interview, you said that your husband paid fifty rubles not to the pharmacy but to the doctor."

"No. My husband would tell me about it."

"Did your husband bring foodstuffs to the doctor?" the judge said.

"No."

The defense counsel burst in at this point. "I don't see any discrepancies in the testimony. The record doesn't say that Bayda gave money and foods."

Josepha Bayda confirmed. "He never took anything from our house."

"Please tell me," said Stern, "do you know what disease your son had?"

Instead of answering, she started sobbing and wiping tears with the edge of her flowery scarf.

"What happened?" interjected the judge. "Why are you crying, victim?"

"He was a cripple! Quite a cripple!"

"And now?"

"Now he's he-e-e-ealthy!" she said, drowning in her tears.

"Why cry if he's healthy?" the judge asked.

"Because he was a cri-i-pple!" the mother cried, still in distress.

"Thousands of Soviet doctors treat their patients free of charge," said the judge Orlovsky. "It's their duty to cure."

Josepha Bayda: "I'm grateful to the doctor!"

"How long did Doctor Stern treat your son?" said Stern, referring to himself in the third person.

"Two years. And we never gave you anything. Please forgive me, I never even came to thank you," the victim said sheepishly to Stern. "I myself was ill."

After the mother, her son appeared before the judge. A tall handsome Stephan, contrary to court orders, greeted the defendant and stared at the judge with dislike.

"In '71 I went to Mikhail Isayevich," he said, respectfully using the very Jewish patronym of Stern. "Every week I skipped one school day. Traveled from afar. And then Mikhail Isayevich said, 'You might fail in all subjects. Better come to my house on Sundays.'"

Prosecutor: "Who was buying drugs?"

"My father."

"Was he paying the doctor?"

"I cannot know that."

"And you?"

"I have no money at all."

"Witness, are you healthy?" interjected Dr. Stern.

"Of course!" Stephan almost yelled. "Thank you!"

"How long will you remember your doctor?" said Stern again.

"All my life!"

I looked at the boy and thought, women like his mother probably had been rescuing Jews from the Germans. Sushko might have done it, too.

Later, when Stephan had already returned to his village, Mikhail Stern's joyful voice rang defiantly: "I was eager to perform a miracle, and I did it. Eunuchoidism—is a terrible word. Recovery from this disease doesn't happen too often. I spared neither time nor effort, nor drugs, nor my days off. If I have been such a money-maker and a cheapskate as I'm depicted here, nothing could have stopped me from cashing in. But I treated him free of charge."

Prosecutor Vitaly Krachenko had pushed aside the testimony of the Bayda family given to the district investigator and wrote in the indictment something quite the opposite. Why was he not afraid to flagrantly disobey the law?

After all nineteen episodes of fraud had been considered, the defense counsel stated that none of the episodes had evidence of fraud or breach of the patients' trust. And why was defense counsel Axelbant, this rich Moscow lawyer, putting pressure on the poor prosecutor Krachenko? After all, he was not just an executor of the Party royal will. He also had his deep-seated feelings.

Once in the early stages of the trial, I walked in the Stern's garden to take a look at the results of the search of Jewish gold. When it was not found, that did not mean for Krachenko that the Sterns had no gold. Two dozen investigators for three months had been looking in all twenty-five districts of the region for witnesses among his patients. The prosecutor knew that for a physician to survive only on his meager salary was a challenge and many asked patients for money. Forty witnesses, selected by the prosecutors out of two thousand passed in three weeks in front of my eyes in the courtroom. One thousand nine hundred sixty of the questioned patients had insisted that Stern had refused to take money when they begged him.

On the sixth day of the trial a local refusenik, Mike Mager, told me that one guy from the parking lot was lamenting, "Ah, Mike, the Stern's car was parked right here with us for a few days, and we didn't know that it had golden bumpers!"

This beaten-up Jewish car had been imagined, in accordance with the expectations of the crowd, to be quickly filled with gold. On the seventh day of the trial August Stern heard a policeman telling a prosecution witness that the gold was hidden in the engine of the car.

Outside the court building, I came across another Ukrainian who, just as the prosecutor, perhaps, had also acquired his knowledge of Jewish gold in early childhood from his loving mother. Leaning against a prison van and looking skeptically at me, this elderly man, pronouncing each word with gusto, told his interlocutors, "He was caught with the gold at the border. Wanted to escape to Israel."

During one of many long breaks and my travels through corridors and outside the court building a quiet old Jew came up to me and asked, "Is it true that the Sterns feed you caviar every day?"

"Sometimes even for breakfast," I said. "But always, for lunch and dinner. And their mastiff gets all of the leftover caviar and doesn't want to consume anything else."

"You laugh," he said sadly, "but we live here."

"Then why aren't you afraid to come up to me?"

"Ah! Whether I approach you or not, we already know what will happen to all of us. After this trial, the Jews in this city will be eaten alive. I didn't allow my family to come within a gunshot of the courthouse."

"That's why the two brothers of Doctor Stern never came to the court?"

"They are frightened to death."

It was time for me to return to my seat. He shook my hand and then let me know, "The other day neighborhood boys called my youngest son to play soccer. When he arrived, they were kicking around the field a skull taken from an old Jewish cemetery."

THE INTENSITY of emotions grew with every passing day. On December 13, Orlovsky said in a trembling voice, "Day after day, right from the very first minute, I, the judge, have been disparaged badly. They have grabbed me by the throat." And here he demonstrated his talent. "Some individuals," he said, "are interested in distorting the meaning of what is happening here. They want to keep us from an objective examination of the case under the law."

I whispered to the KGB man next to me, "About whom is he talking?"

He shrugged.

After another long recess, the judge suddenly explained: some of the individuals present in the room were law students. The next day one of them came into intimate contact with us. It was thus impossible to take a picture of Stern even when the convoy was putting him in the prison van. Out of desperation, we decided to photograph the van and the crowd around it. We moved to the other side of the street and circled around Victor. He promptly opened his coat, and, as we parted, pressed the camera trigger two or three times. Immediately, as if out of thin air, in front of us materialized one of those law students, "Follow me to the police! You have no right to photograph a military vehicle!"

"You just assumed," I said boldly. "And anyway, who are you?"

The "lawyer" turned red and ran away. We already knew him. He was always somewhere near, even at the cafe, where we sometimes went during the lunch break. As soon as Victor handed his camera to a reliable person, the "student" came running back to us, now with two heavy-breathing men in uniform. One of them said, "You were filming a military vehicle. You all have come along to the police station for identification."

"It's an ordinary truck," I said naively.

"Didn't you see the red military star on the door?" said the smart student triumphantly.

At the District Police Department, Victor was led to the second floor. The three of us were brought to a room on the ground floor. Soon there came that same lieutenant colonel, who on the first day of the trial successfully went incognito. It turned out he was the commander of this department.

Rather than order some corporal to do the body search, this Colonel Koval did it himself, with exemplary enthusiasm. It was quite a show: the completely petrified Lasaris, his hands raised, the flaps of his unbuttoned coat and jacket swung open and parted far to the sides, there with the burly colonel fussing around this suddenly pale, skinny statue. After removing from this Moscow Zionist his notebook and a few pages of transcripts of the proceedings, the relieved officer was obviously thinking of the success of his highly professional actions. He scoured Goldfarb and me with careless negligence, which saved my own precious records of the proceedings.

My companions were released. Victor was fined 30 rubles for disorderly conduct, while for an hour and a half I explained to the amiable head of the city's passport office why tiny Israel so cruelly attacked millions of peace-loving Arabs. He asked me if I knew the Arabic language. This meant that he was told something about my recent past. After that, we met several times in court. Always dressed in civilian clothing, he called me by name and patronymic, shook my hand as a good friend, and solicitously inquired about the source of funds I lived on. Maybe my Moscow well-wishers were magnanimously considering the use of the penal code article on the parasitic way of life as my first punishment—the article provided for no more than three years in prison.

THE STERNS' PHONE was disconnected in the early days of the trial, and late in the evening we dictated from the city call center our statement to our Moscow friends. An operator listening in on the line, as usual, covered her mouth with her plump palm and repeated the same remark in a theatrical whisper, "Israel is again at booth 13!"

We stated that much of the witnesses' testimony, as recorded in the preliminary investigation, was untrue and Orlovsky accused us of intending to pervert the course of the trial.

Maybe, by allowing our calls, the KGB was killing two birds with one stone. It showed to the word that the trial was open to public scrutiny and helped Boris Antonov from the Novosty News Agency to adjust his coverage of the trial to make a better piece of propaganda targeted at foreign audiences.

The judge and the prosecutor had made their contribution to these efforts. When Stern said that after receiving an invitation to emigrate, he began preparing for the arrest, Orlovsky used one of his favorite words: "This isn't related to this trial. The comrades"—a contemptuous glance in my direction—"will transmit ... They get paid for it."

On another occasion, the judge said, "Hostile radio stations broadcast that Stern is ill, that he spits blood. Some of the people sitting in this hall pass along such information ..."

One evening the Stern sons were summoned to the regional prosecutor's office. "Convey to your friends," said Ivan Timchenko, the Deputy Chief Prosecutor for Vinnytsia Region, "the possibility of criminal liability for transmitting defamatory information to the West."

The following evening several Moscow refuseniks signed a statement seeking to protect us. It said: "A campaign of intimidation and threats has been conducted against three Muscovites... They are accused of transmitting defamatory information to the West... Such a charge may serve as the grounds for imprisonment... The actions of the court are an attempt to turn the trial into closed proceedings."

A few days later Goldfarb and I were not allowed in the hall and were led to Oleg Gotha, the head of the criminal investigation bureau of the Leninsky District Police Department. The conversation lasted three minutes.

"I have to warn you about your improper behavior in the courtroom," he said, but instead of answering my question as to what constituted our bad behavior, he added, "If we continue to receive complaints from the public in the hall, the police will take action against you."

ON THE SIXTEENTH DAY of the trial I sent the editor-in-chief of the local Vinnitsa *Pravda* a letter beginning, "Judging by the silence of your paper, the readers of Vinnitsa are less interested in this trial than Londoners." I informed him that Antonov's reports appeared in *The Times* in London, asked him to take into consideration the interests of the local population, and report about the trial. It was strange, I stressed, that a large news agency was interested in such a run-of-the-mill story and notified the foreign public of so miniscule a case of bribery. I asked the editor to help me to find the invisible Boris Antonov from the Novosty News Agency in the courtroom.

On Friday, three days before sentencing, after a long wait the hearing was canceled again. The trial was already over. The prosecutor demanded that the judge sentence Stern to nine years in prison. Stern's defense counsel Axelbant, referring to the same string of witnesses, demanded a full acquittal.

Judge Orlovsky, in a new, well-cut suit with medal ribbons, declared to the jam-packed room that lay judge Laktionov was ill and the final testimony of the defendant was delayed until Monday morning. A little man with curled lips and legs sat in the first row every day. Everybody knew he was an alternate lay judge waiting for such an occasion. Someone forgot to inform him.

The judge turned to me, his voice like acid, and said, "You can write it down!"

"Thank you!" I said and wrote it down.

Saturday and Sunday were days of anxious waiting.

Then, on the night of Monday, December 30, 1974, Ida Stern and her sons barely slept. In the morning we naively thought that we arrived at the court half an hour before the start of the hearing. Only Judge Orlovsky, the prosecutor, both lay judges, as well as activists from the taxi fleet knew that the trial had been rescheduled to take place an hour earlier, at nine a.m. We certainly would not have been allowed in, and Stern would have addressed his last plea to the judge and the taxi drivers, who filled the hall to capacity, and not to his sons, his wife and the world imperialism.

But it did not happen, thank God and the Russian laxity, which in the future will more than once serve the good of Mother Russia— we did not see the defense lawyer in the room. In the hallway the judge nervously chastised the court clerk, and the poor thing was looking for excuses and claimed that she could not find Axelbant at the hotel. Thus, the Jewish lawyer sabotaged the operation to combat misinformation. Knowing nothing, he came to the court at the usual time, as did we.

Stern cried out for justice. He denied all the allegations against him, and finally, throwing caution to the wind, he said, "This hasn't been a normal trial of a bribe-taker and a fraud. Some people wanted to turn this court into a bloody feast."

And again, there was a break until the end of the day, instead of the expected verdict. They were still waiting for Taratuta, the Regional Party Secretary, the Stern sons assured me. He had been in Kiev for a few days, at the Plenum of the Ukraine's Central Committee.

That important Monday the taxi drivers enjoyed the trial so much that the next day they returned to hear the delayed verdict.

It was December 31, New Year's Eve, the busiest day in the life of a Soviet taxi driver, and yet they were there. For nearly one and a half hours, the hostile audience, standing, listened to Judge Vasily Orlovsky. The verdict scrupulously preserved even that which had nothing to do with the conviction, including the willful exposure of the young "in the presence of their mothers, focusing their attention on the genitals of their sons."

The taxi drivers liked to hear about the genitals. One nudged his neighbor and they smiled happily. They also liked "That's not enough! You're stingy!" and "So give me the money!" and, of course, the "advertising as foreign, scarce and expensive drugs that were ordinary Soviet medicines."

The case was moving to the end. The tired cabbies whispered and shifted from foot to foot. Pale Stern, not hiding contempt, was looking at the judge and made signs to his wife and sons.

"... It is taken into account ... ," the judge finally concluded in a hoarse voice, "that the defendant had not been tried before, and therefore the panel of judges considers it possible to pass the minimum sentence provided under Article 168 of the Criminal Code of the Ukrainian Socialist Republic." Orlovsky cleared his throat, threw out his chest, and breaking the monotonous patter, said solemnly, "The panel..." He again made an expressive pause, and in the ensuing dead silence we all heard "Bastards!"

"Who said that!?" cried Orlovsky and took off his glasses. "Who dares offend the court!?"

"I do," said August Stern.

"No," his mother said. "I did."

"Leave the room immediately!" the judge ordered her.

Ida Stern, her head held unnaturally high, went to the door. At the door she paused between two policemen and loudly said, not to the judge, but to the standing audience—all eyes fixed on her— "Murderers!" and left the room. All eyes bored now into the judge.

At this point I even liked Orlovsky. After all, for contempt of court, he could have punished this little woman in accordance with the Criminal Code. However, the judge put on his glasses and finished reading the verdict with obvious relief, "... has sentenced Mikhail Stern to imprisonment for a term of eight years, to be served in a maximum security hard labor camp, with confiscation of all property."

Immediately, without pause, as if a call to battle, there rang the doctor's sharp voice, "Shame on those who sow hatred of the Jews!"

All of us were let out of the courtroom only after Dr. Stern, the prisoner Stern, had been taken away in a van with a red star on the green door.

IN THE TRAIN on my way home I was alone. Goldfarb and Lasaris left for Moscow a few days before the end of the trial. I wondered whether the Ukrainian friends told that Jewish child that the skull they used as a soccer-training ball was from a Jewish cemetery. This unhealthy thinking stopped as soon as I was strip-searched. There was an element of legitimacy at play in this act, with a real witness, not an informant or police. This guy was a railroad big shot, and it was absurdly unreal. I had never seen such impressive insignia on a railroad uniform. In the end, with the window wide open, they left me naked in the conductors' tiny compartment alone with this official, as he had to sign the protocol. He got up from his seat and closed the window with the words, "We're all in winter coats, and you can catch pneumonia." He caught my look of surprise and added, "I wish you success in all your endeavors" and quickly went out, finally allowing me to dress.

Upon arrival in Moscow, it took a couple of hours to confuse my shadows. I was not going to return home. Natan Sharansky had been already enjoying his homeless life in my apartment. His family lived near Moscow, and he had now a chance not to tramp

Dr. Mikhail Stern at the Andrei Sakharov tribunal in The Hague. 1980.
(Rob Bogaerts, Anefo)

for three or four months while I, hiding in Lucy Litvinov's apartment, was finishing writing my clandestine book *Why a Physician Was Tried*. My portable miracle of East German Socialist engineering, an Erika typewriter, was able to print up to four carbon copies of my manuscript on very thin paper, with no margins, and no air between the lines. To my surprise, it was read by some people I never knew. In May 1975 Sharansky managed to pass it to someone from the West. But we were blind—we could not even know whether my backstreet *samizdat* crossed the border.

The Stern case got worldwide publicity, and it was realistic to assume that he would be released before his sentence was finished. It happened sometime in March 1977, within twenty-seven months after the trial, much sooner than the deeply disillusioned Vinnitsa Party leadership and I anticipated. On that occasion the APN correspondent Boris Antonov finally addressed the Russian audience with an article that revealed the intrigues of world Zionism. A couple of months later Mikhail and Ida Stern came to see me in my apartment unaware that I was faraway on a secret trip to the unregistered Pentecostal church in Krasnodarsky Territory.

As for my manuscript, during the 1979 International Andrei Sakharov Human Rights Hearings in Washington, a woman in her sixties from a leading Jewish organization approached me and said that it had disappeared from a drawer of her desk. I went numb, but my only thought was: focus on your present problem. I had to concentrate on my task. In a few minutes I would speak through an interpreter on behalf of thirty thousand Russian Evangelicals who needed to emigrate in order to escape persecution. Perhaps the lady was surprised at the calm with which I listened to her. The moment she gave me her name, it escaped me. We never met again.

АРКАДИЙ ПОЛИЩУК

ЗА ЧТО СУДИЛИ ВРАЧА?

"...Настоящее дело для вас, членов судебной коллегии, не представляет
никакой сложности. Это самое простое дело о взяточничестве и мошенничестве.
Но вокруг этого дела, ничем не примечательного, не отличающегося от других
подобных дел, подсудимый и заинтересованные лица создали искусственно на-
каленную обстановку, обострили эту обстановку. Эта обстановка, как вам известно, даже сопровождалась различного рода шантажами, провокациями и кле-
ветой. И все это было направлено только лишь не в интересах объективного
рассмотрения настоящего дела.

Подсудимым была выдвинута версия о том, что это дело результат, якобы,
стремления его сыновей выехать за границу, что привлечению его к уголовной
ответственности способствовали его злейшие профессиональные противники, с той
той целью, чтобы избавиться от него, и, даже, что, якобы, привлечение к уголовной ответственности связано с национальностью подсудимого. Но эти его до-
воды, как голос вопиющего в пустыне, не нашли абсолютно никакого подтвержде-
ния в материалах судебного следствия.

Как известно, сыновьям подсудимого Штерна представлялась возможность
выехать в Израиль, одному еще в мае, другому - в ноябре. И сейчас никто им
не препятствует воспользоваться тем правом, которое они получили. Что каса-
ется дела, то оно возбуждено по сигналам, поступившим в прокуратуру области
лишь после того, как выяснилось, в результате проверки, что получение денег
от больных под различным предлогом Штерн ввел в систему, используя свое
служебное положение, что Штерн не сделал соответствующего вывода из фактов,
которые имели место в шестидесятом году, когда по этому поводу производились
проверки, лишь только за отсутствием достаточных доказательств он не был
привлечен к уголовной ответственности. Что действительно нашло свое отраже-
ние в материалах дела - это систематическое получение денег от больных, оно
подтверждено материалами предварительного и судебного следствия. Допрошен-
ные в судебном заседании простые советские граждане - колхозники, рабочие,
пенсионеры, подростки - со всей непосредственностью, просто и убедительно
рассказывали при каких обстоятельствах, почему и за что давали подсудимому
деньги. На поставленные вопросы они отвечали, что никто не просил давать их,
такие показания на подсудимого, что они его не оговаривают, что они показы-
вают то, что знают, и то, что они делали.

В судебном заседании было установлено, что подсудимый действительно
свои знания, бесплатно полученные в медицинском институте, свой практический
опыт, свою самую гуманную, самую полезную для человечества профессию использовал как источник личного обогащения. И где? В стране, где конституцией
закреплено право на бесплатное медицинское обслуживание в интересах укрепле-
ния здоровья советских граждан.

Штерн нарушил клятву Гиппократа, он потерял чистую совесть и доброе
сердце врача, а свою твердую руку использовал как лапу, на которую ложились
четвертные, десятки, пятерки, оторванные от больных, от детей и инвалидов,
от пенсионеров. Штерн не брезговал ни смородиной, ни яйцами, ни курами, ни
клубникой. Штерновская кухня перерабатывала все... Штерн наживался на чужом
горе, на чужих страданиях... Особая опасность преступления в том, что подсудимый использовал больных.

...Прошу признать подсудимого Штерна Михаила Иваевича виновным в пре-
ступлениях по статьям 168 ч.II и 143 ч.II Уголовного кодекса УССР и пригово-
рить его к 9 годам лишения свободы с конфискацией имущества и с отбытием
в исправительно-трудовой колонии усиленного режима.

Такой приговор будет справедливым".

Так 26 декабря 1974 года закончил свою речь государственный обвинитель
Григорий Криворучко, заместитель прокурора Винницкой области.

Арест и тюрьма

Улица Полины Осипенко так круто сбегает к реке, что с осени до весны
из-за скользкой грязи и снега подчас просто невозможно подъехать к дому, где
живут Штерны. Покосившийся дом мало чем отличается от соседних, таких же
двухэтажных, потертых временем. Верхние дома упираются в улицу Ленина,
центральную в Виннице, нижние - вот-вот, кажется, соскользнут на Листвый

TEN

Different Courts Without a Difference

ONE MORNING IN APRIL 1975, soon after my finishing my book and returning home from Lucy's, Sharansky was planning to dictate a statement of Andrei Sakharov's with which he had been entrusted from my phone to someone in Canada. Before 7 a.m. two men from the telephone exchange woke me up. They said they had to switch something in the metal box above my front door. One of the technicians stepped onto the ladder, opened the box, made a single quick movement inside it, and before setting a foot back on my floor, said, "For systematic use of your phone for anti-Soviet purposes, it's been disconnected."

In a second they were gone. If someone wakes me up too early, I make the dumbest mistakes. I cursed myself for opening the door and fatalistically waited for Anatoly. Two hours later a neighbor knocked. He asked, "Does your phone work?" In former times this Party secretary of the Moscow Composer Publisher had not shown any interest in my life, but recently I had constantly been hearing the click of the tiny metal flap that covered his door's peephole—he followed my comings and goings. My composer friends told me long ago that this neighbor was a known snitch.

To the envy of the vast majority of Muscovites, all tenants of my privileged co-op had phones. The only problem with ours was insignificant: all of them had been paired. I gleefully explained to the snitch that the ungrateful KGB shut off his phone. He frowned and left. My mood improved a little. Sharansky found me standing on a stool studying the ill-fated box above my door.

"It had to happen," Anatoly said in a businesslike way.

"Of course! You used my long absence very productively. You're supposed to know what wiring should be reconnected here in order to blow up the KGB headquarters."

Sharansky climbed up on the stool and became cheerful at once. "These idiots simply disconnected the wiring from the plug."

In a couple of minutes he was delivering Sakharov's statement to Toronto.

What happened after that should be the subject for a symposium of American experts on Russia. Obviously, some KGB bureaucrat checked off a victorious operation and moved on to other urgent matters. From that very morning, for twenty-nine days and nights in a row, we successfully used this detoxified phone for our nefarious activities. Only after nearly a month of this did the report of my newest crime reach some decision-making official. Most likely, the head honchos were never informed about this serious blunder of their subordinates. This time my neighbor was victimized again. Our two phones were disabled somewhere at the telephone exchange.

Before long, I was on a train again, this time with a lawyer, who happened to be a close friend of Simon Verbitsky, my pal at *Asia and Africa Today*. A Moldovan refusenik, Sender Levinson, was accused of profiteering with foreign fabric he received in parcels from Western sympathizers. His older sister sold three pieces of this poplin to her co-workers at a factory producing silk and was released from the pre-trial custody after he, on the advice of his KGB minders, took full responsibility for the crime and admitted that she had acted at his insistence. This lawyer, Valentine

Shereshevsky was his name, had been hired to defend them.

"Can you imagine," he said to me, "that the parents were even allowed to visit their children in the local jail so they could determine whom to sacrifice unto the beast—their son or their daughter?"

"It's a plot for Shakespeare," I said.

If he didn't confess, the minders said, his thirty-year-old sister would be sentenced to six years in prison and, even if released in good health, she'd never find a husband. "So touching!" I said. "In this town the KGB 'shrinks' know what is brewing not only in your kitchen pots, but also in your brain."

"Actually, this is for Orwell," the attorney said.

"What secrets did this former soldier manage to acquire years ago, while constructing apartment buildings for officers?"

"This—now this, is something for Nikolai Gogol," Valentine said and turned the conversation to rumors about refuseniks living in luxury and regularly receiving checks and parcels from the West. So far I had received only one $25 check from some American in front of the synagogue. He had patted me on the shoulder and said something soothing. Even now I did not feel comfortable talking about this. I had exchanged it at the Central Bank for a certificate in dollars, felt as rich as Baron Rothschild, and went to a Beryozka store, stocked mostly with foreign goods.

Valentine expressed pretended outrage, "Beryozka, the beloved birch tree, celebrated in poetry, prose and songs, a symbol of our patriotism, doesn't even admit ordinary citizens with their rubles in foreign currency shops!"

I agreed. "Nothing is sacred anymore."

"So, has this been your only income since you stopped receiving your fat salary?"

"No, once I received from London an album of Salvador Dali's paintings and felt only joy. One fellow wanted to buy it, but I was afraid of bringing greater joy to the KGB by going to prison for profiteering, just like Sender Levinson. As an honest citizen, I took the album to a secondhand bookshop."

"How much did they pay?"

"200 rubles, half of my monthly salary."

"For Dali, this personification of decadent capitalism, I'd give you your entire monthly pay."

"What do you think," I asked, "how many copies of this album are there in Moscow?"

"Maybe none."

"So, that's why I wouldn't be able to sell it."

"Yeah, were I the buyer, after revealing this jewel to my guests, I'd soon serve as a witness at the trial of a nouveau riche named Polishchuk."

"Are you so open with me because Simon Verbitsky is our mutual friend?"

"Just a nice coincidence."

I asked him why was he traveling with an enemy of the state. Wasn't it an open challenge to the authorities?

"No. You're a client, too. You've brought me your pregnant 'relative.' Her husband has been arrested for economic crimes."

"The KGB knows what kind of a relative I am."

"This game is in their interests," he said. "We, defense attorneys, and people like you legitimize these courts just by being there."

"Isn't it funny?" I said. "I can meet with you but cannot see my buddy Simon."

"It's hilarious. Simon and I will laugh to death when you end up in the Gulag."

"Did he tell you about our foreign correspondents?"

"Yes."

"Would you take my case?"

"The KGB might not allow it. It has its own list of defense

lawyers."

"Clearly I wouldn't agree with their choice."

"Life is unpredictable," he said.

I remembered what had happened to the Muscovite-refusenik Gendin in Moldova, but I did not want to tell my fellow traveler about it. In Chisinau prison, they struck him over the head with a steel shovel, doubled the time, threatened to kill him and, to save his life, Gendin heroically escaped and fled to Moscow shortly before the end of his thirty-day prison term.

In Bendery, on the dusty railroad station square, Valentine woke a coachman in a rumpled black cap dozing on a narrow bench of a four-wheeled droshky, his hand holding a whip rested on his knee.

"Royal carriage! The chariot of Pharaoh!" exclaimed the lawyer and waved goodbye.

This was the end of our communication. Stomping down the battered road, I realized that man's best friend was not a lazy dog but a hard-working horse. Bendery, a city with a population of almost one hundred thousand was just fine without buses, trolleys, and trams.

Beside the gate of the Levinson's shabby house stood a sad old mare tied to a poplar tree. She was harnessed to a platform wagon, which had also lived a long and distressing life. Sender Levinson's father was a private entrepreneur from prehistoric urban times.

The first thing he said was, "Please, don't be angry with me for saying this, but you didn't have to come here along with a lawyer. It makes it look like a political process."

Fear—a bad adviser, I thought sadly, and explained patiently that the KGB had already spread the rumor that Sender would be tried solely for profiteering by dealing in foreign goods. After Sender's arrest, investigators searched exclusively for the contents of overseas parcels and did not even glance at the seditious photocopies and film of reproduced Hebrew textbooks laid out on the kitchen table. Several Hebrew teachers were already serving time just for that.

Sender's father pleaded not to send information about this trial abroad. It was too late to ask. It had long been known in the West that this was a lynching of a Jewish activist.

During the four or five days I stayed there, his parents were mostly silent and looked at me with rueful hope. Between themselves, they spoke softly and reticently in a mixture of Yiddish, Ukrainian, and Romanian. I talked mostly with Sender's sister, his heavily pregnant wife, and their three-year-old son. The sister told me that at first she sold only one piece of poplin to her girlfriend at the State silk mill, but when the other two girls learned about her brother's parcels, they begged her to sell poplin to them, too. They preferred this vulgar cotton cloth from overseas to the beautiful silk of their factory.

In the first seconds of the trial, upon the judge entering the courtroom, I felt an urge to share something immediately with humanity. I gave Valentine a furtive glance. He was already looking at me, covering his misplaced smile with a fist. I wanted to slide off the chair on to the floor, so nobody would see me smirk or to address my heartfelt inner monologue to this plump middle-aged woman: "Citizen Judge! You are a woman, and you want to be beautiful. I love your dress; it's made from the very same poplin, which cannot be bought without the right connections. You know that. Both defendants deserve nothing but praise for the compassion they have shown toward these tormented women by selling them this fucking poplin."

The judge was still asking the defendants formal questions, and I had enough time to straighten myself up, and to start following the proceedings.

The sister, instead of answering the prosecutor's questions, was crying and repeating, "Sender, I'm so sorry!"

Her brother shouted, "Stop dodging, say that I coerced you to sell the poplin!"

The prosecutor looked at him like a grateful dog looks at the man who is about to throw him a bone. The stony-faced judge did not intervene until Sender said, "I'm being tried because I want to go to my historical homeland."

The three witnesses were shaking with fear. Valentine tried to explain to the judge that a person could not be accused of profiteering if he did not resell anything, but merely sold his own goods. In response to the defense, the prosecutor listed the American cities from which the parcels came. His passionate final words he devoted to the struggle against world Zionism. He even recalled propagation of Hebrew textbooks that had been pointedly ignored during the investigation. His last sentence, though crude, certainly reflected the essence of Sender's crime. "This case isn't just about pieces of fabric; it's about the defendant's political failure."

Sender Levinson was sentenced to six years imprisonment, his sister to three years. However, the KGB did not disgrace itself. Due to the amnesty announced earlier on the occasion of International Women's Day, she was released right at the courthouse.

We were exiting after the trial—me and the Moldovan refuseniks—when a brawny man leaped out of a large crowd of men with stern faces and pulled from the refusenik Joseph's breast pocket a pen with a red cap. This ballpoint had been presented to Joseph by a foreigner in Moscow. Evidently, the police were instructed to look for microphones.

I did not join the excited local refuseniks outside. I had my own problem to solve.

The night after the verdict, the Levinson's house resembled the house of the Sterns in Vinnitsa. At midnight no one was going to bed, and even the three-year-old boy was as grumpy as had been the three-year-old grandson of Doctor Stern. And here, just as there, this noise pleased me. These shrieks and squawks wisely reminded everyone that life was going on, and one could not put off until tomorrow what should be done today—that is, to put the child to bed.

When the unlocked door opened and Sender's close friend Dima entered, no one paid attention. It was as if Dima had never left the house. He turned to me and whispered, "You stumbled very naturally against that baby buggy."

"I dropped my notebook right on the baby's tummy," I whispered, embarrassed. "The whole town heard his protest against our anti-Soviet action."

Our successes were measured, alas, not by acquittal or reducing the sentences, but by being a noisy witnesses to the injustices and crimes of the regime. Our actions could well have been called anti-Soviet propaganda, punishable by seven years of prison often followed by internal exile of five years. Nevertheless, inspired by this, Dima wanted to outwit the KGB again, this time, by putting me on the train going in the direction opposite to Moscow—to Odessa, where another good friend of Sender, Leo Roitburd, would be happy to help me. So far I had yelled from every rooftop that we weren't hiding any secrets, and our strength was rooted in this openness.

"We have to go," Dima said. "Nobody is outside. I noticed in court—during the breaks they avoided you like a leper."

The KGB remembered its bad experience in Vinnitsa. To disguise the true nature of this trial, they apparently were ordered to ignore my presence in Bendery.

The city was asleep, and we got to Dima's house without any incidents. I had never seen such gigantic burdocks. Heart-shaped, they sprung from the entire ground of his garden like dark-green parasols with broken-off handles.

"You might hide here," he smiled.

"I'd be scared to live here," I said. "On moonless southern nights like this I'd see a venomous creature under every leaf."

"We wrap and bake potatoes in burdock leaf."

That was a discovery. Bendery was known to me as a home-made-wine-and-jam town.

We entered the house. Dima did not turn on the electricity. Holding my hand, he guided me through the dark room to an already prepared makeshift bed on the floor, behind an armoire.

"Nobody will see you through the window. In the morning, I'll show you what I do for a living." He put a small piece of polished wood in my hand. "Now—you can touch my creation."

"This is a head with a beard," I said. "You're a wood carver."

"Yeah, so far I've carved figures from the old cherry and apple trees' roots. In Israel I'll try to become a sculptor."

The first thing I saw in the morning was a calm old Jew with an elaborately carved curly large beard and the steep forehead of a thinker. He lay on the floor next to my palm and stared at the ceiling from under his thick eyebrows. Dima picked up his creation, placed it on the table, and quickly carved on the back of the head "From Dima E. 29.V.75". Today, it hangs over my desk in Washington DC, and I love it still.

ELEVEN

The Sweet Taste of Freedom

W E HAD NEVER met before, but Leo Roitburd, his wife Lilia and their eleven-year-old son welcomed me to Odessa as though I was a close friend who survived a perilous trip across the world. Depressed, I told them that even if the Moldovan KGB were to get a hold of my notebook, there was nothing new in it—for them, or our sympathizers in the West. Leo suggested that I rest for a couple of days, take a dip in the Black Sea, and only then return to Moscow. After all, no foreign correspondents with their severely limited opportunities to travel within the Soviet Union could fully understand the daily humiliation and poverty of unemployable Bendery refuseniks.

"Have you seen the KGB people around our entrance?" their boy asked.

"You're very observant," I said to him. "What adult in full possession of his faculties would come running to your family to hide from the KGB?"

He looked at the laughing adults with amazement that they were so brazenly open, and my spirits were healed.

When we calmed down, I said, "I have to call my mother to say that I am resting on Black Sea beaches. And she will tell me, 'You're lying again, my little boy.'"

Leo explained how to get to a payphone booth. The KGB had

unplugged his phone, but ignored the miracle of technology that had recently captured the imagination of Russians—street telephones used for long-distance calls. I reached it in ten minutes and saw two men hurrying to seat themselves on an empty bench close to the booth. It was a very important moment of my life, a surprise, a sudden realization that fear had given way to an almost physical sense of freedom—I opened the door to the booth and asked them, "Do you also want to call your mom?"

At this point, the Roitburd boy bumped into me. He grabbed me by the shoulder, stood on his tiptoes, and reached for my ear. "They were following you," whispered the panting kid, "hiding behind buildings, trees, and in gateways."

"Well, you must be mistaken," I said aloud. "They are good guys, just playing hide and seek!"

I underestimated the temperament of the young Odessite. "No—no!" he cried. "They were spying on you!"

"They," with the glassy eyes of despair, were examining cigarette butts under their shoes.

"Let's make it easier for their hard work," I said. "Don't close this door. I will talk with my Mama, and you keep asking them if they clearly heard everything."

And he did it with the exuberant enthusiasm of a child. It had been a long time since I felt so serene and relaxed, even though my mother did accuse me of lying again and demanded that I come home soon.

To convince her, I really needed to soak up some sun. At the city beach my brain and body melted like ice cream. I was fine in Leo's swimming trunks, but my KGB escorts were sweating in their pants and hot boots on a red-hot bench at the entrance to the beach. I opened my eyes, covered them with my hand from the sun, and leisurely said to the young Leningrad couple lying on a mat next to me, "Do you see those poor things glued to the bench?"

"Yes," the girl said. "What about them?"

"I suppose they are my shadows. Maybe they should call their boss for permission to remove their fire-breathing pants."

"You don't look like a criminal," she said with a giggle.

I told them about the trial in Bendery. They were surprised by my openness and that I did not lower my lazy voice.

"Some other people are listening to you, too," said the young man, jerking his head in the direction of other beachgoers.

I said, "I'm no longer afraid."

The girl spoke again, "That's wonderful! Someone needs to stop being afraid."

"I can declare to the entire beach the names of other people sent to prison and hard labor camps for the same reason as Sender Levinson."

Everyone was silent and sober for a while.

"When are you leaving?" she asked.

I flattened the burning sand, and wrote with my index finger "tomorrow."

Her companion smoothed out the word "tomorrow" and wrote "Time?"

I wrote "evening, at 6."

He erased the sand.

The next evening they were waiting for me at the railroad platform. With three red roses! I was stunned and could only say, "You're crazy!"

"What's your name?" asked the girl.

"Arkady. Arkady Polishchuk."

"Thank you. We'll remember that."

When the train started, I, still greatly delighted, asked the conductor, "Do you have something for these roses?"

"Crystal vases," he said with a growl, "are placed only in cars for members of the government."

"An empty bottle?" I asked plaintively.

"It also costs money," he said sternly.

"I'll pay for it, as if it's full of vodka."

He brought me a used vodka bottle, half filled with water and muttered, "We don't have enough water even for the restrooms."

I kept my promise and paid as if it were full of vodka.

Soon after the train started moving, I was searched by three men posing as ticket inspectors. This time, the attempt to confiscate my notes was more theatrical than after Stern's trial: one of the actors looked at my innocent ticket, ineptly portraying suspicion; then he passed it to a simpleton, who clumsily mimicked him. The third man did not look at it, just said, "You have a counterfeit ticket," and delicately pulled my sleeve toward the sliding door. A policeman and the conductor joined us in the corridor and the troupe solemnly escorted me to his small compartment. I was stripped naked, they did not find my notes, and in strict accordance with their orders, let me return to my berth, the "counterfeit" ticket in my hand. In Moscow the conductor said conspiratorially, "Take good care of the flowers!"

Two days later, to my shock, Leo Roitburd was arrested at the Odessa airport before boarding a plane bound for the capital, where he intended to meet with other refuseniks. It happened in front of his son, to whom I promised to show Moscow. The trial was held—what a shrewd innovation!—at the airport. Before the start of the proceedings, an expert delivered to passengers a passionate lecture called "Ideology and Practice of Zionism." Leo was magnanimously sentenced to two years in a labor camp for attacking a six-foot tall policeman who could not remember where exactly he had been struck by the bully Roitburd.

left: Citadel wall and old quarter of the city of Derbent, Republic of Dagestan. Circa 1880s/1890s. Photo: Dmitri Ivanovich Yermakov via Wikimedia Commons. *right:* Yuri Yukhananov. 1975.

IN A WAY, I was prepared for the next trial, in 1975, of a young man named Yuri Yukhananov, several years before my ultimate rebellion. I had first known Yukhananov's fellow tribesman Asaf Ilisarov. Asaf was an expert in Arabic dialects and befriended me when was translating some text for my magazine. Asaf claimed that he was a genuine Jew, not like me—an assimilated Muscovite who did not know a thing about being Jewish. There was nothing personal in this assessment. He looked down on all Jews who entered Russia after, according to his estimates, eighteen hundred years of wandering in the wilderness of European civilizations, systematically, step by step, losing their Jewish values and physical appearance. Such was this pundit's view of history.

A Caucasian highlander with wild eyes and noble facial features, he laughed like a happy kid when I told him that if he grew a mustache, he would look like the Egyptian dictator Gamal Abdel Nasser. His clean-cut head, with its very short curly hair and slightly graying temples, was a little too big for his puny body.

The first time we met, I asked Asaf if he had been born in Azerbaijan. He looked at me like a shining mountain taking in a swampy lowland and said, "No, I'm a Tat from Derbent, the former

Iranian gateway to the Caspian Sea."

I thought that Tats were Muslims, worsening my moral and intellectual standing. Nonetheless, he continued, "Many Tats didn't have anything to do with Jewishness, so it's better to call us Mountain Jews. We lived in Northern Persia long before Jesus Christ was born, if he ever was born. Fire-worshipping Zoroastrians didn't force us to abandon our religion. Only centuries later did Iranian shahs coerce us to convert to Islam. Those who didn't were killed or had to run for their lives into uninhabited mountains. We didn't interbreed for at least fifteen centuries. And this is why you don't look like me."

I heard something tender, like sympathy in his tenor and saw compassion in his dark eyes.

All I knew was that the Tats were a small tribe, perhaps a twenty-thousand-strong ethnic group living in the southern regions of the Soviet Union, in Azerbaijan and Dagestan. Asaf was accepted at a military academy in Moscow because nobody there knew that Dagestan Tats were actually Jews. "We were accomplished warriors and served in the Persian cavalry," he said with such pride as if he had just dismounted at this door of his tiny Moscow apartment where we now stood.

Right away I asked, "Can you ride a horse?"

Asaf ignored my tactless question as we went inside, but to prove something, he opened a closet and pulled out a uniform with captain's epaulets draped it on his narrow shoulders, and placed on his head an officer's cap with a cockade blazing over the shiny visor.

Yuri Yukhananov definitely did not want to serve in the military. Just a year earlier, in 1974, the military-medical commission of his and Asaf's hometown Derbent again found him unfit for service. The nineteen-year-old had a congenital spinal defect. However, after he filed an application to emigrate, it suddenly became clear that Yuri was perfectly healthy, and the Motherland was eager to take him into the ranks of her defenders.

That was why Yuri, his friend Boris, and I were now on the way to an attorney.

I naively tried to draw their attention to the red building of the Moscow City Council and the gloomy gray building of the Institute of Marxism-Leninism, located opposite each other on both sides of Gorky Street, the central street of the capital. However, they were much more interested in the monument erected between these two temples of communism. The young men fell in love with this handsome founder of Moscow, Prince Yuri Dolgoruky ("Long-handed"), and even more so, with his mighty horse.

"You have horse-riding in your blood," I said, "so, tell me, could a prince ride a gelding?"

They rushed to examine the appropriate part of the horse. It was perfectly smooth.

"Do you youngsters remember Khrushchev?" I asked. "He was the one who ordered that the balls of this poor creature be cut off. In his educated opinion the whole assemblage looked too natural."

"Lenin wouldn't do such a stupid thing," said Yuri.

"He wouldn't erect a monument to a prince in the first place. Stalin was the one who ordered it. However, Khrushchev's directive represented historical progress; if Stalin didn't like this stallion, he would've ordered the balls cut off of the sculptor, the architect, and a good hundred other people involved in this crime against the Soviets."

"We don't prance on horseback anymore in Derbent," Boris said, "but our grandfathers did, in tall lambskin hats and long cloaks."

Their visit to Moscow was successful. The lawyer said that even if the court did not dismiss the case based on the diametrically opposed medical records, he would argue that the court demand

Yuri had a new examination at a major military hospital. We were also lucky with Alexander Lipavsky, a very good doctor. This refusenik was an experienced specialist precisely in the field of congenital spine problems. Dr. Lipavsky examined Yuri and explained how he should behave in the hospital.

We had been friendly acquaintances—Lipavsky was interested in my work at the magazine and in my opinion about Soviet espionage in Africa and Asia. I had trouble refraining from telling him about our correspondents, but managed to keep my mouth shut. Who knows, maybe this silence protected me from prosecution. Two years later, in March 1977, we learned that he was a KGB stooge.

A few days later, Yuri, Boris and I were hiking between two sixth-century walls, clambering along a small dirt trail two miles straight from the Caspian Sea up into the mountains. The walls protected a narrow passage, about three hundred yards wide, leading to a fortress that towered over Derbent. Using the knowledge I had obtained in the past from Asaf Ilisarov, I called them the descendants of a Persian colony. "Yes," said Boris. "We defended Persia against the Steppe Khazars. Jews are the oldest people in the world."

I allowed myself to say, "On this planet there are many oldest peoples in the world."

We stopped and through a passage punched in the ancient wall saw endless rows of vines and fruit trees. "It's a Jewish collective farm, one of four such farms in Derbent," said Yuri. "Jews for centuries cultivated the land here."

For centuries, I thought? In a Muslim country? I found that pretty unusual. I remembered one of the oldest European anti-Semitic clichés—Jews never wanted to cultivate the land.

"Mountain Jews had been making cognac a thousand years before the French," said Boris.

"Don't tell this to the French anti-Semites," I said.

"The Qur'an does not allow Muslims to produce wine and tobacco," Yuri said. "Now they drink and smoke, and don't believe in Allah."

At this point, a group of tanned vine-growers, men in sun-bleached working clothes and wide peaked caps, and women in long dark dresses and small headscarves, approached the passage. Loudly discussing something in an unfamiliar language, they came to us, said hello in Russian, and all the men shook our hands. The women did not, but smiled silently. The older man said in the affirmative, "Yuri, your guest is from Moscow."

Yuri nodded.

"Are you a lawyer?" the man asked.

"No," I said.

"And when will the trial start?"

"The day after tomorrow," said Yuri.

The man turned back to me, "How many years, do you think, will Yuri have to stay in jail?"

"This year four Jewish boys have received sentences of two to three years for refusing to serve in the military; in Kiev, Kharkov, Moscow, and not far away from here—in Krasnodar," I said.

Yuri's lean face showed nothing but determination, but I changed the subject. "Please tell me, in what language were you talking?"

Everyone laughed. One of them exclaimed, "Muscovites!"

The older man explained that the Tats speak in a mix of Persian with ancient Hebrew and resolutely returned to the topic of conversation. "Isn't it better to go into the military than to prison?" he asked.

"After three years of service he won't be allowed to go to Israel for at least another five years."

The men shook our hands again; one of them patted Yuri on

the shoulder, and they left.

"So," I said, "you rule your womenfolk with an iron hand. They didn't say a word. In Israel, the girls will show you who the boss is."

"We wouldn't mind," said Boris. "Old folks still remember how their grandfathers could have up to three wives."

We passed several more holes in the high stone walls, the ruined defense towers, and stopped at the remains of an inn with a large courtyard called the caravansary. Whenever I glimpsed back, the shining sea was always in my view. Wherever I looked up, I saw the forbidding mountains.

From the remnants of the fortress we went down to the old city. From above, its narrow streets and flat roofs looked like the curves of cracks in a pile of flat stones.

In the middle of a steep and winding street, the peculiar smell of brandy hit my nose. I was sniffing the air when Yuri said calmly, "Ah, this is the famous Derbent cognac."

This country still called this brandy "cognac" with impunity.

My face obviously radiated confusion, and Yuri explained in a dull voice that when a Moscow commission suddenly descended on the Derbent Cognac Factory and there was a lot more of it than was indicated in the documents, the best Soviet cognac had to be quickly poured into the sewer pipes. "We have lousy drainage, as you can see—all around here there is just bare ground; that's why the odor seeps everywhere."

"It would be better," I suggested, "to send several rail cars with that cognac to people you trust in a big city."

"There was no time."

"Didn't the Moscow auditors know how to sniff?"

"We don't know the details," Yuri said.

"Money doesn't smell," said Boris.

I remarked that those were the two-thousand-year-old words of a Roman emperor, who talked of a fee for the use of public restrooms.

"You will smell our public restrooms, free of charge," Boris said, perking up. "Yuri lives now with me and five hundred neighbors, under one roof."

My gloomy protégé did not say a word.

Soon we reached a strange structure with walls unevenly plastered with clay. The long building did not have doors facing the street and looked rather like a fortress. We walked through a low gateway into a huge courtyard, probably the only passage into this hot and dusty quadrangle. Countless narrow doors, some of them open, and small windows faced each other from all four inner sides of the structure.

"This is the old Jewish quarter," Yuri said. "Very old. A family is living in each pencil box."

Slovenly dressed women, often with young children, sat beside the doors. I did not see a blade of grass. Boris pointed at the center of the quadratic court: "These are our latrines."

Several small sheds plastered with the same clay stood there atop a three-foot-high common foundation, probably sheltering tanks with an unambiguous purpose. Children had been jumping from this podium down onto the dusty ground and repeatedly climbing back onto it, rushing between the sheds to the opposite side of the foundation, and jumping and climbing onto it again. It lasted forever.

Regal mountains rose far beyond the flat roof of the ancient structure, looking with disgust at the squalor of it.

THE TRIAL DID NOT last long. The Moscow lawyer immediately said that the case could not be considered without the expert opinion of the Regional Military-Medical Commission, as the documents of the case contained conflicting conclusions from local medical experts. The judge, without further ado, said that in the next day or two, Yuri would receive an appropriate referral from the city enlistment office and would have to go to a military hospital for the examination.

In the small courtroom there were only a few of Yuri's friends. Neither his parents nor the secret police were there. The old vine-grower, whom we met on the steep road to the citadel, ran, breathless, into the room when we were departing. He said, "The Russian military can be very difficult for a Jewish boy; thank God, we don't look like Jews."

Late in the evening, Yuri came to my hotel with two pieces of important news. One, his father had invited us to lunch at his home. And two, an officer from the enlistment office went around to Yuri's friends and told them that he must urgently report to the military commissar. He had repeated the same phrase, word for word, to each of the friends, "It's in his interest." In the end he did find Yuri and led him to his boss.

The lieutenant colonel promised to give Yuri, no later than the next afternoon, a referral to the main hospital of the North-Caucasian Military District. He had sounded almost paternal. "You'll go by train to Rostov—it's a ride of about twenty hours. If you have no money, ask your father to buy a ticket for you. You have to get there as quickly as possible. Remember, it's in your best interest."

"What does all this mean?" Yuri asked me.

"The KGB knows you're not faking. Maybe they've decided not to pursue your case. The brave military commissar has already soiled his pants; he was the one who, on the KGB's instructions, arranged the latest conclusions of the local military-medical experts."

"And why would the KGB do that now?"

"They began to understand that if you were to go to jail, all of your medical records will reach tricky Jewish doctors in the West, who will raise hell, and you'll become the size of a major Hollywood star, and will be invited to appear there in the role of Superman."

"That would be neat," Yuri said.

He promised to remember the KGB and send discreet letters from the hospital to our volunteer mail recipient Lucy Litvinov, in whose apartment I lived for several months, about his health and medical procedures. I promised to show everything to Dr. Lipavsky.

But first we had lunch at the house of Yuri's father. Boris walked us right to the door.

"His father is a rich man," he said. "He's afraid that they'll put him in prison and take away all that he has acquired. That's why he kicked Yuri out of his house."

Yuri never breathed a word about his family.

"I'm sure," continued his buddy, "he's now paying a lot of money to all the big shots of the city—from the Secretary of the City Party Committee to the last clerk in the court."

"No one kills a cash cow," I said. "They need him free and prosperous. They would be satisfied if his son alone were put behind bars."

"But all the local officials are afraid of each other and can arrest my father at any moment," said Yuri in a sudden outburst.

Never in my life had I seen such a large number of carpets in one human dwelling. They were on the floors, on the walls, and on the large low sofas. It seemed to me that they even covered the low ceilings. The lamb melted in my mouth; homemade sugary sweets and hourglass-shaped glasses of strong tea brought back memories of a banquet at an international conference in Baku, the capital of neighboring Azerbaijan. Yuri's mother smiled silently, carrying abundant treats and looking at her son; I repeated, "Delicious!"

His father spoke about the weather and the carpets. Perhaps they were the main source of his income. He didn't say a single word about the trial, but was clearly flattered to see in Derbent an expensive Moscow lawyer and a representative of rebellious Jews. Yuri kept quiet, and I was not too talkative, either.

When we were leaving, his father said, "Derbent is one of the oldest settlements in the world, many times older than Moscow."

Probably he wanted to show that he was a cultured man.

Already in the street, his outcast son said, "My father is a good man."

Two weeks later, we received his first letter: "Dear Lucy, the food here is tasteless, but good. You were right—I am the youngest here. Doctors treat me well. They think that this problem with my back will stay with me all my life. I walk around in a beautiful garden with a true general, also a patient. We have become friends and talk about bears and big cats who live in our mountains. His name is a military secret. This is all. I have to go for a procedure."

In none of his three letters did Yuri send kisses to Lucy, though, as was correctly noted by the observant Dr. Lipavsky, a good boy should always do so in a letter to a girl. Saniya (such was Lipavsky's nickname) winked at me, as is customary with experienced men when it comes to women, and asked who Lucy was. I said that she was my childhood friend, did not have anything to do with emigration, and reluctantly agreed to receive Yuri's letters.

I trusted him, but to protect her, did not tell Lipavsky that I had been hiding in her apartment while writing a book about the trial of Dr. Stern.

Everything was going according to our plan until Lucy received permission to leave for Israel and went to the United States instead. Her departure deprived me of my last line of communication contact with Yuri. Judging by the absence of any news from him, there was every reason to assume that the examination in Rostov found him unfit for military service, and after a while he probably emigrated. Otherwise, he would have found a way to get in touch with me.

Thus the adventures of Yuri Yukhananov ended like a Hollywood blockbuster—with a happy end. Our hero defeated all his enemies and withdrew to the accompaniment of fanfares to the fairyland of his ancestors. I don't think Hollywood would have come up with such an unrealistic scenario in which a KGB provocateur provided some professional advice to our hero.

Thirty-eight years later I found two Yuri Yukhananovs in the United States. One phone number, in Iowa, no longer existed, but dialing the other, in Queens, New York, I got through. A recorded female voice said in good English that the Yukhananov family would call me back, and I left my agitated message. No one responded to my reminder about water under the bridge, I decided not to bother them further.

MEANWHILE, in the late fall of 1975, another, in a way, unique trial was awaiting me. It was initiated not by the KGB, but by me and my co-conspirator, the architect Gary Berkovich, though he was really the one who dragged me into this ridiculous adventure. He had been fired on suspicion that he was preparing to apply for emigration, but in fact, at that stage Gary had only befriended the family of refuseniks at whose door we were once arrested. He wanted to figure out if America really needed two more architects—him and his wife Marina. While the suspect tried to solve this dilemma, he was punished before committing the crime. Thus his bosses unwittingly set Gary's thinking in that direction. That is why he, being an assertive and restless individual, had the nerve to sue his state architectural enterprise to demand back his job as well as back pay for the months of his enforced absence from the drawing board.

To my amazement, a Moscow judge agreed to accept this odd case for consideration. To suspect the judge of sympathizing with Gary was ridiculous, but his foolhardy attempt to sue the authorities had worked. Maybe the KGB strategists thought that if Gary remained in the country and continued to insist on reinstatement, a swarm of fired Jews might copycat his legal moves. My accomplice was soon somewhere on his way to America. The judge and the KGB certainty couldn't imagine that before the departure of this full-fledged anti-Soviet family, I would become an obedient tool in the hands of this rabid Zionist. He supplied me with the power of attorney to continue the fight for his unpaid wages. I had to tell the judge that Garik borrowed money from me to feed his children, and promised to return it with the help of the Soviet court, the most just court in the world.

I said, "The judge will laugh her head off and tell all her friends at the KGB about our brazen escapade."

"That's good," said Gary. "Let the world know about our fight."

"Your scheme is designed for idiots. Everybody will understand that we're just teasing the Russian bear, and for all we care, we can kiss your money goodbye."

"So what?" Gary was unrelenting. "Aren't you tired of cowardly Jews, who are flogged at thousands of meetings for having the audacity to express their desire to emigrate? You're going to remember this trial until the end of your life."

I said, "Because of its unheard-of absurdity."

In fact, I liked the scheme.

An impregnable secretary refused to pass a copy of my power of attorney to the judge and recommended that I send it by mail. She took it to the judge only after I said, "She won't be grateful to you for such a delay."

A minute later the unhappy secretary invited me into the

judge's small office. The young woman behind the desk asked, "Are you serious?"

"Absolutely," I said.

"Why are you doing this?"

I tried to relax my facial muscles. "I need this money and hope that you will take this case on its face value and not as a provocation."

She studied my face for a second and asked, "Where's your friend now?"

"Probably walking day and night around the Roman Coliseum with his children, five-year-old Slavik, and ten-year-old Lana, and his wife. After all, they both are architects."

"So, they're not in Israel."

"No. He wanted to see the American skyscrapers."

"But they were given an exit visa for travel to Israel."

I had to check the level of her awareness and tolerance. "That's an official game, you know, a privilege given only to Jews. But for many, where they go is less important"—I caught myself and instead of "than from where they go," I said, "everybody knows that."

She was not irked and said, "Okay, I will accept your claim for consideration as an ordinary civil case if you promise not to inform foreign correspondents about it and not to bring your friends here."

I couldn't believe my ears. "Fine. I promise. Thank you."

She smiled wryly, "Another judge would consider you a provocateur and report you to the proper authorities."

The judge was certainly not a coward.

"Usually this courtroom is full of ordinary plaintiffs and defendants in all kinds of civil cases. Don't use this audience as a platform," she stressed, "for expressing your views."

I promised to speak only to the merits, which are only about the money.

"If you don't keep your promise," the judge said, "I can always stop the proceedings and do other nasty things."

"I don't have any reasons for that."

"May I ask you a personal question?" she said reluctantly.

I nodded.

"Where do you want to go?"

"Nowhere," I said.

The judge shook her head and refrained from the next question.

She underestimated the power of two inevitable words—"emigration" and "Israel." While I was speaking about Gary's unpaid wages, I dropped these two stink bombs in the jam-packed courtroom. Deathly silence reigned. Only two representatives of the Design Institute of Marine and Riverine Structures were loudly indignant. The chairman of the Institute's trade union and the head of personnel, interrupting each other, proclaimed noisily and at length that Gary Berkovich committed a spiteful act against the country that nurtured him, brought him up, and gave him an education.

The judge called them to order. "The defendants will get an opportunity to object to the plaintiff," she told them.

I kept my promise, was brief, and asked that the three-month income Berkovich was denied, should be returned. The unionist continued expressing his contempt for traitors who go to the "fascist state" of Israel. I could not help asking, "Well, what if the destination were not Israel, but fraternal China, would you mind then?"

Dumbfounded, he looked at the judge, who then asked me to shut down my fountain of eloquence. I apologized. He said that Berkovich had been fired by the unanimous wish of all his colleagues who angrily rejected his attempts to cajole them. To my delight, he said, "This brazen renegade brought a big cake to work and invited everyone to take part in a farewell tea party. He cut the cake and laid its pieces out on every desk. All our employees, without exception, rejected this pitiful attempt at yet another provocation and unanimously dumped every piece of that cake in their waste baskets."

I yelled, almost hysterically, "It's not true!"

The judge looked sternly at me and covered her mouth with her palm. I apologized anew.

With the same fervor the head of personnel confirmed everything the union leader said. Now it was my turn again. "Both representatives of the administration didn't mention the very reason for our presence here—the money," I said. "Fortunately, they clearly admitted before this court that Berkovich was fired not because of dissatisfaction with his performance, but at the request of the perturbed masses. I have nothing to add to their honest acknowledgment and at this point could conclude my testimony."

I made a dramatic pause, glanced scornfully at the other actors of our theatrics, borrowed from them a powerful weapon of demagoguery, and continued when the judge had already begun to sort through the papers on her desk. "The political short-sightedness of the Institute's senior staff contributed to the successful departure of Berkovich to Israel."

They did not expect such audacity from traitors. I saw fear in their faces and enthusiastically carried on, "Actually, he could've continued working for the benefit of Soviet society until his departure. In such a case we wouldn't have any financial claims against the Institute today. Why had these comrades twice failed to appear in court? There could be only two explanations for such anti-social behavior—unwillingness to pay 840 rubles or disrespect for the Soviet justice system."

I caught the judge's interested gaze, took a deep breath, and introduced the facts related to the skills of Berkovich. Recently, I stressed, he had designed two successful projects for large passenger river stations. One of them was already operational in the big city of Ufa.

"This work involved the entire collective of the Institute!" shouted the head of personnel.

"Exactly! Finally, we hear the plain truth from the defendants. Yes, the entire staff worked on both projects"— I paused dramatically again—"which bear Berkovich's signature."

Never before had I experienced such pleasure from my public speaking.

"Well," the judge said dryly, "proceed to the cake, if, of course, it's relevant to the case."

"It is," I said. "The treatment of the cake by the Institute's representatives reflects their unwillingness to..."

I clearly had skidded, and while I was agonizing about a politically acceptable formulation of my rebuttal, the judge to my delight, cut me off, "Plaintiff, don't deviate from the essence of your claim!"

"Okay," I said quickly. "Everybody ate this dirty Zionist cake."

"It's a lie!" yelled the trade union leader.

"And washed it down with Indian tea," I said gloatingly.

"We protest!" he yelled again. "Berkovich was trying to demoralize our healthy collective!"

The judge, both hands over her mouth and nose, was clearly enjoying herself and briefly lost control of the situation.

I said, "In fact, Gary mentioned the only architect who didn't eat the cake."

"Who?" barked the personnel boss.

"Sorry, I can't help you identify this good man," I said. "All I know is that he was a Jew who was frightened to death."

At this point the judge whom I now adored, interrupted our squabble and declared a break before announcing her decision. The people in the courtroom started lively debates. I sat quietly, knowing what the verdict would be.

She returned in five minutes to announce, "The claim of Berkovich and Polishchuk against the Design Institute of Marine and Riverine

Structures is rejected for insufficient evidence."

To relax after this strenuous ordeal, instead of taking the bus, I walked leisurely toward my home and mused about the two bureaucrats frightened by my unexpected politically correct rebuff; by now they were perhaps thinking of reporting to the KGB the judge's amusement and anti-Party behavior. Following my habit of recent years, I glanced back and noticed behind me a young man whose burning eyes had caught my attention back in the courtroom. I cursed the judge for deceiving me. So, she had the KGB's blessing, I thought, and quickly took hold of the door handle of the nearest house; I wanted to see the reaction of my shadow to this sudden move. To my surprise he came up to me. Tails do not usually start talking to the subjects of their sleuthing and I joked, "Did you decide to emigrate?"

"Yes," he said with beads of sweat standing out on his forehead. "Sorry, I think ... I changed my mind ... Fear ..."

"It's all right," I said, "I have a similar problem in my family."

I appealed the district's court decision to the Moscow City Court. It dismissed my complaint without listening to me though I was present, along with a lawyer turned refusenik. I was not disappointed. Judges certainly considered our very presence there to be a political demonstration and reported the outrageous event—to the KGB—contributing to my growing file.

TWELVE

More Dangerous Than Jews

TWO SHABBILY DRESSED MEN, both wearing thick rimmed glasses, apparently villagers, stood outside the Moscow synagogue. Some refuseniks glanced at them warily, each man a sore thumb among the crowd.

That night they did not sleep in the railroad station, but in my apartment. That night, Nikolai Petrovich Goretoi and Feodor Sidenko stood on my balcony and told me about the flight of their persecuted church from city to city, from the West of Russia to the Far East and back to the West again—from the shores of the Pacific to the Krasnodasky Territory near the Black Sea.

"We have no place to run to anymore," said Nikolai Petrovich, looking at the dark roofs nearby and at the nocturnal panorama of Moscow.

For me, hearing their stories was like discovering an unknown planet.

"Well, what a company!" I said. "Three myopic men are staring at nighttime Moscow at the flight altitude of a swallow, talking about things that no eagle would be able to discern."

They had begun talking about emigration soon after the war. But they didn't know the mundane word emigration and called it an "exodus," just like the exodus of the Jews fleeing the Egyptian Pharaoh. "Since that time," said Nicholai Petrovich, "we have been

Nikolai Petrovich Goretoi in internal exile next to an arctic reindeer in the village of Chumikan on the Sea of Okhotsk (part of the Pacific Ocean). 1966. The Chumikan population in 2012 was 1091 people; in 1966, thanks to exile settlers like Nikolai Petrovich, it was larger—1361 people. In this frigid subarctic climate, the residents are hunters, fishermen and several not very successful gold diggers. The nearest railway station is 330 miles away, the nearest port is 453 miles away.

From: *Get Out of Your Land and Go: Interviews—autobiographical testimonies of believers in a stage of their exodus from the USSR to freedom* (Bramante: Urbania) 1988, cover image.

ready for the miracle of a Christian exodus from the Red Pharaoh. He's been trying to destroy our faith since he seized power. He's putting us in prisons and madhouses, he's taking away our children and sends them to orphanages."

"To me the Jewish emigration is also a miracle," I said. "It weakens this dragon. But you, you're trying to kill it—you're true fighters."

"For Christ," Feodor Sidenko added.

And I made another discovery—they loved Jews. Nikolai Petrovich Goretoi, quoting the Bible from memory, was patiently explaining to me that the Jews were God's chosen people and therefore should be particularly close to the heart of every Christian.

"Chosen for what?" I said. "For suffering?"

"I know," he said, "you're thinking about the persecution which the Jews were subjected to for the rejection of Christ."

I could not help but observing, "If only for that! Jews had been persecuted millennia before Jesus came to this world. History has proved that there are more occasions to hate Jews than for a Russian to drink vodka."

The ingenuous Feodor Sidenko laughed hoarsely, "Russians drink more than anybody else in the world."

"Do you?" I asked.

"No, we don't drink, don't smoke, don't steal, don't swear, and don't beat our wives."

"Such a boring life!" I said. "Now you have convinced me that you are American spies and more dangerous for this society than Jews who do all that you mentioned, maybe, except beating wives."

Feodor liked my silly jokes, though I was not joking.

The remainder of the night Nikolai Petrovich Goretoi spent on a bed-chair in my small office; Feodor Sidenko could choose between two floors—next to Goretoi's bed or in the living room next to mine. At first I hypocritically offered them my large bed. To my relief, they delicately refused.

After that day many Evangelicals passed through my apartment. Their unsuccessful attempts to file applications for emigration with local authorities led them to Moscow. Wherever they were from— the Far East or Western Ukraine—they taught me how to pronounce the words of grace to the Creator before a meal and to kiss the lips of ill-shaven men when they meet. The first lesson I took with joy. Initially, the second one required some effort. I still remember the young Ukrainian villager who opened his thick-lipped mouth wide for a slobbery kiss. Thank G-d, his unique manner of greeting was the exception to the rule.

In the morning we continued to learn about each other and about differences in our vocabulary.

I said, "Our acquaintance is the finger of fate."

They said, "This is the hand of the Lord."

I did not see a big difference in these formulations. They definitely saw one, and explained to me that it was God who sent them a clever Jew as an assistant. To explain, rather incoherently, what strengthened my interest in Evangelical Christians, I said, "I don't know of any Protestant country where Communists were able to seize power. Catholics and Orthodox Christians cannot make a similar boast."

"Only an educated Jew could make such an observation," remarked Goretoi.

"To get better acquainted with you," I said, "I've read a few books about dangerous cults of Pentecostals and Baptists. You, horrific sectarians with terrorizing rituals and ties with foreign anti-Soviet centers, look a little Jewish to me. The bullshit published about you includes the same age-old stories used in the libels against Jews—the same immortal dead or half-dead babies, global conspiracy, and espionage."

At first, Feodor Sidenko had a poor understanding of our historical similarities. He grasped it after I said that as a ten-year-old I fought with boys who called me a kike.

"In Nakhodka, where we lived for a long time, Pentecostal children were stoned or just thrashed by other children," Feodor said.

"Our kids didn't use their fists," said Goretoi.

"This is maybe the only difference," I said. "Maybe your morals are higher than mine. This Jew could never turn the other cheek."

"Arkady Abramovich," Goretoi said softly, "sometimes it's not for mortals to know that they are doing the Lord's work."

Meanwhile Feodor studied the image of me on the wall,

depicted as a huge centaur.

"It's by my friend," I said. "A well-known painter."

The centaur's powerful arms and brawny chest didn't necessarily look like mine, but the head had all my unmistakable features including outstanding nose, weak chin, and curly gray hair.

"Why did your friend portray you as a horse with glasses?" Feodor asked. "Nikolai Petrovich would draw you a lot more like you."

I tried to explain, "Long before the Lord sent Christ to people, some folks believed in stories about such creatures—the upper half as a man, and the bottom like a horse."

Feodor shook his head disapprovingly. "What savages!"

The next day I came home frustrated by disturbing news about Malva Landa, a well-known human rights activist. My guests had already returned from a meeting with local underground Pentecostals and were waiting for me to join them for dinner. Malva's case was one of the most ridiculous I ever heard, but they were not surprised when I related her story. The KGB innovators, keeping an eye on the West, decided to try her, not for her human rights activities, but for setting her own room on fire. The smoking retiree Malva Landa had maliciously done just that. A neighbor's room in her communal apartment was slightly damaged, much less than hers.

"We will pray for her," said Feodor.

"Sakharov," I said, "was ready to pay for all the damages. The authorities could also deduct the money from her pension."

"Nothing can surprise us," said Goretoi, and he told me about a documentary filmed when they had lived in the Far East. In one episode a group of weeping women and children was wandering the streets of Nakhodka and, as the narrator explained, "The savage rites of Pentecostals led to this mass hysteria." The coffin behind which they were walking was not shown. The cameramen also shot in broad daylight the "secret" ritual washing of Pentecostals in the icy Pacific Ocean. They were caught red-handed while addressing their prayers to their overseas patrons, the voice said. To every politically literate schoolchild it was clear that the sect was praying for the safe arrival of American spies.

"At least in this slander there was a smidgen of truth," said Goretoi. "Arkady Abramovich," he continued, "you're leading a secular, non-religious life, and maybe it will be difficult for you to understand how our prayers guide us. Many believers had heard a prophecy that Nakhodka would be a place from where our exodus would begin. It was a revelation, a divine instruction. We heard it long before we began moving, fleeing persecution, to the Nakhodka port on the Pacific."

They started to gather there, on the edge of this world, not just because they had been wandering all over the country like gypsies— far and wide. Not just because they hadn't found a place where they could glorify Christ without fear of prison. No, it was this prophecy that encouraged at first hundreds of them and later thousands.

I had my secular explanation for the prophecy but was not going to soil their spiritual world with my dirty boots.

Goretoi continued, "I was the presbyter, and at first we had three hundred people, large families with small children, and the old, a lot of them, living alone. We had shared with these old women everything we had."

Feodor Sidenko was surprised that Nikolai Petrovich Goretoi was talking about such a common thing. "We always share all that God has given us, our last piece of bread and the last of the firewood."

Goretoi smiled. "Unlike you, Arkady Abramovich may not be aware of the Christian commandment 'Thou shalt love thy neighbor as thyself.'"

"My neighbor is a stool pigeon," I said glumly.

"It's a Jewish law as well," said Goretoi. "It's in the Old Testament."

I thought of Israel's Arab neighbors, but said, "I'm ignorant and envy you."

"It's me who's illiterate," said Feodor. "I attended school for only four years, and then had to earn my bread."

"From the KGB's point of view you're more educated than I. They're afraid of your biblical armament, Feodor. Having failed to destroy the faith, they try to blow it up from inside, placing their agents in charge of all religions."

"Therefore we don't register our churches with the godless state," said Goretoi.

"To the KGB you represent the regular folks, freed of official ideology, and this is a danger to the very existence of the ruling mafia."

"What's a mafia?" asked Feodor. "A clique?"

"A gang. You're capable of blowing up the regime's demonic religion with a word and leaving it without a flock. Next to you I'm like a roadside stone next to a roadside bomb."

"I know," he said. "That's why they sent me ... to a hard labor camp ... and a psychiatric prison."

We slept little for the second night in the row—my guests continued to tell me their story. The very first list of Nakhodka Pentecostals wishing to emigrate was made by Nikolai Petrovich Goretoi in 1961 when he was forty years old; with their children, the number exceeded one thousand. At that time, I was already working at Asia Africa Today. That same year he was sentenced to five years of imprisonment and five years of internal exile in sparsely populated areas with severe climatic conditions. Two members of his church were also imprisoned. There was no mention of the emigration list at the trial—the most powerful dictatorship in the world did not know how to handle this phenomenon. I doubt if any Russian Jew at that time would have dared to raise his voice about emigration.

"Do you remember," I asked Goretoi, "the article of the Criminal Code under which you were tried?"

"Of course, Article 227." I heard surprise in his response. "Creation of a group harmful to the health of citizens."

I took a copy of the criminal code off my bookshelf. "Your article is preceded and followed by articles about all kinds of sexual and deviational crimes."

Now I clearly had Nikolai Petrovich Goretoi's attention.

"The previous article, 226." I read: "'The establishment and maintenance of brothels and pimping. Keeping of dens for drug addicts. Operation of gambling dens.' Article 228, immediately after yours, named simply and to the point—'Production or distribution of pornographic materials.'"

Feodor Sidenko chuckled hoarsely, "So we Christians are some sort of sexual perverts."

"Right," I said. "Not for nothing did Lenin compare religion with a venereal disease. That's why your Article 227 immediately states, 'Creation of groups, under the pretext of preaching religious beliefs, causing harm to people's health, sexual promiscuity, and involvement of juveniles in such activities.'"

"Where was the outrage from Christians in the West about this?" Goretoi said, shaking his head.

Three years into Goretoi's penal servitude, when I already was a managing editor of *Asia and Africa Today*, Feodor was renovating the kitchen of a foreigner. Feodor called him a Japanese consul, but I doubted the diplomatic status of this Japanese man who worked at the port of Nakhodka. In his funny Russian he praised Feodor Sidenko's work and was surprised when this Russian refused to drink Japanese vodka and had no use for the words that this foreigner had been taught by dockers. Feodor told him that his church wanted to leave Russia and was ready to go anywhere, even to Japan. The man asked him to bring the passports of those who wanted to leave.

What foreigner willing to help would ask for a Soviet internal passport? The next day, as a precaution, naïve Feodor brought only four passports. The Japanese passed them on to the police. Feodor and a member of his church, Vasyli Patrushev, were arrested and sentenced to four years in a hard labor camp. Today I can only guess what desperate souls owned the two other passports—my numerous recordings of conversations with the Pentecostals are gone or have deteriorated. Feodor Sidenko was single. Patrushev had a large family, and he certainly did not want to expose his children to the risk of being left without both parents.

Then, ten years later, when I had already stopped writing, but still was the managing editor of the magazine, Feodor Sidenko again intervened in high-level politics without knowing it; he had been subject to a 'preventative arrest' before the visit of U.S. President Gerald Ford to Vladivostok, some one hundred and thirty miles south of Nakhodka. A month earlier, in late October, Feodor saw soldiers planting fir trees along the highway leading to the Vladivostok airport. He realized that the Soviet Union was readying for something important. This planting was particularly intense near some shoddy barracks, like the ones where he had spent four years behind barbed wire. This time, Feodor was prudently locked up in the Vladivostok Psychiatric Hospital where the doctors began giving him daily shots.

"Those twenty-six days in the nuthouse were worse than four years in the camp where many were maimed while logging," Feodor said with a sigh. "At that hospital we all were mutilated." He sighed again. "Some kind of a poison."

I didn't dare ask him for details, but now for history's sake, I wish I had.

During two days of talks, Gerald Ford and Leonid Brezhnev made serious progress toward a comprehensive ten-year pact for curbing nuclear weapons and toward world peace. In twenty-six days Feodor's health was undermined for life. He had no way of knowing how many people were arrested in the Far East in order to strengthen peace in the world. All Feodor knew for sure was that the fir trees planted along that highway didn't take root, and by mid-November, a week before the arrival of Ford, they had turned yellow and crumbled. The authorities had to re-send soldiers to urgently paint branches of the dead trees a beautiful green color, pleasant to the eyes of the foreign visitors passing by. Efforts toward world peace prevailed again.

Soon I had some more guests, Pentecostals and Baptists of the same undeviating kind.

One, a Latvian and former naval officer, told me how he was discharged, while on a ship at sea, after he had a revelation and began to believe in Christ as his personal Savior. While taping his story, I could not help cracking up. "I imagine the reaction of the deputy commander for political correctness when you announced this good news!"

"He turned pale," my interviewee replied, "and began to stutter and swear. He was afraid he could lose this good job, suitable for slackers."

"Was the sea quiet?" I asked.

"Oh yes, it smiled," he said.

I liked this brave mariner very much. Ruthless time has washed his name out of my memory as a lazy wave washes a drawing off the sand.

THIRTEEN

A Jewish Invasion of the Communist Sanctum

T HE MORNING OF October 19, 1976, twelve Jewish refuseniks showed up at Brezhnev's Reception Room. I was the only one who, formally, was not a refusenik because I had never visited the Visa Office and had never been officially denied an exit visa. All the others were long-term refuseniks. Already, there were more than a dozen petitioners. I asked a gray-haired woman with a black headscarf for whom she was petitioning. She sighed, "My son. Appealing for a pardon. Sentenced to be shot."

What could I say? I asked, "Where are you from?"

"From the Far East. The Port of Nakhodka. He wouldn't hurt a fly ..."

"How long did it take you to come here?"

"I don't know," she said.

I thought of Goretoi's church and the Pentecostal exodus. She was from their town and maybe even had heard about these dangerous sectarians from neighbors, or had read about them in a local newspaper.

Petitioners watched with a mixture of awe and amazement as twelve Jews placed their non-kosher kefir, milk, boiled eggs, bread, and sausage on the low shining tables and sat in leather chairs meant to induce deep reverence for the head of state.

Upon release from Butyrskaya Prison. *From left to right:* me, Michael Kremen, and Victor Elistratov. November 5, 1976.

"Would you like some kefir or milk?" I asked her.

"They will arrest you, my dear, for such a thing," said the old woman.

All the Soviet presidents stared at us from the paneled walls, some indifferently, others reproachfully. She looked at our group again and was horrified. "Sorry, dearie," she said. "I'll move."

"It's okay," I said. "I understand."

Her wide armchair remained unoccupied until a Biblical prophet with flashing eyes left his chair on the opposite side of the room.

"Aren't you frightened by this Zionist sabbath?" I asked him.

"I'm a Jew," he said, nervously stroking his huge raven-black beard.

"It's written all over your face. Petitioning for an exit visa?"

"Yes. Have been for two years."

"Lucky you!" I said. "This gray downward parted beard is Vladimir Slepak, asked for a visa eight years ago, unemployed; next to him—Victor Elistratov, refusenik of seven years standing, now a happy stoker, in the past a highly qualified engineer. Join us, and in the unpredictable future the majority of us will get permission to go; to balance this yielding to the West, it'll be accompanied by a prison term, by my guess, for a couple of us."

He remained silent for five minutes and then said, "My name is Isaac Elkind. I'm in."

"You can sign our petition," I said.

"How long can we stay here?" he asked.

"The KGB is now weighing its options. There are foreign correspondents outside, waiting for action. Otherwise, we would've been arrested upon arrival."

"I overheard your conversation with that woman," Isaac whispered. "I'm a lawyer. Several times I defended those accused of murder and never learned anything about their execution before being told to stop writing petitions for the dead."

I leaned close to his ear and whispered, "One of us is a KGB informer. A blackmailed refusenik. Thirty minutes before entering this door, we kind of dragged the poor thing to join us."

"Why?"

"We wanted him to be punished."

"Who?" he said.

"We'll tell you after this ordeal is over."

A woman in dark business attire entered the hall and commanded in a stern voice, "Citizens, immediately leave the Reception Room of the head of the Soviet state! Otherwise, police will do what's necessary to restore public order."

We tried to pass our petition to her. Her face contorted with rage, and she said that we should apply for exit visa individually, not here. Thirteen men said almost in unison, "We did."

Soon all seats along one wall were occupied by silent men in plain clothes. They did not talk. They stared at us. One guy obviously got his job for his powerful physique. Never in my life had I seen such massive shoulders and such a display of muscles visible even under his coat. All thirteen of us together wouldn't have been able to take him on, even with clubs. I said to my comrades, "Psychological attack a la World War One. Only without marching, bayonets, and drummers."

At 5 p.m. we saw the first uniformed man, a police major, not some lousy lieutenant. That was a good sign. He said, "Citizens, reception hours are over. Please leave the Reception Room!" The prophet Isaak returned to his chair on the opposite side of the room. We did not move. The fellows in plain clothes did not move, either. They probably hated our guts. Was it fair? They stood hungry, overworked, and sleepy—a couple had been nodding off already—protecting law, order, and the Motherland while these traitors were drinking Russian kefir and eating Russian sausages. Endlessly!

This peaceful coexistence lasted thirty more minutes. Every ten minutes the same major would enter the hall with exactly the same pronouncement to the same rotten "citizens." After the third warning he returned with a new legion of plainclothes men. Each Jew was carried by two or three silent fellows to a bus parked in the backyard. Lovingly carrying the lawbreakers instead of dragging them was an unusual humanitarian action and the most humiliating to the dignity of the law enforcement rank and file. It also was a positive sign.

The foreign correspondents probably still remained on Kalinin Avenue, and once in the back, our handlers could again act in the time-tested method—they brusquely lay some of us on the asphalt before pushing us inside the bus. Finally, we all were sandwiched between the seats occupied by our guards, who were dressed like villagers. We began telling them why we came to the Reception Room. At first they remained silent. After a while they began telling us that America supported Russian Jews financially.

One guard with a neck of a wrestler turned to me and said, "If America unleashes war against Russia, Israel and traitors like you will fight against us."

I got angry. "I'm not a traitor; look for traitors among your friends."

Vladimir Slepak elbowed me. He didn't know the roots of my boldness; it wasn't boldness at all, it was a prudent calculation, a cool-headed assessment, a reckoning. I possessed a nasty state secret.

"What do you know about Jews?" I raised my voice. "Nothing. You were all brainwashed back in kindergarten!"

"I see you're bold," the guard smiled crookedly, "Want to receive a long sentence?"

Vladimir elbowed me again, "Don't waste your eloquence."

"Nothing personal," I said. "The whole country has been brainwashed; I too was brainwashed at your tender age."

"Shut up!" said Vladimir.

After that I changed my tune and said, "You're a petty officer."

He was surprised. "How d'you know?"

"I'm a fortune teller."

The faces of these staunch atheists, sitting behind and in front of us, moved halfway from hostility to curiosity.

"You were born," I said, "far away from Moscow in a poor working class family."

Judging by their faces, I had scored a point or two. "At the age of fourteen or fifteen you joined the Communist Youth Organization, though you were a lazy student."

The petty officer hemmed, "At sixteen."

I paused. "If you take your hat off, I'll tell you where you served."

He turned to his colleagues-in-arms, who nodded, and he took off his worn, cloth cap.

"Okay," I said. "Now it's better ... you served as a border guard."

"At what border?" one of them asked acidly.

"It's a State secret," I said.

They laughed. I admitted, "I might be wrong. It looks as if you served in the occupation forces in East Germany or Czechoslovakia."

"We're not occupiers," said my guinea pig, "we're liberators." But it was clear that at least one of my guesses was correct and I could continue. "You were good at political education studies and joined the Party."

Their commander rose suddenly from his side seat behind the driver and came back toward us. "Stop talking with the detainees," he ordered without raising his voice and went back to his seat. My prestige as a fortune-teller was saved.

"How did you know that he was a petty officer?" whispered Slepak.

"The age and commanding manners," I said.

We continued traveling on the Dmitrov highway, crossed the Moscow Beltway, passed Severny, a new settlement more than forty miles from the capital, and after a sign that read "Boarding House" entered a deserted forest tract with the sign "Restricted area. Entry forbidden." The road was empty, except for a black Volga sedan which had been following us all the way from Moscow. The commander looked at his watch, grabbed a walkie-talkie and said, "Yes! It'll be done!" and announced, "Now all of you will leave the bus!"

We had several seconds to consider the situation in its proper perspective: three-dozen KGB rank-and-files could wreak havoc right here, on the roadside, in the darkness of a forest. We decided not to leave the bus. We caught hold of the metal handles of the seatbacks and demanded to be taken to any railroad station.

It is a painful experience when your delicate fingers, clutching at a metal handle, are exposed to crushing blows and at the same time four or five hands are trying their best to tear you away from this handle. I was astonished to see how long Vladimir's fingers were able to endure this.

We were losing the battle. Some of us, in order to avoid the beating, finally acquiesced to leave the bus. Those defying the order were thrown out. Josef Ahs, a quiet physician, barely resisted; from the open pneumatic door I saw him lying in the half frozen dirt. Two guards were kicking him. I was trying to set my hands against the door when someone kicked me in the small of my back. I fell out of the bus, and another guy leaning over me, yelled, "You Jewish cunt!" and struck my side with his boot.

I raised myself a little and spit in his face. A long-distance spittle strike, this sweet reminder of childhood competitions landed on his chest. He couldn't anticipate such an offense, and I had a second to get up on my feet. He hit me in the ribs with his heavy boot. I felt a sharp pain and thought, you shouldn't do this! I also thought, they were avoiding hitting us in the face, wasn't this another promising sign? A minute later I saw Josef Ash's swollen eyelids and Zakhar Tesker gingerly touching his broken nose. Actually, those soldiers were well disciplined; on this deserted night road they could have crippled all of us.

Suddenly a military truck with blinding headlights emerged from behind the turn. It slowed down and a baby-faced lieutenant yelled in a high-pitched voice, "What's happening here?"

"We are police!" yelled the bus driver, "handling delinquent kikes! Go—go!"

Then another resisting fool—Boris Chernobylsky tried to stop the truck. Soon he also was lying in the slush.

At this moment the Volga sedan, which had stopped two hundred yards from the battlefield, reminded us of its existence. Its headlights flashed twice, and the squad quickly went back into the bus. This stubborn kike Boris now stood in front of it with arms akimbo, yelling, "Bandits! Cutthroats! Cowards!"

Three cursing men jumped out of the coach and pushed him away while the driver backed up the bus a bit and made a U-turn. Furious Chernobylsky tried climbing on the back bumper, but did not succeed. He threw a stone and fortunately missed the target.

We were left in an unfamiliar place, probably a military area, and we had five chilly night hours to search for a railroad—the first train would only run at about five o'clock in the morning. After walking some six miles we met a collective-farm watchman in a long sheepskin coat. The old man was scared; our scratched faces and dirty torn clothes did not inspire trust. Nonetheless, he gave us good directions, and an hour later we reached an empty station.

On the train many of us, including the drained informer Tsypin, plunged into a deep sleep. Those who could not sleep decided to continue our assault on the Reception Room in the morning. In Moscow everybody went home to get some rest, except Zakhar and me. We needed to get an x-ray, to furnish evidence. But to whom?

A doctor in the Sklifosofsky Institute said that I had two cracked ribs and recommended to wind a towel around my trunk. He refused to give me an x-ray film or a written reference. An exhausted night nurse of this principal trauma center muttered, "If we give a reference to every hoodlum beaten in a street fight, the country would soon run out of ink and paper."

They certainly had shortages of x-ray films and painkillers.

The KGB strategists thought they had taught us a measured lesson. But we were poor students and again took them by surprise. Even more than that—now seven more refuseniks joined our ranks.

On that day, October 20, 1976, boredom reigned in the Reception Room. Upon our arrival all petitioners were sent off the field. They saw with their own eyes the Jews who invaded the Holy of Holies of Communist rule, where visitors had to experience the thrill and awe. To minimize the attention of foreign journalists, we were permitted to stay undisturbed there until the Reception Room was closed, an hour earlier than usual.

The details of this arrest have vanished from my memory—I was exhausted by pain and the sleepless night. All of us, except Boris and Josef, were brought before a very unhappy judge who, however, knew that all seventeen of us deserved leniency. That day, for sure, he had canceled consideration of all other cases and waited hours for our arrival. In five minutes, without asking questions, he sentenced all of us to fifteen days of imprisonment. A police wagon nicknamed "Black Raven" took four of us to a suburban branch of Butyrskaya prison. We knew nothing about the fate of others. Three weeks later we learned that Boris and Josef were in the main building of this prison, near the Garden Ring, the inner beltway of Moscow with neither gardens nor trees. No doubt, Chernobylsky and Ahs were selected for a harsher punishment because they were not known in the West. During interrogation, both had been promised four years of imprisonment. Yet after four months behind bars they became well known and were released without trial.

We were lucky to be locked up for just fifteen days. The Soviets still dreamed of the abolition of the U.S. trade restrictions that had been enacted as a direct result of persecution of Jews wishing to emigrate. The Kremlin tried to minimize the scale of the Western protests and the punitive machine became unpredictable.

Pictured here are eighteen Russian Jews who participated in our invasion of Brezhnev's Reception Room and those who were arrested during the following days. Many of us are unshaven as this photo was taken just after our release. In the midst of the first row there are two women, the wives of Chernobylsky and Ahs. Their husbands were selected for a much longer term. On the left is Leonid Tsypin, a KGB provocateur who also was "imprisoned" for two weeks.

From left to right, first row: Arik Rachlenko, Leah Chernobylsky (wife of Boris Chernobylsky), Mikhaela Ahs (wife of Josef Ahs), Vladimir (Zeev) Shakhnovsky, Evgeny Yakir;
second row: Anatoly Sharansky, Yosef Beilin, Igor Tufeld, Zachar Tesker, Alexander Gvinter;
third row: Leonid Tsypin (KGB agent), [?] Zelinii, Dmirti Shriglik, Victor Elistratov, Leonid Shabashov, Arkady Polishchuk, Vladimir Slepak, Aharon Gurevich, Isaak Elkind, Michael Kremen.

Moscow, November 1976. (Association Remember and Save)

A *New York Times* article by David K. Shipler, "Moscow Jews Say They Were Beaten After a Visa Sit-In" (October 20, 1976) reported that "some of the plainclothesmen wore the red armbands of *druzhinniki* or auxiliary police, but the Jews said they were convinced the assailants were policemen or agents of the K.G.B., the security police." Anti-semitic remarks were made, referring to Jews trying to take over the world, and men were beaten using "very sophisticated tricks," not damaging the face but clubbing the men "over the neck in such a way as to make the body limp." This happened "about 35 to 40 miles" outside Moscow. "'They ordered us out of the bus,' Mr. Polishchuk reported. 'We said we wouldn't leave. It was very dark. We didn't know where we were and we were afraid.' The plainclothesmen pushed and dragged the Jews from the bus, he said, and for what some of the demonstrators estimated was 30 minutes, chased them through the woods, pummeling and kicking them."

FOURTEEN

How to Catch an American Spy

S OON THE SOVIETS got tired of balancing on barbed wire and
went full-force. In January 1977, a TV-documentary titled *The
Buyers of Souls* was shown nationwide. In that quaint work of art,
Anatoly Sharansky earned special attention as a well-paid agent of
international Zionism and imperialism.

Then in early February, Dr. Alexander Lipavsky miraculously
found a room in Moscow's overcrowded center and invited Anatoly
to share it with him. Well done, I thought; this physician has
been good in helping others. Recently, he had managed to dig
up, somewhere, some perfect sausages for a few Siberian exiles.
The living together lasted only a few days. Lipavsky left on family
matters, disappeared, and came back some ten days later, yet no
longer in the flesh. I learned about it in a subway car. Two college
students next to me were reading an article in the *Izvestia*. One of
them said, "Spies should be shot."

His friend nodded and glanced at me. I borrowed their paper
and my face probably expressed consternation. I muttered, "What
a bastard!" In that article Lipavsky called Sharansky a CIA agent
and confessed that he also had collaborated with the CIA. My
neighbors now stared at me.

I exited the train at the nearest stop and glanced back at the
passengers. They kept looking at me, so I twirled my finger at my

temple to show that they were not quite right in the head. One of them made the same gesture at me, and the other one shook his fist. Were we moving back to the days of Stalin? Was I like them a quarter of a century ago, not understanding the absurdity of public accusations of espionage and sabotage well before the arrest of the culprit? Nothing seemed to have changed. The whole country still needed cult-deprogramming counseling.

Since the beginning of March, Sharansky had been continuously shadowed by a large retinue of agents breathing down his neck. One day, a small group of refuseniks left their usual meeting point near the synagogue, and accompanied by a KGB swarm, was walking toward the Old Square. The somber agents were walking behind us, on both sides, and ahead. A short man, apparently their chief, brazenly stepped into the narrow gap between Sharansky and me. I asked him, "Doesn't it bother you that we are walking next to you?"

His reply was quick and businesslike: "Don't meddle with my work!"

We stopped at a public restroom, and Anatoly went inside. The chief nodded to one of his men to follow Sharansky. When they returned, I tried to distract Anatoly from depressing thoughts and continued my horseplay. "Was he actually watching your human right movements at the urinal?" I asked.

Nobody was entertained. The chief pulled a walkie-talkie out of his inside pocket, moved slightly behind the group, and apparently started reporting the current situation on the front line. Our escort was clearly waiting for an impending order from higher authorities, perhaps even the Politburo. The finale to this production dragged on. For one more month, Sharansky continued to do his terrible harm to the country. Only on March 15, 1977, was he arrested. It was the quick capture of a spy in the act, Russian-style. The short-lived experiment with soft sentencing was over.

The spy's wealth was still stored at my home—a shapeless

winter hat with flaps, torn boots, and a scratchy army blanket.

The KGB certainly would have preferred to expose an impressive Zionist spy network sprawling the globe, but other than Lipavsky and the red-bearded snitch Tsypin, the unwilling participant in our action the previous year at Brezhnev's Reception Room, there were no other fish in the KGB's net. So, in the spring they began interrogating everyone who had signed, along with Sharansky, the various appeals to the authorities and the West. Some of the signers were scared, others, despite a formal non-disclosure agreement, shared their experience with friends. It all came down to looking for the authors of these often old documents, and nothing about state secrets and espionage.

When it was my turn, I arrived at the KGB's Lefortovo prison on the edge of old Moscow where Anatoly had already been kept for a couple of months. A somber investigator ordered me to sit down in the long room at a little table in the corner, diagonally opposite to his desk. A square piece of rough paper, which covered the top of this thin-legged table, quickly brightened my mood. I stopped thinking of those who had been kept here for years with no trial. The paper was a shooting gallery target skillfully shot through the center and the adjacent circles. The vulgar torture of the recent past was now replaced by simulation—a paper target aimed at the faint of heart. I felt a rush of amusement steeped in adrenaline.

"There is nothing here to smile about," said the investigator sternly. "You're here to give evidence of the grave crimes against the state."

"This paper tablecloth just reminded me of a textbook Chekhov observation," I explained innocently.

He did his best not to look dumbfounded, which led me to believe that he was a lousy student at school.

The door opened suddenly, conveniently obscuring me in

my corner. A second later, I grew worried when I saw the green back of a soldier step forward toward my interrogator. Instead of escorting me somewhere, he sat by the window, ignoring my presence, adjusted a pistol at his side, and fixed his eyes on a wall. The interrogator headed for the door, adjusting his tie on the way, and I calmed down thinking of a push button somewhere under his desk. Soon I understood that it was not needed.

I counted the number of bullet holes in the target and the number of points scored by the shooter. To attract the attention of the soldier, I mumbled Chekhov's "You cannot put a loaded rifle on the stage if no one is meant to shoot it."

He did not react. Then I tried to irritate him. "I guess, someone punched these holes with a nail."

The tin soldier's face did not change, and he continued staring towards the wall.

Then I added, "A rusty nail."

When the interrogator returned, the serviceman disappeared, and the questioning continued. Soon it began to resemble a damaged gramophone record with the needle stuck in the same annoying creaky scrap of a tired old song. A dozen times he said, "You signed such and such an appeal in such and such year, month, and day. Is this your signature?"

A dozen times I repeated, "Yes, it is."

And so it went. He asked, "Who wrote this document?"

"I don't know," I said.

"Was it Sharansky?"

"No, it wasn't him."

"Why are you so certain?"

"Because when he lived at my place, he never wrote anything."

"Then, who was it? You?"

"I don't know."

"Stop playing the fool. When he lived in your apartment, you weren't there. Do you refuse to give evidence? This is the KGB prison, and for failure to cooperate with the investigation you can end up over there," he said, nodding at the small barred windows with metal canopies across the prison yard. The investigator's accent confirmed what's been said by others interrogated in this prison—the KGB did some horse-breaking of their own provincial cadre in order for them to conduct these investigations of such an important case. The horse behind a big desk now looked rather timid than wild.

"Do you call evidence," I said, "the letters sent to the Soviet authorities?"

"Maybe, it was you who wrote this?" he repeated again.

"I don't recall writing it."

Everything was infinitely repeated; only the dates and some addressees were different. This dragged on for four or five hours—maybe more. The same stone-faced soldier kept disappearing and reappearing, causing the investigator to hurry off somewhere. Surely, he was receiving instructions from his superiors who were listening to this questioning; maybe a microphone was behind that portrait of Felix Dzerzhinsky, the first head of the Soviet secret police.

After the last visit to his supervisors, he said, with a face contorted by anger, "We know everything about you, where you go, whom you meet, and what you do. We don't have to look for new material to bring a case against you. I'm not talking about a trifle such as turning your apartment into a den for people associated with foreign intelligence services, but we decided to give you another chance to think about yourself and your family. Go home, and be here tomorrow morning at nine sharp."

"The boss isn't pleased with you, my child," I thought. "Which is good."

On my way home, when I stopped wondering why I was not put in a cell at least for one night, I thought about my interrogator's face. With his big round cheeks and almost lipless mouth, he looked like the target on that rickety table.

In the morning, the "target" continued to run to his boss, leaving me alone with a new, now-costumed soldier with a black tie and scuffed shoes. This new actor helped to banish my night terrors. With the weathered face of a soldier on outside guard duty and his tin stare, in his cheap black suit he looked like a doleful mortician who had lost his clientele. I could not expect a better sedative.

Apart from this detail, the day was similar to the previous one. Only once did the interrogator break the monotony of our encounter, get up from his desk, and with pursed lips, quickly walk up to me. "Do you acknowledge your signature on this document?" he asked, placing on the target an open letter in support of the U.S. Senator Henry ("Scoop") Jackson and Representative Charles Vanik's amendment to the current law on trade with Russia. I kept silent. I would not admit to signing it. He repeated his question. I said, "Many people who've been refused permission to emigrate have signed it. It's quite natural that they support the amendment."

The narrow line of his lips disappeared—the "target" smiled for the first time in two days. "Therefore you acknowledge that your signature is proof of your participation in this anti-state conspiracy in America's interest," he said.

"No," I said. "Conspiracy requires secrecy. These are open letters."

"Don't pretend to be naïve," he said. "With your gray head you're behaving like a child."

"These letters," I said, "simply ask the world to help us to emigrate."

He sounded like a boxer who had just knocked down his opponent. "You're asking the American Congress to exert more pressure on the Soviet Union and impose higher tariffs on our imports. You call this blackmail the most effective course of action toward the USSR?" He began yelling, "You're asking them to penalize our country and our socialist economic system! You want America to have power over our internal policy!"

Instead of getting scared, I was becoming angry and blurted out, "I dislike this amendment anyway."

"What?"

I repeated, "I dislike this amendment."

"Okay! Here is a paper and a pen. Write it down!"

I wrote, "I dislike the Jackson-Vanik amendment because it demands a privilege of emigration only for Jews."

"What do you mean?" he asked.

"I mean that every citizen of every country should have the right to freely leave it and come back when he wants to. Is it a crime?"

"Lefortovo prison is not a place for political demagoguery. We'll see you again very soon."

As I was leaving and the door slammed behind me, my elation quickly petered out. "Some hero!" I thought. "What made you so happy? You chickened out of mentioning Evangelicals in this written statement. It was a unique chance to do so."

It was already dark when I reached the courtyard stretched along our co-op building. An obese old man, a retiree from the Bolshoi Theater, approached me. He looked around and said, "I don't see your boys in a car today."

"They aren't mine, they're yours," I said.

His voice cracked. "You're always joking."

"I've already chatted with them today," I said.

The old musician was breathing heavily when he repeated, "You're always joking." He lowered his voice. "Some villagers have been sitting on the bench near your entrance for several hours.

Waiting for you. How could you not be afraid!?"

"I'm afraid," I said.

A couple of times my neighbors had seen how this former wind player, on a cold winter evening, despite a severe shortness of breath, came out of his warm apartment to bring homemade sandwiches and hot tea for "my boys" sitting in a cold "Volga" near my entrance.

But I felt more pity than contempt for him. He did it out of fear, not out of love. The object of his all-consuming devotion was his Jewish boy well over thirty, a cellist, who was constantly touring Europe, earning hard currency for the government. His loving father, to secure the future and employment of his child was simply demonstrating his loyalty to the state.

FIFTEEN

The Assault on the American Embassy

T HAT EVENING, a Ukrainian who had already stayed at my place for a couple of days, and two new guests from Siberia discussed with me and Nikolai Petrovich Goretoi the eternal question—how to make the authorities openly recognize the existence of the thousands strong Christian emigration movement.

The Ukrainian had come to my place with a bunch of Baptists and Pentecostals whom preacher Nikolai Kunitsa brought from the Ukrainian city of Rovno. They had tried, time and again, to apply to emigrate. This most recent time, their applications—written on rough grayish pages of exercise books—were torn up and trashed right in front of everyone; my guests, in turn, heard the same question from an official, "Are you a Jew?" After a well-calculated pause, the official, who was female, had said, chuckling, "First you have to convert to Judaism and after that show me tangible evidence." Obviously she had circumcision in mind and enjoyed her own stimulating joke. She repeated this to all of the men, with minor variations. No doubt this officer was instructed to humiliate these bumpkins, and these amusements were probably cooked up in cooperation with her thoughtful boss. She knew that these modest provincials would not complain to her superiors out of shame.

When they returned to my place, frustrated, I said, "Maybe

it's not such a bad idea to complete this idea of hers. Just imagine returning to that office after circumcision. Tell her that you did it because Jesus Christ was also circumcised. She might become terribly upset."

I explained to the Siberian newcomers that we were being overheard by KGB bugs and asked them to take a stroll along Prospect Mira (Peace Avenue). Before leaving the apartment, Goretoi filed a brief speech to the ceiling. "We are members of the one Church of Jesus Christ," he explained for the benefit of the KGB. "Wherever we live and worship Him, we are brothers and sisters in Christ."

I interpreted to the godless ceiling: "This means that Evangelical Christians submit an application for emigration as one family, all together, in one list." After that I shook my head. "Often only one member of a Jewish family applies."

"We cannot afford this," said Goretoi. "We are one family."

Scattered out across hundreds of towns and villages, they felt more confident together, on one single list. I admired their faith-based courage, borne of many years of despair, but feared that the KGB could easily turn it into a hit list.

When we got off the elevator, my new acquaintances examined the unreliable cables over this metal box. They had ridden this unpredictable conveyance for the first time in their lives here in Moscow.

"Next to you I look like a terrible coward," I said. "I still can't forgive myself for not mentioning you during my interrogation."

"Don't worry, Arkady Abramovich," said Goretoi, "our whole church has been praying for you."

"Thank you!" I said. "I need it."

We walked slowly along the dark deserted street. "Just sending your applications or passing appeals to foreign correspondents isn't working," I said, stating the obvious. "We ought to try to bring it directly to the American embassy."

"I've been thinking about that while still in the camp," said Goretoi, "since Feodor and Patryshev gave their passports to that Japanese Consul."

"It'll be hard to break in," I continued grimly.

"You shouldn't come with us," said Goretoi. "If you're arrested, no one will know about us."

"We need foreign reporters," I said. "They love messy melodrama. Just to get in touch with them may take an indefinite number of days. That's where Sharansky would be handy with his English. For you to come at a set time to Moscow is always a problem ..."

One of my Siberian guests remarked, "For several years we've been beating our heads against this wall."

"Will you go?" I asked him. "They can bring criminal charges against all of us."

"Members of my church are in prison," he said. "Children in school have been beaten."

"They are forcing our kids to write in newspapers that their parents are cruel and stupid fanatics," the Ukrainian guest said. "It's a deadlock. We should try to break into the embassy."

"At first I'll approach the officer in the booth," Goretoi said, summing up. "Try to break through, after we start talking."

At night we wrote an appeal to U.S. President Jimmy Carter. I had already accumulated a mountain of facts about the persecution of Evangelical Christians; it rested upon the stories of people living thousands of miles apart, stories of imprisonment, discrimination, and humiliation. Frequently recorded on tape, they were supported by copies and originals of court sentences and orders, decisions of local authorities, receipts of countless fines, and defamatory newspaper articles. It all had to be squeezed into two thirds of a page. My frail Erika typewriter was able to produce only four copies, and I had to type two more. In the morning they were distributed to all participants of the upcoming suicide mission, and a single copy was laid between the pages of a Pushkin volume.

Before going on reconnaissance, I joked with them: "Christians, practice running fast."

While I was waiting for the elevator, Goretoi dashed out of the apartment to the landing. "Already in training?" I asked, chuckling.

"Arkady Abramovich, yesterday you were strolling in ragged shoes on the wet asphalt. We have to buy you shoes."

"Are you kidding me? Don't you have enough worries with a dozen sick elderly and your own eleven children? No, thank you very much, I cannot accept such a gift."

"Arkady Abramovich, be realistic; you won't be able to get to my church in these crumbling boots."

He was right. I sheepishly agreed, and we dropped by a shoe store in my neighborhood. Wearing my new shoes, I went to a grocery store opposite the embassy, looked through its window and then at my watch, as if waiting for a date while trying to understand when and how the policeman changed duties at the gateway. We needed to find out if our plotters could run into the embassy's yard alongside an entering diplomatic car, and if we were lucky, to identify at least some of the undercover spies who circled the neighborhood for hours, looking like ordinary citizens.

The next day, I was watching the progress of our assault from that store. As Goretoi approached a policeman in the booth, several men in civilian clothes appeared out of thin air and dragged my friends to an adjacent yard. I jumped out of the store and ran across Bolshoe Sadovoe Koltso (Big Garden Ring), one of the busiest streets of old Moscow. Dodging honking cars, I finally made it to the curb, where a pair of lovers walking leisurely turned into wolves. Shadowing me, they turned quickly into a semi-vacant lot where a bunch of plainclothes and uniformed police were studying my guests' passports while packing them into a van emblazoned with flowers on its sides. But the most surprising thing was that my cries and demands to release them were simply ignored. Shouting, "I'm a witness!" I tried to get into the van, but two policemen stretched out their hands, and without uttering a word, blocked me from reaching the wagon door. I continued shouting, "They did nothing wrong! They were just looking at the embassy! Citizens have the right to walk here!"

After the van carried my friends away from this wasteland, I was left behind, along with that couple of spies, now back in love. Still looking reproachfully at me, they walked back out to the street, again holding hands.

I hurried to a former general, Peter Grigorievich Grigorenko, one of the few remaining free members of the human rights organization, the Moscow Helsinki Watch Group. The old man said, "Arkady, they still have plenty of opportunities to arrest you. Who knows, maybe you now belong to some criminal case they're cooking." He could hardly move, and his hands were shaking. Long incarcerations had taken their toll.

Grigorenko's wife, Zinaida Mikhailovna and I visited police stations around the American Embassy. The policemen looked at us with suspicion, as we explained that my visiting relatives were arrested for no apparent reason near the embassy. In fact, we just wanted to make sure that this detention wouldn't go unnoticed.

It was late evening when veteran refusenik Victor Elistratov spoke with Reuters and BBC reporters from the telephone booth into which we had both squeezed. They asked him if we had the statement we wanted to pass to Americans. I nodded. Passing the information to the correspondents would happen later, in person, and I silently thanked the KGB for giving their plainclothes robots the enigmatic directive to ignore me and not even search me.

A year later, on June 27, 1978, seven Siberian Pentecostals, from the Vushchenko and Chmykhalov families, broke into the U.S. Embassy and remained there for almost five years until the Soviets allowed them to emigrate.

A precinct policeman had visited me from time to time, but recently, after our failed attempt to break into the American Embassy, he began coming frequently. He was well past fifty and had the rank of a major. I had never seen an officer with such a high rank at such a low position. On his chest there were two order stripes clearly earned during the war. He was never rude, and knowing that he had nothing to do with my situation, I treated the old soldier with respect. Once he said, "Please come with me to the police station. They want to talk to you."

At the station, a man, looking at me askance, warned that if I would not soon find a job, I might get a two-year prison term for leading a parasitic lifestyle. I told him that recently I found an elevator operator job, but the KGB did not allow the manager of the building to hire me.

"The KGB has nothing to do with this," he said dryly.

"Then, please explain to me why this woman was shaking in her shoes when she turned me down the very next day after promising me this sophisticated position."

"Sign here," he said, "that you have received this warning."

After that, the policeman asked me twice more to go with him to police station. I refused and said that if those people needed to talk with me, they could send me a summons to come to their office and not to use the police for their own ends. To my surprise, the major did not insist.

"They are listening to every word we say here," I warned the man and saw a shadow of sadness in his eyes.

Once, he came smiling. "At the Visa Office they want to talk to you," he said. "You have to arrive there at ten o'clock in the morning." I explained that if they were serious about a visa, they would send me a summons.

One Sunday morning, in the midst of my attempts to find out what happened to the detained Pentecostals, he said, "Today you must go with me. Otherwise, I will have to arrest you."

He saw my reluctance and added, "It's not at the police station. We're going to a school nearby."

As we walked, I asked if he knew anything about Sunday schools. The major shrugged. I asked if he had read Mark Twain.

"No," he said, glancing over his shoulder. "Please don't talk to me."

Clearly the soldier had had some troubles because of my stubbornness, and I shut up.

Like two peas from the same pod, the school was similar to the one I attended, where, at a tender age I had shed a lot of my own and others' blood when I was called a kike. The major unlocked the door, and we went to the fourth floor. Before locking me in a classroom, he said, "If you need to go to the restroom, knock on the door."

"How long will we be here?"

"I know nothing."

Planning a press conference about the disappearance of four Pentecostals, I had been hurrying from one activist to another, and the KGB had probably decided to slow me down. We spent all day there until dark. When he unlocked the classroom, I said, "You were left without lunch and dinner."

To my delight, on the bench at my entrance I found, Nikolai Petrovich Goretoi with Olga Matyash from his church, and Vladimir Stepanov from the Far East. All participants of the action at the embassy gate left the police station only feeling slightly shocked and with a heavy fine for disorderly conduct. After a night in a police bsement, all four were put on trains and sent home."Maybe," I said, "the embassy's Russian personnel informed the KGB that Americans saw the detention, and to escape publicity, you were pardoned."

"Maybe," said Goretoi. "But maybe you made a lot of noise after we were arrested."

"The next time," I said, "they will accuse you of an attempt to disarm the Marines, capture the embassy, and raise the Israeli flag over it."

In a couple of days, the deferred earlier trial of Malva Landa was to be held in the Moscow suburb, where she lived before her room caught fire under suspicious circumstances. This time, I had a chance to introduce Goretoi to Andrei Sakharov. The legendary academician intended to come to this macabre KGB revenge trial and told me that afterward he could talk with the Pentecostals. Usually, Sakharov shied away from new acquaintances, especially the people who came from afar; he feared for their safety. He had already been told twice about the disappearances of these courageous souls.

The Pentecostals and I were moving through a crowd of men in plain clothes and police uniform, vigilantly looking at us, when I saw a familiar face. Yes, it was Alexei, my buddy in ice dancing to whom a few years ago I poured out my anti-Soviet soul. The good man held out his hand for a handshake, but I did not want to jeopardize him and said, "I'm sorry, you mistook me for someone else," and proceeded to the stairs leading to the second floor.

"Malva's my mother," said Alexei to my back. I turned around, and we shook hands. "I've already been fired from the university," he said.

"Why?"

above: A.D. Sakharov and E.G. Bonner at home with Anatoly Sharansky (*left*). Moscow, no later than March 14, 1977. The very next day Sharansky was arrested, accused of being a CIA spy. Photographer unknown. (Sakharov Archive)

below: Malva Landa, Moscow, spring of 1977. The oldest Russian human rights activist, one of the first members of the Moscow Group to promote the implementation of the Helsinki Accords in the USSR (1976). In May 1977, during her trial, I introduced a group of Pentecostal leaders to A.D. Sakharov. Photographer unknown. (Sakharov Archive)

"For being unable to re-educate my mother."

"Sorry for the foolish question."

"We always knew where your bitterness would lead you," Alexei said.

In the courtroom, soon after I pointed out Sakharov to my companions, the court clerk gabled that for technical reasons the court was again postponed. Alexei darted out of the room. Sakharov, the Pentecostals, and I went for a short walk through a spring grove nearby. He asked them to tell him about themselves, and they did at length. When Goretoi asked him about his attitude toward religion, Sakharov replied, "Positively viewed, and with respect."

After that he hurried to the city. We feared for Sakharov and wanted to accompany him at least to the train, but he resolutely refused, saying that he could perfectly get home on his own.

SIXTEEN

In the Cultist's Lair

I WAS READYING to travel to underground churches, when my old pal the police major delivered a summons from the Visa Office. He said in a congratulatory tone, "They're going to give you a visa."

I looked at the little rectangle. It was hard to believe. I had done nothing to deserve such a gift. Questions churned in my head. Why are they suddenly releasing me from their fishbowl? The fake foreign correspondents, without fail, were still continuing their faithful KGB service. Did they happen to find that crumpled piece of paper sealed under the insole of my ice-dancing boot, now regrettably fallen into disuse, with addresses of Evangelicals to whom I planned to travel? Could it be some trap? What should I do?

All I knew was that I had to rush.

As soon as the policeman left, I started packing my suitcase, then caught myself and tried to fill my briefcase instead, without making it suspiciously fat. Before leaving the apartment, I turned on the light in the kitchen in the faint hope that this hackneyed trick might make the KGB have to spend a couple of nights before figuring out that I was wasting electricity.

This morning nobody was there on duty at the entrance, but I did not want to tempt fate, and on the way to the railway station, skipped buying food for the trip. So far everything had been fine, except for the fact that no one in the church of Nikolai Petrovich Goretoi was waiting for me.

On the train, I climbed up on the top bunk, turned my back to my fellow travelers, pretended to be asleep, and focused on what was happening. My first thought was ridiculous: they had decided that locking me up could make me a celebrity and could be more damaging for their enterprise than kicking me out of the country. If nobody stopped me on the platform of Temryuk, one and a half thousand kilometers away from Moscow, then indeed they were choosing to let me out of their cage.

No one knew about my sudden departure. Three members of the now nearly moribund Moscow Helsinki Human Rights Group knew of my plans to travel to Pentecostal and Baptist churches, but two of them, Alexander Ginsburg and Natan Sharansky, had already been in prison for several months, the general was ill, and his wife was busy taking care of him and their fifty-year-old helpless son with Down syndrome. If the KGB found out that I went on a trip without notifying anyone, they might be tempted to settle scores with impunity, maybe by "finding" me dead on the tracks. I hoped that my thoughts were not clouded with delusions of persecution. I decided that I should just go on behaving insolently and shamelessly, since only my dear friend Tom Kolesnichenko could imagine that I would be such a reckless fool.

This was June 2, 1977. We had planned that we would meet in Starotitarovskaya only in the middle of June. Our list of Christians asking for exit visas had already started to snowball, and I would be with believers not only from neighboring towns and villages but even with some from Ukraine and the Caucasus.

Clearly my arrival in Starotitarovskaya, at the southwesterly edge of Russia, would not be a cause for celebration among the local population still overheated after a recent public trial of the Pentecostal "fanatics." The police visited all of them and demanded that they attend a political lynching at the District House of Culture. There, signatures on notices were obtained from all members of the church, including the old and the sick.

The next day I left my top bunk only by early afternoon, when the train was approaching Temryuk. A lively old woman said, "Here we were arguing about you, son. Tell us, who's right? Were you drunk and forgot your suitcase at the railway station in Moscow or somebody stole it there?"

I explained that my wife had already taken all our suitcases with food to Temryuk. The experienced old lady shook her head, "Yeah, you men cannot be trusted even with empty bags; you'll sell your last pants to get a drink."

In Temryuk, there wasn't anyone in mufti rushing toward me with an arrest warrant, and I began thinking about the thirty-five kilometers that lay between this district center and the Starotitarovskaya Cossack village. The southern air was filled with the aroma of sprouting greens. I had not eaten since the morning before and bent my steps toward a café called Red Poppy next to the station. Several men and a barmaid—an artificial blond with lush hair—looked at me with displeasure, hostility and suspicion. Behind the barmaid hung a handwritten sign, "We do not sell alcoholic beverages. Only champagne." The bar customers stood at the ready with empty glasses, which she filled below the counter with a yellowish drink from a hidden flagon. Judging by the grimace on her face, it was heavy.

While walking back to the barmaid, a curly-haired mustachioed man passed by me and asked hospitably, "A visit to Cossacks?"

I nodded. "Yes, Starotitarovskaya."

"I'll take you there."

"Thank you." I pointed at his blue pants with red stripes. "There are still some fearless Cossacks over there."

"You can read about us only in textbooks now. There is little left of us, hereditary Cossacks, but now many out-of-towners—Armenians and even Baptists—live there."

"Where did the Cossacks go?"

"Scattered haphazardly or laid low, became Party workers and accountants, no longer warriors."

Pride was evident in his words, and to please him, I said, "You probably have a sheepskin hat and a sharp saber at home."

The Cossack smiled. "My grandfather surrendered the saber. If he had tried to hide it, he'd have ended up in some godforsaken place."

When a girl brought me a goulash and two glasses of tea, he twirled his drooping mustache and nodded at her. "A good-looking Cossack, too."

She blushed.

"What's a Cossack without a horse?" I said, and she chuckled appreciatively.

"We came here two hundred years ago," he said, "to defend Russia against the Caucasus highlanders and the Turks. Hence—close to the Black and Azov Seas and a short hop away from Crimea—just to live and be happy with life."

After I finished eating, he said, "Okay, time to go. You should've tried this grape wine, almost as strong as vodka."

"I'm afraid to go with you," I said, clicking on his empty glass and grinning crookedly.

"Don't worry, Cossacks are good drivers. I won't charge you for the ride."

When our risky travel began, I asked—avoiding the word "Pentecostals," unfamiliar to locals—if he knew those "Baptists."

"Dangerous nuts," he said. "A prison is the place for them, and an orphanage for their children."

"What would you do if police took your child from you because you wanted to keep your horse and sabre?"

He looked at me with surprise. "The Baptists are cunning. They don't behave like Russians, don't drink, and want to move to Israel. No wonder they are suspected of spying."

"And what would one spy on in your village? Homemade wine? Moonshine?"

"They meet with foreigners in Moscow."

"KGB agents walk behind every foreigner over there. Well done, Baptists! Learned foreign languages in a Cossack village!"

He guffawed.

I explained that one million spies come to the capital every day from every corner of the country to spy on sausage and clothes.

He tittered.

To learn the state of our prosperity, I continued, it's enough to see our queues for oranges; the queues to Lenin's Mausoleum reflect our state of mind.

Along the straight-as-an-arrow, partially paved road, now and then stood fruit trees and red poppy flowers, bright in the sun, on tall upright stems.

"Beautiful land," I said, "and spacious. There is enough space here for everybody, even for believers in God."

"Recently we gave them hell," my driver said. "People wanted to beat them. They prayed for three hours. We laughed, didn't allow them to leave. Many demanded that the cultists be evicted out of Krasnodarsky Territory. One of them, probably their priest, wanted to say something, but we didn't give him a chance."

"Weren't you interested in what he could say?"

"No. I don't want my children to listen to these illiterate savages. There were a lot of our children there—just give them a pretext to skip school.... All the district bosses were there, too."

If this dashing Cossack only knew that he was taking me right into the hornet's nest. When we were halfway, he did ask, "What's the name of your friend? Maybe I know him."

"Goretoi ..." my voice cracked. "Here—ah he ... probably goes by ... like a Cossack, Mykola ...

"His surname is naturally Cossack," said my driver approvingly. "But Mykola is Ukrainian. We would call him Nikolai. No, not familiar."

But misfortune happened anyway. I asked him discreetly to stop at the beginning of the street, but he said, "No—no" and took me straight to Nikolai Petrovich Goretoi's house. And, of course, the Lord had arranged for the good Nikolai Petrovich to be standing right at the wooden gate of his mud-brick hut.

"Wait!" my Cossack said, "That's him! That priest with thick glasses!"

"He's a pastor, a bishop," I said.

"You lied to me!" he yelled.

"No, I didn't. He isn't a Baptist. He's a Pentecostal."

"Who cares? A sectarian is a sectarian!"

"Does one need to be a Baptist—to reject this fairy tale of building a paradise on earth? This is their crime, nothing else."

Goretoi was talking to someone inside the house, but the short-sighted pastor could hardly see me in the truck, though he could hear our argument.

"And who are you?" persisted the angry Cossack. "Why did you come here? To stir up trouble?"

"You go down to the KGB!" I said. "Right from here! Say that a suspicious Muscovite went over to the enemies of the people and brought a briefcase full of Bibles."

"Is it true?"

"No, you can't buy a Bible in this country. It's more dangerous than your grandfather's sword. See in what a beggarly house this spy and his bunch of underage spies live? Wouldn't you want to leave the country if your children were thrashed almost daily in school?"

"What do you need them for? You don't look like a believer."

"I like them. They lie less than you and I do, they work hard and don't steal, they are less afraid of the authorities than we are, and they teach us not to fear death."

"And you're no longer afraid of death?" His bright eyes were full of scorn.

"Of course, I'm afraid. But they prefer it to spiritual death."

"And what is spiritual death?" the Cossack snickered.

"You'd better ask them. Nikolai Petrovich would be happy to explain it to you. Let's go over to him; he'll be glad to talk with you."

"You're kidding."

"No. I'm serious."

He shook his head.

"Recently," I said, "these 'fanatics' brought me a newspaper from the Far East. A seventh-grader named Love is reported to have begged the authorities to take her away from her parents, and to put her into an orphanage. Isn't that lovely?"

"Okay, you better go," he said, clearing his throat. "The neighbors might become interested in what I'm doing here for so long."

"Thanks for bringing me here," I said, extending my hand. "What's your name? I'll ask them to pray for you and for those you love."

His mouth twisted. He shook my hand without saying a word.

In the rays of the unobtrusive sun, we were having dinner in a courtyard, at a homemade table of long narrow boards. I peered at the children, made faces at them, and then tried to look perfectly innocent; they stared at me and smiled at each other—we had fun. Their mother, Varvara Nikolaevna, busy at the stove, said through the open window, "Arkady Abramovich, you would make a good father."

The children told me how they stopped going to school a month ago after the principal trumpeted at an assembly that if he were given an AK assault rifle, he would have shot all of the sectarians. "What a gifted educator of the young generation of builders of communism!" I loudly proclaimed.

The kids thought it was very funny, and when they finally calmed down, Goretoi said that the inspectors from the Board of Education visited families of Pentecostals on three consecutive days to persuade the children to return to school.

"See how humane they are?" I said. "And you keep complaining."

The children continued giggling.

"I have long noticed," I said, "that my inappropriate jokes are enjoyed only by unreasonable children."

Varvara Nikolaevna apologized for serving meatless potato soup and bland kasha. I asked the master of the house to bring his wife to Moscow during his next trip, so she could cook me such a delicious meal.

"Maybe one day," he said, "she'll cook for you in America. If the KGB is serious about your visa."

This cheerful mood at the table looked unreal to me. I already knew that back in Nakhodka their little children as well as those of his deacon Nikolai Bobarykin were forced to go on stage and give evidence in court. They were questioned to establish the "facts"— the creation of a prohibited fanatical sect.

"There were enough crying children in the courtroom to form a kindergarten," joked Goretoi.

"Or an orphanage," corrected Nikolai Bobarykin, approaching me from the gate with Feodor Sidenko. Both kissed me on the lips.

"We knew," seventeen-year-old Ilia said, "they wanted to take away our dad."

"This five-year-old," his father said, "yelled louder than the

Nikolai P. Goretoi and me in his vegetable garden. June, 1977.

judge when the witness Sidenko told him ..."

And here Feodor almost gleefully repeated his offence in his hoarse voice, "All of this is gross bullshit!" Children roared with laughter again as he continued, "For contempt of court the judge sent me to a forced labor camp for six months."

I knew this judge had violated the law and sentenced Nikolai Petrovich Goretoi to five years of camp and five years of exile when the law provided only for one or the other.

"Especially after that trial," Ilia said, "other children threw stones at us. This school is better than in Nakhodka."

His father turned to him. "Show Arkady Abramovich your head."

Ilia got up from the long bench, walked over to me, and bent his head. Parting his thick black hair, I counted nine whitish scars. "Twelve years ago?" I asked.

Goretoi, his wife, their son Ilia, and me with those who just joined the "hit list" by putting their names on a list of those desiring to emigrate. Ilia is on the far right; I counted scars on his head.

"They caught us outside our house," he explained. "The older children were beaten at school. We were building a cute little house of stones."

"Does your head still hurt?"

"Now—no."

I knew that Pentecostals were stoned in other cities, but for the first time I heard it from the children themselves.

"That's why," Goretoi said, "most of them don't have a chance to finish high school." He passed to the sharp-eyed Valery a buttered enameled bowl. Valery deftly climbed the cherry tree by which we were sitting. Soon the bowl stood in front of me, full of cherries. I said, "No way!" and pushed it toward the children.

"What's the matter with you, Arkady Abramovich?" their mother exclaimed. "Really! You're our dear guest!"

"I can't," I said. "You don't have enough fruit here for this underage legion."

"Don't you see our plum tree and two apple trees?" she said.

"They won't begin to bear fruit for two months," I said, sounding ridiculous.

"Sooner," said Goretoi.

Looking at the curly potato field, I began to devour cherries. Soon some legionnaires joined me. I thought, just talking with these children around this table gives you a picture of the life of Evangelicals in the Soviet Union. The sixteen-year-old Klava Pishchenko tried to comfort this depressed Muscovite. "Here we're treated better," she stressed.

"How many brothers and sisters do you have?"

"All ten of us were beaten up in Nakhodka. After such a beating I was sick for six years."

"You look healthy now."

"I'm fine now, only sometimes have headaches."

The children calmly continued to eat cherries. The adults, too, showed no particular feelings. It was their life.

Then we heard another voice from the gate: "Welcome to our church, Arkady Abramovich!" It was Enoch, the oldest son of the Goretois. "My barefooted scouts have told me of your arrival, but I was standing in the clay and couldn't tear myself away from the work. We're building a house for a brother from our church."

"Enoch," said Nikolai Petrovich, "in a couple of hours send the children to every family; as it gets dark, we'll gather at the home of Vera Shchukin."

In mock surprise I raised an eyebrow. "Conspirators?"

"It's the norm," Goretoi said with a grin. "I assign the time and the place of each prayer meeting two hours before it starts."

The faces of the children who were to participate in this criminal offense were carefree. I said, "Your kids' untroubled faces impress me more than Eugene Bresenden's letter to justify his emigration, about Siberian police throwing tear gas canisters into a room with worshipers."

In my head crept some bombastic words about what I could learn from these children, and I said, "At your age, I was a slave; I was born a slave, but you were born free."

"And when you were nine years old?" Valery, the cherry picker, was clearly trying to make sense of what this gray-haired Muscovite was saying.

"At your age," I admitted, "I dreamed of becoming a border guard defending the Soviet Union from spies and saboteurs."

All the kids started smiling and looking at each other again. Maybe they began understanding what I had said so abstrusely.

The long days of June meant it started to get dark after nine. When a street lamp lit in front of their house, Varvara Nikolaevna said, "It's aimed at our door."

"Maybe the builders installed the lamp crookedly," I said.

"Ours is the only house with a street light on a long street—is that by chance, too?" She looked at me like a mother amused by the naïvete of her child and nodded toward the house across the street. "We're being watched from there."

"I wanted to smash this lantern with a slingshot," Valery said with a sigh, "but father forbade me. He said, 'Let it shine, so our grannies won't trip.'"

"Thank the KGB," I said, "for not following your grannies' movements with a military searchlight mounted on an all-terrain armored vehicle."

"This year, almost every day, shadows have been following us everywhere and police, for no particular reason, have broken into our homes," said Goretoi, "but today, on the occasion of your arrival, they are nowhere to be seen."

"The local KGB should pray for you every day," I said. "Without you, they would've stagnated here, without an increase in rank and salary."

After this lively exchange of views on the role of light and darkness in the spiritual life of mankind, we all crossed the kitchen garden planted with heavenly potatoes, passed by green onions and fragrant dill, and, through a narrow opening in the fence, began making our way to the house of Vera Shchukin. One by one or in pairs, we used the most roundabout paths between houses. The village was asleep. Almost all windows were now unlit.

I wiped sweat from my forehead and whispered to Goretoi, "Muggy."

He said nothing. I couldn't stop talking. "For how long have you been aware that this gathering is prohibited by articles 142 and 227 of the Criminal Code?"

"For as long as I've believed in my Savior," he whispered.

When we entered the one-room house, its windows had been already sealed shut, carefully curtained, and a dim kerosene lamp was burning. People quietly took their seats, our shadows darting fearfully on the walls and ceiling. In the semi-darkness, folks kept coming, and children and women huddled on the beds and on the floor with the little ones on their laps. Children giggled and jostled each other in the ribs. The men were pushed up against the walls. Two old women sat close to the invisible gap between the door and its frame, in hope of catching a breath of fresh air. On stools sat an old man, white as chalk, and two pregnant women. One of them, with a hand-copied New Testament, offered me her chair, but I shook my head and clung to the wall. When nearly forty persons had squeezed into the house, the deacon turned on the light, and ducked outside to check if it escaped to the street.

I was already seized by euphoria when the service began, to my surprise, with individual prayer; each participant, young and old, prayed as he or she wanted and about what he or she wanted. Everybody was talking to the Lord. For me, this steady hum was a symbol of the democratic structure of Pentecostal church life, which was out of place not only in the Soviet regime, but also in the hierarchical structure of Russian Orthodoxy. Whether it would fit into the life of a synagogue I had no clue.

In ten minutes my clothes were soaked through with perspiration. But it almost did not bother me. I was a part of this service, just like the kids who sang and prayed like everybody else, though maybe I was more like that baby babbling something very important on her mother's lap.

Three sermons were preached, and Goretoi was just one of the preachers. In Moscow he repeatedly quoted the Bible by heart. Now he opened a book with this tarnished gilt cross on its cover, the only copy his church had. Goretoi inherited it from his Orthodox mother; it seemed to me that his eyes were closed when he read a long passage. Later he passed it to the next preacher. After every sermon, prayers were offered. All earthly suffering of these people, prisons and beatings, poverty and humiliation—it all became small and insignificant; they were with God and no one could erase from their faces the expression of joy, peace, and hope. Time and again everybody was singing psalms. Overwhelmed, only after a while did I realize that they sang softly, so no one outside could hear. The service was interrupted only once, when Goretoi suggested to the hunched old woman at the door that she go outside to catch some fresh air. She refused and the preaching and singing continued.

I knew I would not see printed songbooks and would instead hear the hymns that had somewhat changed as a result of repeated oral transmissions, or which were composed by Goretoi and other preachers. Every handwritten hymnal, from a thin notebook up to a volume of three hundred pages stitched together, was subversive literature. Each was a single copy and labor of love forbidden by law. The torn-out notebook pages were bound in illustrated home-made covers. The front, inside, and back sides of some covers were adorned with postcards of great artists of the remote past who could not foresee that their clandestine "religious propaganda" would be used by courts as evidence at the trials of Christians in the second half of the twentieth century.

We were returning home after midnight, again in silence, when the village and all the birds of the world were long asleep. The kids were right, their life was easy here; today they prayed at home, right in front of neighboring houses. In Marxist terms, this was historical progress. In the South Siberian winter of Barnaul, they went out of town for ten miles to pray in the open steppe, in the icy wind; in the Far East they trudged to the harsh hills; in other parts of the country, they gathered late at night deep in the woods.

Soon the Goretoi family was also asleep, except Varvara Nikolaevna and me. She asked if she could speak with me. We went outside and sat under the cherry tree, talking softly and eyeing the large shining moon oddly sliced by the sleepy branches.

We knew we would never meet again.

She asked me with a sigh, "Do you want to count how many times we've run away from one place to another?"

"Fifteen?" I guessed.

"No, more than that," and she started counting on her fingers, listing the cities, towns, and villages. She counted twenty-one places.

"With small children."

"There is nowhere else to run in this country," she said.

"And how many times have you been fined?"

"That's impossible to count," she said. "With all of the money we've paid in fines, we could've built a skyscraper for you in New York City."

"That's very generous of you, not a very tall skyscraper though."

"Why? Every time, we're fined half of our monthly wages. We're used to having to pay for everything, even for Christian funerals, and getting fined just for praying."

"Maybe you're right—since 1918, a million fines a year multiplied by sixty—we could build a Pentecostal city. Would you allow my tribe into such a heaven? Muslims don't."

She giggled exactly like her children did. "Ask Enoch and his Nadia about how, after their wedding in Ukraine they were interrogated. The police informed the managers at the enterprises of all people caught at that wedding and fined almost everybody." She looked tired. "They demanded information on salaries of all present."

"Let's postpone further talk until daylight," I said, suppressing a yawn. "But just answer one question—how do you manage to feed them?"

"There were times when we collected spikelet from collective farm fields after harvest and dug edible roots out from under the snow. Wherever we lived, supervisors knew that we would agree to take the worst jobs."

"Medicines cost money, too."

"The Lord has sown various herbs, roots and leaves for us. Talk with Nadia, and she'll send parcels with healing herbs for you to America. They say that only cactuses with prickles grow there."

"But why! Pork stew is also growing there. During the war, as a child, I adored this canned American fruit."

We fell silent and listened to the night. I said, "We've done well today, without police and with cherries. It's time to go to bed."

"No," Varvara Nikolaevna said firmly. "Tomorrow you will be busy talking to people from other places."

"Oh, Varvara Nikolaevna!" I begged again, "I need to go to bed."

"No—no! First I have to tell you what my husband wouldn't

want to talk about."

"Okay."

"Enoch worked here at a cement plant. At first we were surprised that Enoch was hired as an electrician, but after two weeks, when he went to the paymaster, he only got pennies. The plant needed an artist, and they gave this job to my husband; you know, he was an art teacher when we met. To impress me, he even drew my portrait."

"Did you like it?"

"Oh, I fell in love with it. Before him, a couple of drunkards created problems for the plant director when he needed some posters and slogans."

"I would go on a binge, too, if I had to do such work," I said. "I just can't imagine this pious pastor writing 'Onward to the Triumph of Communism!'"

"We had to make a choice. In Nakhodka our children went to bed hungry; after his arrest, everybody was afraid to hire me even as a cleaning lady. By the way, I think, he and Nikolai Bobarykin were sent to the same camp because their camp commander had good connections at the top. Everyone knew that both sectarians had magical hands. Nikolai built the officers' houses, and my husband drew paintings for them. And slogans."

In the morning Goretoi painted a wider picture. "I once refused to write a banner with the words of Stalin's favorite poet, 'Lenin lived. Lenin lives. Lenin will live forever.' I told the camp's deputy chief, 'I cannot do this. Why should I deceive people? He's been long dead.'"

"You're a rascal, Nikolai Petrovich!" I chuckled, "How many days in a punishment cell did you get for this revelation?"

"You lose track of time in the cooler," he shrugged. "No more than a week—they needed me."

Goretoi used to say that one day he would draw a landscape for me, but inexorable fate decreed otherwise. It was not given to us to know that two years later, when I already was in the United States, half-blind Goretoi would again make posters and draw pictures, only in another camp. This time he was sentenced to seven years of hard labor and five years of exile, not only for religious propaganda but also for anti-Soviet activities. That was how the government labeled his struggle for emigration.

We must pay tribute to the Perm-37 camp commander who, as the head of a famous camp for political prisoners, demonstrated political blindness and ordered Nikolai Petrovich Goretoi to draw unprincipled lyrical landscapes and even the portraits of his children, from family photos, of course. No doubt, these paintings still adorn the homes of the camp commander's children and grandchildren, maybe even in America.

Goretoi asked me not to roam the village. Everyone I wanted to see would come to me themselves. Though, judging by my smooth arrival, at the moment, the police followed new instructions to just hang back, and nothing threatened us. With two underage bodyguards, I went to see the construction of a house for a church member and the kneading of the clay.

"We bring this stiff clay from a quarry," Enoch said, looking up at the blue sky. "To knead it with bare feet is difficult. Eh, well, sometimes the Lord sends rain to help us make it softer. In other places, if lucky, we would hire a horse from a collective farm to do the job. Here we use our children."

He threw another shovelful of sawdust into the clay, and I pointed at the mountain of sawdust. "From the farm?" I asked.

"Pay five rubles to a tractor-driver, and he'll bring the farm chairman himself. They throw it in a landfill, anyway."

Two other builders laid the mixture of clay with sawdust in the four sections of the mold constructed from wooden boards, and then, tapping on the sides of the mold with shovels, released four raw adobe bricks to dry.

Sometimes a shortfall of communication helps. A few days later, my luck, the guests began to arrive. The young and the old, men and women, came to see me every day. I was struck again. They seemed to have lost the instinct of self-preservation inherent in any creature. They had entered their names and addresses in the thousands-strong list of traitors who had decided to notify the omnipotent authorities of wanting to leave the sacred Motherland of world Communism. This list would serve as irrefutable evidence of their guilt in future courts, but these people did not have a choice. They knew that the state was determined to destroy their faith.

Only the haste with which they left the village shortly after being included in this joint list may have signaled their anxiety, but there could be other reasons I wasn't aware of, such as work and families. And, in case of arrests and just as mementos, we took pictures.

Later I regretted not having taken a picture with a heavyset and vigorous woman from the Kiev region. Somehow, this ruddy Ukrainian villager reminded me of the women I saw in West Africa, whose beauty was defined by their weight. Thanks to her, I heard someone speak in tongues for the first time. Of course, with my atheist background, I immediately tried to determine what language was given to her by the Holy Spirit and was amazed to hear a few words of German. After the common prayer on the knees, I at once began my cynical calculations. She looked no more than thirty; even if she were thirty-seven and was born a year or two before German tanks rolled into her village, it still would be unlikely that the occupiers had enough time to play with this toddler.

Today, I would not dare to be so skeptical, but even then I liked that I could not find a rational explanation for this phenomenon.

Here, one of Nikolai P. Goretoi's sons, Victor, is carrying exactly the same kind of primitive bricks, the production of which I observed in the Cossack village Starotitarovskaya nine years before this particular photo was taken. At that time, Victor Goretoi was one of those children who solemnly guarded me on my way to the construction of a new house for a member of their church. He also was one of the boys who kneaded clay barefoot for such bricks.

From *Get Out of Your Land and Go: Interviews—autobiographical testimonies of believers in a stage of their exodus from the USSR to freedom* (Bramante: Urbania) 1988. This collection of photographs and documents was published in Italian by a Catholic organization in Rome that dealt with the persecution of Christians in communist countries. See also the photo of Goretoi on page 195.

Soon she took me in the yard and said that God knew what he was doing when he sent this Jew to help Christians. After that the woman whispered that she and her husband observed the Sabbath and did not eat pork. I was smart enough not to ask her how a true Ukrainian could survive without salted and garlicked pork fat, although my tongue itched to do just that. In parting, she mentioned the recent dispersal of a Christian wedding in Kiev. Then, without hesitation and to my horror, the beauty planted her impressive seat firmly on the fragile rear end of a motorcycle, said, "Praise the Lord! It's a miracle they didn't arrest you here," and waved for a long time, not trying, thank God, to turn around to face us. I thought about my grandmother. A neighbor hung her after the Germans entered Kiev.

One of the youngsters brought me out of my reverie and back to Starotitarovskaya. He asked his older brother, "Is she pregnant?"

"No, she's not," responded the more experienced fellow. "A pregnant woman's belly is smaller."

"Maybe she has three babies in her tummy," insisted the younger expert.

Their father heard them and said, "We have to include the names of the unborn in our list, but only the Lord knows whether they will be boys or girls."

"I don't think," I said, "that if tomorrow your church is allowed to go, the Soviets would say 'No, this newborn was not listed in your family's names and cannot go.'"

"Arkady Abramovich," said Goretoi, "you idealize the KGB. We have to include the names of the unborn."

When tasked to find names suitable for both boys and girls, I pleaded, "The ending of all Russian female names is always different from male names."

"Don't be picky," he said, "please, choose similar names."

"What if they are twins or triplets?"

"Arkady, don't shy away from hard work."

I came up with four names—Valentin or Valentina, Alexandr or Alexandra, Yevgeniy or Yevgeniya, and Pavel and Pavla.

"Not enough," said the pastor firmly. "We have to supply such names to other churches. Haven't you heard the little ones speaking about triplets?"

After a few more minutes I squeezed out of my brain two more unborn babies, Gabriel and Julian; they sounded more Jewish or Armenian than Russian. Silent during our conversation, Enoch suddenly asked, "Arkady Abramovich, what should I name my next child?"

Goretoi looked at him with undisguised interest.

"I like a Valentine," I said. "It sounds like the strumming of a guitar."

Many years later I met with her. She had become a teacher in Boise, Idaho.

THE NEXT WEEK, on June 16, 1977, a dusty green jeep pulled up in front of the house. Two men in dark suits and mottled ties emerged from it. The driver remained in the car. Peering from the window, Goretoi said, "What an honor! One of them is from the District Party Committee, the other—from the KGB. Dressed as for a state holiday, which means they are visiting you."

Goretoi invited them to sit down at the unpainted table under the cherry tree. As it turned out, they came to see him, not me, but I joined them. The already familiar strange procedure repeated itself—they totally ignored my presence. It seemed that Moscow would not be dealing with me for as long as I did not shoot a cannon at the KGB headquarters.

One of the guests said, "Nikolai Petrovich, we're here to remind all of you to take part in tomorrow's local elections."

"You know," Goretoi quietly said, "that all members of our

church renounced their Soviet citizenship, so we cannot take part in this event."

"We're all adults," said a guest, whom I took for a KGB officer, "and you still remain Soviet citizens. If you don't participate in the elections, your neighbors are going to be very angry at you."

I thought of my failed attempt to leave the Party.

"We cannot do that," repeated Goretoi. "You know that we're asking the authorities to let us emigrate."

"You forbade the members of your group to participate in the elections," the Party official said, raising his chin.

"No, no one in our church has the power to deprive its members of their human rights," was Goretoi's nuanced reply. "Their behavior is predetermined by their faith in Jesus Christ. And His guidance is the only voice they trust. You follow Communist Party directives, we follow His directives."

The KGB man said amiably, "We don't want you to be accused of organizing a boycott."

"We're here to talk only about your civic duty," said the Party man, furrowing his brow.

"In your group there are old and sick people, and we want to act humanely," the KGB officer said politely. "Your folks don't need to go to the polling station tomorrow, the members of the election commission will visit all of you with ballot boxes. They need just to put their ballots in the boxes."

"We're not a group. We are a church."

I desperately wanted to repeat the historical statement of the witness Feodor Sidenko at the trial in Nakhodka, but instead of saying "All of this is gross bullshit!" I caught myself beating a drum roll on the table with my fingers. Everyone looked at me. I got up. "If you don't have questions for me," I said, "I'll go inside and play with the kids."

When they left, Goretoi said, "At parting, I gave them an

above: The handwriting on the photograph of this small house with three windows says, "Built by the hands of two sons-in-law." It belonged to Pentecostals and was demolished by authorities. Located on the outskirts of the small town Dneprovsk, near the Dnieper River, Ukraine, this house was likely constructed by members of a Ukrainian family with young children and built with the same kind of homemade bricks that I witnessed being made by the Goretoi family and their fellow church members in Starotitarovskaya.

below: This team of construction workers in Ukraine is comprised of relatives belonging to the same church. Photo from 1986. Photographer unknown.

argument from Revelation, 'Come out of her, my people, that ye be not partakers of her sins.'"

The very next day I found myself unlawfully partaking in the electoral sins. Two festively dressed women had not expected to see some unknown citizen in the home of sectarians. They could not tear their eyes away from me and ignored the three old women, whose house they solemnly entered with a ballot box and a bundle of ballots. The authorities clearly did not deem it necessary to notify the activists of my subversive endeavors in the village. Perhaps it was a state secret. At the moment, I was most worried about the suspicious bus on which the two arrived. Such a bus could be used for transporting a police squadron kept somewhere nearby. Maybe these idiots have become victims of their own propaganda, I thought, and dreamt of a violent Christian demonstration.

A hard life clearly had not deprived the old ladies of their sense of humor.

"My nephew doesn't want to vote either," said one of them, nodding in my direction. The "nephew" nodded gloomily two times.

"Why?" asked one of the state's goodwill ambassadors.

"I'm not a local," I said. "Came here to visit my kin."

"As an educated man, you should explain to these not very literate women that every citizen should vote."

"Shouldn't I first explain to you why they don't want to vote?"

"We know why," she said. "Because someone with connections to the CIA brainwashed them, and now they want to move to the fascist state of Israel. They don't even know that they will endure hunger and poverty there. Their sect is banned there, and they will be forced to pray in a synagogue of the Jewish God."

"How awful!" I said. "And for this reason they must participate in local elections?"

The activists started to get nervous. After I asked, "How many candidates are on your ballot?" they looked bewildered. Then one of them said, "We don't need many; we trust our candidate."

"I don't know this godless candidate," said the old woman, who was breathing heavily and spoke at intervals. "I want to die where my church won't be penalized for my funeral. The Lord said to me that in Israel my church wouldn't be fined."

She was the one whom Goretoi suggested get some fresh air during the service.

The activists started to get angry. "I don't know what your god tells you," said one of them, "but here the government tells us that you have to participate in elections."

And again, I saw it firsthand. When it came to their faith, these people, even the sick and old, did not frighten.

"Here we're not allowed to pray." The old woman continued speaking, breaking off after every sentence while her gray hair was quivering. "If I help a sick neighbor, I'm fined. If I teach the Bible to my grandchild, I'm fined. If I talk at the well with a neighbor about Christ, I'm fined."

I was getting tired of the intrusion in the life of these women and said, "I'll interpret for you what she just said: Soviet law strictly prohibits charitable activities, religious instruction of children, and missionary activities."

Then I asked them why they came on a bus. The ambassadors called me a dangerous sectarian, and as they were leaving, I said, "Next time, include Jesus Christ—in the list of candidates."

"Troublemaker!" shouted the perturbed activist.

To my surprise, a quiet old woman, silent during the visit, now spoke, "Love thy neighbor as thyself."

The pale and hunched women all went limp and kept mum: their strength had left them, and I did not ask about the bullet hole in their ceiling.

Some months earlier, authorities had decided to engage a

couple of local ruffians in the fight against sectarians. Goretoi had been sure that they were paid for their cultural-educational work— to intimidate his church. And these drunken pedagogues found a weak link in the community to terrorize, the three old women in poor health. When two men with a hunting rifle had opened the ramshackle door of their house with one kick, the women recognized both as well-known local rowdies and thieves. They ordered the women to stand up against the wall; one of the ruffians aimed the rifle at them and barked, "Give up your damn god, or we'll shoot you down like old dogs."

He lifted the rifle, shot at the ceiling, and ordered, "Give me all the money you received from America."

It was the end of winter and the old ladies brought from the cellar four heads of cabbage and a small sack with potatoes.

He said, "We aren't beggars," and asked in a conciliatory tone if they happened to have some vodka. The women said that they drank only water.

The authorities did not bestir themselves until after Nikolai Petrovich Goretoi had written a statement to the police, naming the two bandits. Thereafter, the same KGB officer who had just visited us stopped by Goretoi's house to say that the delinquents were arrested and would soon be brought before the court. No one ever talked to the old women who were ready to testify, but the pair disappeared from the village for a couple of months.

UPON MY UNEVENTFUL return home to Moscow, I went to see Andrei Sakharov with a draft of my document on the Christian emigration movement. His wife Elena Bonner was one of the three still-free members of the Helsinki Human Rights Group. In their small kitchen, we were busily writing on and passing between us a piece of paper. I suggested that if I said that I had visited the Pentecostals on behalf of the Group, it would show that it was still alive and kicking.

Moscow-Helsinki Group Document #23, written by Arkady Polishchuk, page 1. Scan by Google Books.

At the conclusion of our silent conversation, I moved our secret correspondence to the side and said, "Nowadays this thousands-strong list could easily become a roster of those sentenced to ten years of prison; that is, if they are not accused of organizing a revolt." After that I hesitated for a second or two and added, "They have authorized me to be the official representative of the Christian Emigration Movement in the West."

"These walls have big ears," said Elena Bonner.

"That's why I am saying this," I said.

It took me several days to cram all the facts into the Moscow Helsinki Group's Document #23 on the Christian Emigration Movement. It rested upon the testimonies of people living thousands of miles apart—stories of imprisonment, discrimination, and humiliation—told to me and to several Russian political prisoners who got to know these Evangelicals in hard labor camps and prisons. Frequently recorded on tape, these witness accounts were supported by copies and originals of court sentences and orders, decisions of local authorities, receipts of countless fines, and defamatory newspaper articles.

When I returned home from the Sakharovs, the same police major with grey stubble on his tired face waited for me at my entrance. Again, I signed for a notice from the Visa Office. And again something was holding me back from going there, from this crucial step.

In fact, while the Visa Office formally was a branch of Ministry of Internal Affairs (eg. the Police Ministry), it was actually a KGB hand. When I finally showed up for an exit visa, the official greeting me coldly said, "Your visa has expired."

For some reason I said, "thank you" and moved toward the door. But she interrupted my movement and interjected, "Do not hurry, our boss wants to talk to you."

And we went to the second floor. I never found out who he was, the head of the Office, or his deputy for that matter, who introduced me matter-of-factly.

"This is Polishchuk."

A tall, heavy-set man stood up gracefully from behind his desk and held out a green rectangle in my direction. "This is your expired visa," he said. "Take it to the embassy of Holland." The man looked at me skeptically and in conclusion said, "You keep traveling somewhere."

It was clear to me that he meant my visits with the Pentecostals. Nonetheless, even this revealing remark was nothing in comparison to their treatment of my expired visa. It wasn't until I was already in the street that I looked at it. It was valid from July 1 to July 10, 1977. Today was the 11th of July.

The high level bureaucrat in the Visa Office did not intend to punish me for such a serious violation of the law. All of a sudden, I

My invalid Soviet exit visa which I brought to the Netherlands Embassy. The central page pictured here carries the seals of the embassy inside this already worthless Soviet document.

was above the law. What an unintended achievement!

The Royal Netherlands Embassy in Moscow was in charge of Israel interests in the USSR, and their officials were not at all worried that my visa was invalid. The decision to let me leave the country had been made by the KGB. A beautiful lady with an even more beautiful accent asked me when I wanted to depart.

"In August," I replied.

SEVENTEEN

Send-Offs of Various Kinds

B EFORE MY DEPARTURE to the West I lived in a sticky fog, did not think much of the unpredictable future, and thought more of whom and what I was leaving behind. Nonetheless, I wrapped my pessimism in cheerfulness, repeating to myself and others that at the age of forty-seven I had an opportunity to live a second life and make it from scratch.

The noise of the farewell gathering in my overcrowded apartment was heard on all six floors of the Moskovsky Compositor, the "Moscow Composer" co-op. None of the neighbors dared to come say goodbye.

Among battle-hardened human rights activists, Christian dissidents, and Jewish refuseniks there were some people I never knew; they came to ask me to pass their names to Jewish organizations, to request an invitation from nonexistent Israeli relatives, and to smuggle their letters to someone in the West. A couple of newcomers were whispering, although nobody, including the wired ceiling of my top floor apartment, was able to hear about their sensitive problems.

One of them produced a children's "etch-a-sketch" delivered by a foreign sympathizer and began etching a list of his requests. The toy was considered to be sophisticated spy equipment. I refused to take letters, anticipating a thorough search at the airport. Through the noise I yelled that from now on they could speak out loud because they were already photographed by KGB agents sitting in two cars right in front of the entrance. Experienced Alexander Podrabinek told me that a nervous blond man with a mustache sitting on the bench in front of those cars wanted to talk with me.

I ran downstairs to meet Nahl Zlobin. I had not seen my friend for several years and heard that he was already a philosophy professor. Friendship with me automatically could lead to expulsion from any citadel of Soviet ideology.

I greeted him with the words, "They took pictures of you talking to Podrabinek, our main fighter against the use of psychiatry for persecuting dissidents."

"To hell with them!" said Nahl out loud. "Why so many?" he asked, nodding toward the cars.

"They're afraid that we might attack them."

Nahl tossed his head back and began laughing very loudly; I knew this process of freeing yourself from fear.

"Don't forget your friends," he said. "I'm proud of you."

I could only guess how Nahl managed to learn about my departure.

When I returned to my guests, Nikolai Kunitsa was explaining to my mother how important it was at her age of seventy-eight to accept Jesus as her personal Savior. She was smiling and looked lost, as this was the first time in her life that she had met an Evangelical Christian. She did not want to offend this "villager," but the subject probably was ridiculous to her. At the moment her only concern was that she was going to lose her son. Mama looked disapprovingly on two bright-eyed teenaged sons of a BBC correspondent, obviously brought here for educational purposes. The boys were impressed by two glossy jackdaws scared by the presence of noisy humans in close proximity to their cage. I made a promise to Yuri Mnyukh from the Helsinki Group to bring his birds to Vienna, although I was not sure that customs would allow me. He and his wife did not have enough time to overcome all the multi-stage procedures required for birds to emigrate from Mother Russia.

In the morning hours of August 8, 1977, my mom and I, my sister and her husband, along with Goretoi, Kunitsa, and my university bosom buddy Fred Solyanov, were riding in two taxis to Sheremetyevo Airport. In my pocket lay the one hundred dollars I was allowed to buy in the Central Bank, on my knees stood a cage with two birds, and I sang a song about youths on their way to faraway places where they, as new settlers, would help to build Communism.

The taxi driver asked, "Aren't you afraid to go to Israel?"

"Aren't you afraid to remain here?" I asked him.

At the airport, I had to run with two unhappy birds trying to stay balanced in their cage as they were sped toward the customs office dealing with pets. I held in my hand an official permission for them to migrate to the West, with notarized signatures of both Mnyukhs, and a similar permission for me to represent Yuri, Nelly, and their birds. A woman in a bluish-gray uniform, covered by a white doctor's smock thrown over her shoulders, smiled sincerely while I told her how my friends found two dying birds on asphalt pavement, one of which already had recovered by now but the other still had a broken wing. She gave me a form with a stamp allowing the birds to travel, then looked at the door, lowered her voice, and warned me, "Be careful during the inspection!"

A sympathizer in such an unlikely place? I walked away, thunderstruck.

I came out to find my little Mama, who clasped me tightly with both arms. She did not look at me, just pressed her cheek against my chest and stood still in silence. She let me go only when my turn came to go through inspection. "Sonny," Mama said, "we put a vodka bottle in your suitcase. Give it to your friends."

I had lied that I had many influential friends abroad; my only

A.D. Sakharov and E.G. Bonner at their Moscow apartment with Yuri Mnukh (*left*), who almost two months later met me and his beloved birds at the Vienna airport. Taken no later than June 14, 1977. Photographer unknown. (Sakharov Archive)

friend Irmi Bloch, an exchange student from Vienna University, was studying Russian language in Moscow, and she hated vodka. My priceless documents remained in Moscow with her. Among them were originals of fines for Christian funerals, weddings, worship at homes and in forests, protocols of court sentences, and photographs of imprisoned Christians. Irmi and I had become acquainted at the home of a mutual friend, Irina Kaploon. Years before, in 1966, Irina, then a seventeen-year-old schoolgirl and her friend Vjacheslav Bakhmin, twenty-two, were arrested for passing handwritten anti-Stalinist leaflets to terrified Muscovites. Both were released after ten months' imprisonment, without trial or apologies. A couple of days before my departure, I asked her to reflect back on that time: "Were you two crazy?"

She said, "No, we were enraged."

"At that time I was afraid of my own shadow."

She took me to a window, "Want to see your shadow?"

Through the openwork curtain, I recognized the fellow. "Today he's not hiding."

"This is a bad sign," said the seasoned Irina. "They do this to break people before the arrest."

"No, this is a courtesy reminder of my upcoming departure."

After this meaningful conversation, she beckoned me and Irmi into the bathroom and, without a word, moved the folder with my documents from my bag into Irmi's satchel.

MAMA AND MY SISTER, after consulting with some knowledgeable people, had tried to convince me to take more sets of bedding, linen tablecloths, and some wooden matreshkas, so I could sell these brightly painted nesting dolls in Vienna and thus earn some money. I did not want to upset them, but the fact was that emigrants were taking merchandise in the hope of selling it even in Israel, where the population of Russian matreshkas had probably long exceeded the population of Jews. Departing families were not allowed to take belongings loosely classified as antiques, art, or expensive jewelry. Thus, the official art experts did not allow me to take abroad my only treasure—several cheap statuettes and masks I had brought from Africa years ago. They said that the ebony had "strategic" importance.

In that moment a family before me had several swollen trunks. The parents and two children nervously looked at two customs officers studying dresses, suits and other garments, old and new, shoes, obligatory matreshkas, old and new underwear, bedding, toys, socks, toothpaste, family albums, medicine, dictionaries, and worn slippers. After all this wealth had been laid out on a large table, a packer began putting it all back into the trunks. In the middle of this procedure the head of the family gave him, as it appeared to me, several one-hundred-ruble bills. For what? I thought, for this junk? Probably also for customs officers. Bribery and fear walk hand in hand.

Then it was my turn. The officers were looking with suspicion at my cage with birds and wanted to put it through an ugly apparatus, probably a primitive x-ray machine with some cables attached on the side. The thing looked like a caveman's forefather of modern security technology with its metal and explosives detectors, body scanners, and other devices threatening human modesty more than the threat of terrorism. I said "nyet" and resolutely pulled the cage from the officer's hands.

"You're using force," he said. "Do you understand that you can be arrested right here and your visa can be canceled?"

"You wouldn't do that," I said, standing my ground. "It wasn't your decision to let me go."

"OK," he said, "you will miss your flight. It will cost you a lot of money."

At this moment out of nowhere came a little man with a nondescript face, rather, a face like a mask with holes behind which hide the eyes. I told this true KGB personality that the birds could be harmed or even killed by this machine. The No-Face was reasonable. He said, "Take your birds out of the cage, and the officers will check it."

I got panicky. Over the several days that I had fed and watered my roommates, I never took the creatures out of their cage! I had thought about it, surely—the smell was getting more and more putrid. But I did not want to harm them with my inexperienced handling, and the scariest part of all was the very thought of accidentally releasing and losing Yuri's adopted children in this huge airport. Not having a choice, however, I fearfully opened the little wire door, and with sweaty, shaking hands began struggling with the poor things, probably harming them in an attempt to take them out, one at a time. After my brutal victory I pressed the jackdaws in unnatural positions with splayed delicate wings to my bosom, my fingers feeling the beaks and scaly warm legs. I held them there while the officers x-rayed the cage. The parties to this

Many family photos such as this one have passed through my hands. On the backs, as a rule, only the names of family members were written, without addresses. About the Gerasimchuk family, pictured here, I remember only that they were from Ukraine. 1975.

struggle were quickly exhausted. Afterwards, I somehow managed to put the resisting birds back and sighed with relief.

The officers began looking at my belongings, immediately extracting and putting aside the bottle of vodka. After that, they passed to No-Face an envelope filled with photographs. He looked at me, "Who are these?"

"Relatives."

"These are villagers," he said reproachfully.

"Yes," I said. "From Ukraine." In fact they were from Southern Russia. "My parents were villagers too, from Ukraine." My heart sank. I was cursing myself for not leaving the pictures with Irmi Bloch or, at least, not putting them in a family album.

"Many children," he said.

"Yes, I might never see them again," I said, feigning a sigh.

"You have many relatives," he said, shifting and rearranging the pictures.

"And all of them are fools," I tried to distract No-Face.

"Why?"

"They don't want to emigrate."

The wooden grin expressed satisfaction and began putting the pictures back in the envelope.

I was allowed to move to the packer. My only suitcase was lying flat on the floor and he, squatting, was slowly putting back my belongings. The packer placed my priceless photographs with the large families of Pentecostals next to a brand new English dictionary and said in a low voice, "I hate them, too."

"Then why do you work here?"

"You saw how it works. Very good money. I was a teacher. Don't want to go hungry anymore."

Before closing my suitcase, he squinted toward the officers and whispered conspiratorially, "I can put in here whatever you want. I don't want any money from you, I just want to help good people."

What I said to him in response could be found in any dictionary of American obscenities. I had not sworn for many years. Here at the airport I discovered that I had not lost the skills so brilliantly used in my all-boys school.

Three months later, at the International Andrei Sakharov Hearings in Rome, the co-founder of the Moscow Amnesty International branch, Valentin Turchin and his wife Tanya said that the same sinewy KGB packer played a similar trick on them. At first glance it seemed that the secret police had a striking lack of logic; they wanted to throw us out, and yet it would be an achievement to arrest us at the border on criminal charges. In fact, it was not just revenge; they saw a broader picture—to intimidate any potential opposition to the regime.

EIGHTEEN

New Life, Old Stars

A FTER THE AEROFLOT PLANE took off, another man with a wooden face sitting next to me, looked at the cage on my knees and asked severely, "Why are you taking the birds to Israel?"

He obviously knew that on board there were numerous emigrating Jews. They were allowed to fly only with this sole Soviet airline.

"Are you going to Israel, too?" I asked him in anticipation of a burst of indignation.

"No," he said, suppressing his anger.

"Are you, by any chance, an ornithologist?" I asked politely.

"No," he barked.

"Are you a Soviet diplomat?" exaggerated sympathy grew in my voice.

"Who are you to ask me such questions?!"

"I'm sorry, is your occupation a state secret? I can tell you about mine."

With that, he did not talk to me anymore.

Traveling abroad was a rare privilege. Jews encroached on his privilege. In the seventies, almost all Russian émigrés were Jewish or married to Jews. Our society slightly opened the doors that had been shut for sixty years. Jewish spouses were called means of conveyance, and some of the "chosen people" even charged those desperate ones who wanted to get out and—oh, what a historical irony!—were not as lucky as the Jews.

When the pilot announced, "We are crossing the air border of the Soviet Union," I got on my feet, stood at attention like a soldier ready to sing the Soviet hymn, and raised my eyebrows invitingly toward the "birdwatcher." But instead of pursuing this patriotic train of thought, I took the cage in my hand and went to the lavatory.

Upon returning to my seat I closed my eyes and immersed in a strange mental state where events and thoughts mingled like snowflakes in a blizzard. I saw my mother clinging to my chest, the faces of friends, and the guilty faces of my sister and her husband. I saw my former wife. She will remain young and beautiful until the day I die.

When this blizzard died out, I saw clearly in my mind's eye Malva Landa. Recently she made me feel guilty on the railroad platform right before her departure to Trans-Baikal knolls. Sentenced to two years Siberian exile, this sixty-two-year-old geologist said acidly to me, "Some people go east; some go west."

She was right: If you want to fight, do not desert the combat zone.

Then human rights activist Alexander Ginsburg, arrested six months earlier, came to mind. On one of those strange days before my departure, I took Nikolai Petrovich Goretoi, Feodor Sidenko, and Nikolai Kunitsa to visit his family.

While Ginsburg's wife, Arina, was telling us how KGB agents "discovered" several hundred American dollars inside their toilet bowl, her two little boys, as if bewitched, watched Goretoi's hands unwrapping a gift—a large sturgeon. The smoked fish, wrapped in several layers of paper, sawdust, and cloth, had survived a long, red-hot journey in overcrowded scorching buses and sweltering August trains.

The images of my friends and relatives had disappeared into

my sleep when the plane began to descend. After it landed and the passengers stood in the aisle waiting for the door to be opened, I turned to the closed-mouth patriot. "Now I can reveal why I brought the birds here," I said.

One of his eyebrows went up. I showed him a middle finger, shook it, and, after a meaningful pause, said innocently, "With this steel finger I pushed my family diamonds down their tender throats."

He remained silent.

At the Flughafen Wien, the airport outside of Vienna, I passed the cage to Yuri Mnyukh. "They are waiting for you," he said, pointing at a group of men.

After this warning, he deftly checked the birds.

"They're probably meeting some officials from Moscow," I said.

"Oh Arkady, don't be naïve, they already put bugs in our place. When you call us or come to us, please, remember that we can do a lot of harm to our friends in Moscow."

One more victim, I thought—it's really sad.

"We're physicists," Yuri said. "We know how they do it."

Newly arrived Jews were divided into two groups. A larger one was taken immediately to an Israeli plane under escort of Austrian police with machine-guns, as Arab terrorists tried their best to stop Jewish emigration. A minibus took us, a small group of subdued people who did not go to Israel, to a hotel. Instead of a pompous porter in a magnificent livery, like the ones we had seen in foreign movies, we were greeted by friendly prostitutes propping up a peeling wall next to the ragged hotel door.

In an hour I had an uninvited guest. For peanuts, a criminal looking Russian bought my two sets of bedding and one tablecloth. He asked, "Don't you have matreshkas?"

"No."

He looked at me with contempt, but then magnanimously offered to smuggle me to Germany. The guy and his colleagues in the trade were knocking on the doors of all the people who had just checked into the hotel. Everybody was selling them bedding, tablecloths, matreshkas, and cheap jewelry. My wooden dolls were later given as exotic gifts to Irmi Bloch, her relatives and friends.

A couple of hours later, a tired representative of the resettlement agency Hebrew Immigrant Aid Society (HIAS) told me that in three days my group would be taken to Rome and would wait there until America or any other country would accept our applications. I needed to stay in Vienna: Irmi promised to send, through Austrian diplomatic channels in Moscow, my documents on Evangelicals. He sympathized with my problems, but there was nothing HIAS could do for me; if I were to stay here longer than three days, he said, I would be denied financial support and assistance in resettlement. He gave me Austrian shillings to buy a three-day food supply, and I expressed my determination to remain in Vienna no matter what.

It was late evening. I was wandering around strangely quiet streets, nervously thinking of my next move in this unknown world of old imperial buildings, sharp spikes of medieval Catholic cathedrals, and noiseless unfamiliar cars of unseen colors, reflecting streetlights like curved mirrors. If I stayed here, how in the world would I survive? What did I have in common with these occasional passers-by stopping in front of illuminated shop windows?

My thoughts evaporated after I took a closer look at an unlit auto parked in a narrow, neatly scrub-brushed street. Someone was looking at me out of it! The night before I had seen similar outlines in front of my Moscow co-op. My heart began pounding. No—no, we aren't back—we aren't there! Just a couple of hours earlier I had felt sorry for Yuri Mnyukh; now I myself was suffering from the same delusion. I began moving unsteadily toward this car: one step, two, three; I came close to it, placed both hands on its shiny top, and bent forward peering through the glass. The car was empty! Only then the cold light of logic began gleaming in my mind: these seats were shaped in a manner I had never seen before—they recalled the contours of human bodies! European autos had headrests, padded headrests! Oh, these unnecessary capitalist inventions! We did not have these hedonistic devices in Russia, damn capitalists! They scared the hell out of me.

From now on, this terra incognita, Österrreich in the aboriginal language, was not full of dragons anymore. Instead, it was again full of normal uncertainty. Now I could think of Irmi Bloch, still in Russia, and of a phone number of a former prisoner given to me in Moscow. It was nearing eleven p.m., when I saw a telephone booth. I could not control my trembling voice: "Tanya Velikanova said that, if in need, I could call you anytime." I apologized several times.

Lev Kwachevsky said, "Of course, come to us right away. You did not wake us up."

The unconditional surrender of sleepy Kwachevsky to a stranger supported my opinion about Tatiana Velikanova, one of the founders of the first Soviet human rights organizations: if I ever met a saint in my life, it was this unique woman.

I was at his place before midnight.

The very next day he took me to an organization I had never heard of—International Rescue Committee or IRC. His friend Doctor Faust was the head of European operations. They were helping escapees from communist countries. That day the corridor was packed with Poles, some in similar leatherette jackets. It looked as if they all arrived with the same tour bus. I thought with gloating delight, 'Who is going to drive the empty bus back to Warsaw'?

Doctor Faust asked if I was ready to surrender the good financial support of Hebrew Immigrant Aid Society for the modest help of his committee. He repeated twice that normal people do not give up this benefit of their own free will.

In 1936, Doctor Faust had fought against Generalissimo Franco and considered himself a communist. Long before the end of the Spanish Civil War, he was shocked to find out that in the Madrid area the Soviets established several secret prisons. The NKVD experts were torturing and killing Catholics and Spanish nationalists, and very soon they began killing communists who criticized Stalin, not just Trotskyites and anarchists.

"I was then seven years old and worshiped the NKVD," I said. "I didn't like it when it was renamed the KGB."

"It seems to me you would have been one of those who rushed to Spain to help," said Doctor Faust.

"Thank you," I said.

"They threatened me, too. It was an ugly time, for all dreamers alike."

In two days I had moved to a small windowless room with its slanted ceiling under a creaky wooden staircase. Day and night I was sorely aware of neighbors and of their lovely little children running tirelessly up and down the squeaky stairs. Today, I have nothing against children. I even have three of my own. But at that time I was missing the quiet of those probably childless prostitutes who worked in that nice hotel where I had spent my first two or three comfortable nights.

A month later, I left this closet for an excellent room with two tall windows facing Märzstrasse, a short walk from the Schönbrunn Palace. After the squeaky stairs and screaming kids, the rumble of trams under my windows sounded like a comforting lullaby of rustling leaves. There was only one minor inconvenience: my spacious room was some seventy feet away from the communal washroom with two showers and two toilets, located in the middle of the long corridor.

I admired Lev Kwachevsky. He was one of those true dissidents incapable of compromising with the regime. Lev refused to have a defense attorney and thus demonstrated his stand toward the sham legal proceedings, denied any guilt, and defended his right to read and disseminate any literature.

Doctor Faust and I joked with him about his socialist convictions. Lev, the youngest of us, criticized us for being prejudiced on the subject of true social-democratic values, but he was forgiving since he knew about our bad experiences with communist ideology and practice.

Lev and his wife decided to cheer me up, and we went to watch a movie prohibited in Russia. In ten minutes I found out why they were giggling: it was a porn movie. I could not anticipate that a porno would be so boring and unimaginative. It was the best propaganda for abstinence I have ever seen. Twenty minutes later we left the theater, and I confessed that I experienced much more stimulation in the Vienna streets. After three years in lecherous Europe, my new friends forgot that in the virtuous Soviet Union all women wore bras. The widespread exhibition of nipples in the sticky August heat, for want of this habit in Russia, was much more inspiring and arousing for innocent Soviet citizens than for spoiled Europeans.

EVERY DAY I LEARNED something new. For example, it was a six-year-old Russian boy who gave me my first good lesson about Austrian sensitivities. In the recent past, his father, a journalist Boris V., had worked at the APN. A year before applying for an exit visa, Boris bribed someone to obtain a new internal passport restoring his ethnic origin.

Once I waited for him and his son among the trees and flowers of the hillside far above the summer residence of the Habsburg emperors. Nothing could bother me on that bench. I was deeply immersed in my struggle with an English textbook for German speakers when I felt someone's delicate attempts to pull my pants down. I looked in the direction of this surprise attack and saw the unexpected: a powerful brown-grayish goose kept pulling at my pants. Soon, disillusioned but waddling with dignity, he went back to his partner who was quietly observing the scene. Never before had I seen Canadian geese. When they disappeared, I made sure that three-hundred-pound wild boars were not creeping up on me. Irmi Bloch—now returned from Moscow—had already shown me such a fanged family contemplating an assault on Vienna in the wooded hills of her neighborhood.

I placed my textbook on the bench and violently shook my head as I heard a crackling and a boy's voice, "Bang—bang—bang! Boom—boom!" On the path appeared a child shooting at the squirrels, the birds, and at me. The massive toy pistol looked like the real thing.

"Where did you buy it?" I asked his father. "There are no toy weapons in stores here. I haven't seen children with such toys in Vienna. After their recent history, they have demilitarized their society."

"You just don't know where to look for the good stuff," Boris said.

An hour later we began our descent toward the Baroque beauty of the Imperial palace. When we reached the crowds of tourists, many were looking at the weapon in Michael's hand. The boy started shooting at people: "Bang—bang! Boom—boom—boom!" They began yelling at us. Only then did Boris demand, "Stop aiming at people!"

After a fierce struggle he snatched the pistol out of the boy's hands and put it in a plastic bag with Mozart's image.

SOON AFTER my arrival in Austria, I applied to immigrate to America, though I was in no hurry. Irmi arranged my meeting with Cardinal Franz Koenig and organized my first press conference. Thanks to her, Amnesty International groups in Vienna, Salzburg, and Graz began writing letters demanding the release of Christian prisoners. I had already received invitations from Swedish and Norwegian Christian and human rights organizations and had an Austrian travel passport.

Finally the day came when I could visit the American Consul. In the reception room sat one Muscovite, who instructed me in what to say about my communist past.

"It's as easy as pissing on two fingers," he said, "All former communists pass easily. Just tell them that you were forced to join the Party."

He spent some five minutes in the consul's office and, joyous, came out of it, "I'm flying to my relatives in New York."

I liked the consul. He was honest and concerned about my fate. When I said that since childhood I had dreamed of joining the Party and nobody forced me to do this, I drove him into a corner. He apologized and said that he had to reject my request to emigrate to the United States. After the interpreter read the 1952 law on Suppression of Communism, I tried to explain that to leave the Party on your own was impossible and dangerous, though I had tried to do just that. The consul did not understand this nonsense. After I said that I was arrested several times, he expressed his sympathy to me, but had to stick to the law of the country. When I began suspecting that he was unaware of the very existence of the Soviet Union, the consul said that he only recently arrived from Frankfurt and had never had anything to do with communist countries. I mentioned Sakharov and said that he was one of those who set up the Soviet atomic bomb. The consul looked at me in

Participants of the International Sakharov Hearings, November 15–28, 1977, held in Rome. *From left to right*: Arkady Polishchuk; Tatyana Turchina; outstanding Russian poet and prose writer Naum Korzhavin (first arrested in 1947 in the midst of the campaign against Zionism); Valentin Turchin, Tatyana's husband and a well-known physicist. Photographer unknown. (Sakharov Archive)

horror—he had never heard this name. It was pointless to tell him how difficult it was for Sakharov to find me in Vienna, and how he reached me by chance on the overcautious Yuri Mnukh's phone and asked me urgently to go to Rome to participate in the International Sakharov Hearings (which I did, with a train ticket bought by the IRC). We were living on different planets, this consul and I, but we both understood that even among aliens there were some good beings. I went to Doctor Faust with apologies; he would have to spend some more money to support me in Vienna until, with the help of Irmi's diplomatic contacts, my documents arrived. To my surprise, he rubbed his hands gleefully, "Now we have an amazing story for the *New York Times*. Three other countries are ready to take you. I have to call my friend immediately. You'll be a celebrity."

I pleaded, "Please don't call. Sooner or later, they'll let me in just like everybody else."

When *Newsweek* correspondent Alfred Friendly Jr. invited me to a bar, I wasn't aware that he had even left Russia. Preparations for the trial of Sharansky were still dragging on. The KGB had not yet dug up any fascinating spy stories to support its case against him and meanwhile had "exposed" three American correspondents in Moscow as CIA agents. Friendly was one of them. We chatted a lot, and I mentioned that America prevented another former communist from landing on its sacred ground. He asked me not to worry.

A couple of months later, in the middle of September 1978, I received a copy of a letter to the American ambassador in Austria. It was signed by U.S. Secretary of State Cyrus Vance and the chair of the American Commission on Security and Cooperation in Europe, Dante Fascell. Both gentlemen were perhaps unaware of my very existence until recently, but they certainly had developed a high opinion of me. Most probably Alfred Friendly Jr. was the one who influenced their opinion.

But worldly glory is transient, and only one person—my dear Irmi Bloch—accompanied me to the airport bus. Of course, to demonstrate a more dramatic and glorious farewell, I could say that all who accompanied me to the plane to New York cried.

NINETEEN

Russian Jews, a Russian Tiger, and Some Other Russians

I SERIOUSLY NEEDED to work on my English. I sounded like an insecure child unsure of his path on the bumpy road to adolescence while in fact, upon my arrival to New York, I was a man of forty-eight. The KGB had given me this chance to relive my life, to fall into childhood again on this unfamiliar planet called America.

As a newcomer in New York in the hot sticky fall of 1978, I quickly learned that even the skills passed from generation to generation differed in America from those in Europe. They were even farther from the muddled rules of Russia, which are sometimes more or less European, or at other times, more or less Asian and can be confusing for the psyche of the country. It can be blamed partially for Russia's split personality—the entire nation wandering in the wilderness of history's crossroads.

Alas, I was not a very good alien and still occasionally offended some social, cultural, religious, sexual, political, ethnic, moral, medical, gender, and other sensibilities; for example, I still cannot stop myself from offending some women by holding a door for them while saying the politically incorrect "ladies first."

Nonetheless, extraterrestrials are capable of learning a lot. Now l can eat without a knife and know how to make a sandwich out of anything by putting everything on top of everything, and to not drop a crumb from my edible skyscraper of American ingenuity. I forced myself not to cover my mouth with my hand while yawning; such covering might mean that you did not have good American teeth. If somebody tells me "Let's meet for a lunch or coffee," I do not ask anymore where and when—it would be boorish, they do not mean it, it is just a term of politeness, similar to "good bye." I even tried to walk and to talk while keeping my hands in my pockets; later I understood that the trick was invented by people in three-piece suits to avoid rude finger-pointing.

My mind still remained on another planet when Lyudmila Thorne from the Freedom House befriended me. Her Baptist parents escaped from Russia in the early 1920s, soon after the Bolsheviks seized power, and so Lyusia had a soft spot for me. "Improve your English, and you'll be a member of our Lecture Bureau," she said and suggested a language school in Manhattan.

At that school, as the only male in the class, I found myself back in an exotic part of Russia. The rest of the students were young women, most of them from the Black Sea city of Odessa. They called their Brooklyn neighborhood Little Odessa. Every Russian knows Odessa Jewish jokes; many Russians know that the city has given the country a disproportionate number of writers, poets and musicians, a good number of crooks and bandits, and many other colorful characters. One hundred years ago, it was the most Jewish town in Europe. In the Soviet years Jews were heavily represented in the intellectual and criminal categories of local citizenry. They also ran a lot of underground enterprises, which in America would have been mostly lawful and not the subjects of criminal inquiry, imprisonment, or extortion by officials. Nowadays, the rich flavor of the good old Odessa has somewhat faded. While extortion, bribes, the black market, and the Black Sea are still there, the majority of Jews moved from its shores to Brighton Beach and relocated Odessa to the shores of the Atlantic Ocean.

The ladies at the school were puzzled by the very fact that I had been studying English instead of making a decent living like a true mensch, like their mature and responsible husbands, boyfriends, and brothers. They certainly followed the old Odessa Yiddish saying: "If you have money, you are wise and good-looking and can sing well, too." Per contra, the women liked this somewhat strange man, a journalist who no doubt had connections in high places but instead of using them wisely, was learning a new language.

I had no intention of telling them that every month I was receiving a fortune—five hundred dollars from a Californian mission "Evangelism to Communist Lands." The mission, soon renamed "Door of Hope International," needed me; I needed their devotion, support, and network. Soon they arranged some of my speaking engagements in Evangelical churches on the East Coast.

From time to time I would disappear from the classes, and that furnished a wide variety of assumptions from the women. A couple of times I overheard wild whispering about my public, and, of course, intimate life. One of them saw in *Life* magazine a picture of me sitting at the table with the wife of famous exiled writer Alexander Solzhenitsyn at the International Andrei Sakharov Human Rights Hearings in Washington DC. I became an instant celebrity.

The women wanted to do something good for their dissident. They wanted to take care of this lonely man who, poor soul, did not even have a girlfriend; at least, that is what he, under serious scrutiny, kept telling them. At one point one of the ladies in flashy dresses chimed in, "Look at our expensive dresses. All of them are stolen."

"Interesting," I said politely.

"Wouldn't you like to have good clothes for little money?" asked my well-wisher, while a couple of others were nodding and smiling affably. "Just give me all your sizes, from shoes to hat, from shirts to suits, and the boys will deliver."

Another relatively young lady inserted, chuckling, "If you don't know your size, we can take all the measurements ourselves."

They were having fun and were ready to measure all parts of my body without delay. Then they explained: the "boys" go to the best department stores in town and take out whatever they like, not just clothing, but also TV sets, bikes ("you need a bike!"), jewelry, china sets, watches. I gracefully declined.

This was that blessed carefree time when unsuspecting Americans did not yet have magnetic security tags in stores.

This Russian tolerance toward theft multiplied during the years of Communist rule. Many times I had heard the expression, "The state robs us, we rob the state," or, "The only ones who don't steal are those who have nothing to steal," or, a much older Russian saying, "You're not a thief if you're not caught with the loot."

In the meantime my cohorts began asking my opinion and advice about all earthly and heavenly matters. One morning, the defiantly blond and good-mannered Nina asked my opinion about whether it was OK for her to have a lover. She had been married for several years and loved her husband. I said that the affair could undermine her love and pointedly stressed that she already was unfaithful to her husband.

"Why?" she asked fearfully.

"Because it already happened in your mind and heart."

Nina took this "it" very seriously, and I felt how cruel I was being, playing a hard-nosed moralist. I liked her; she seemed to be a good and unspoiled person.

Once Nina invited me to live in her house. My eyebrows shot upwards.

"My husband and I want you to get acquainted," she continued, "with my sister-in-law. She's a programmer, good-looking, and intelligent." Probably, my eyebrows continued moving up and she added, "We just want you to have good meals, relax, and enjoy your life in good company."

"Does she live with you?" I said, somewhat lost.

"Yes, we rent a house near the ocean, at Brighton Beach, near the famous boardwalk. Alice saw you once."

"Where?"

"Here."

"Why did she come here?"

"To take a look at you."

"Come on! You're all crazy!"

"You could become her boyfriend."

I tried to escape this minefield. "What if I'm a sadistic and lazy bum? Is she desperate?"

"Oh! No—no. Alice just doesn't want to live, as she's saying, in a ghetto."

"I really appreciate the invitation, it sounds lovely," I said and explained that soon I would move to California, to work for a Christian mission on behalf of some Christians back in Russia. It might take years and wouldn't make me rich. "Who knows what's ahead... The best thing for Alice is to move from Brighton Beach to America."

"Are you a Christian?" she asked.

"No. I'm a Jew, and most of my relatives were killed during the war. In Ukraine."

"She said that you look like a prince."

"Oh yeah, like a prince of Egypt," I said with a nervous laugh, "just taken from a sarcophagus."

The invitation was never renewed.

IRA FYBISH WAS the first true New Yorker I met. At the Jewish Center in Queens, he volunteered as an English tutor to recently arrived Russian Jews. He knew more Russian words than many of his students, but the only problem with this two-legged talkative bookcase was that he was unable to put three Russian words together. Ira had lived in Greenwich Village all his life; this in itself, for many, would have been a clear sign of refinement and sophistication. The floor of his smallish apartment, his bed, bathroom, and stove were all covered with books, often with titles I was unable to understand. Ira knew everything about everything, and for years, while teaching children with mental problems, he had been working toward a sociology PhD. We needed each other. It was a kind of symbiotic friendship. He was the only American capable of talking with this mute, deaf, and mulish Russian for hours, day after day, with no signs of exhaustion.

At that Center, Ira befriended a pretty lady named Natalie who had been teaching English for several years in one of the rare Moscow schools where children studied English intensively from the first grade. During my second visit she secretively showed me the Old Testament and whispered, "This is the Christian Bible." Mimicking her, I whispered back, "This is also the Jewish Bible; only Jews call it Torah. You don't need to hide it; this is basically the same text. The difference is mainly in conclusions made by different humans."

She looked at me with disbelief and quickly put the dangerous book back in the drawer.

"Did you read it?" I asked.

"No. But I flipped through it—pretty boring stuff. The Torah must be more interesting." She obviously couldn't trust my information. "You know," stressed Natalie confidently, "they don't have bibles in the Soviet Union."

She apparently made this major discovery only in Queens.

Ira was looking for a nice Jewish wife of Russian origin, and Natalie became candidate numero uno. He could not know that such immigrants did not even understand what country they left behind and even less about what planet they landed. Thanks to Dostoevsky's *Crime and Punishment*, he was searching for a mysterious Russian soul residing in an attractive body. His logic was faultless: the less attractive the body, the less mysterious is the soul. I recommended that he read some other Russian writers of the nineteenth century and even quoted Saltykov-Shchedrin's "If I fall asleep and wake up in one hundred years and am asked what is happening now in Russia, I'd say: drinking and stealing."

Less than a year later, in 1979, Ira Fybish married a good-looking Polish Jew. It was she who stood with us at the New York Zoo, in front of an open-air cage with a huge Siberian tiger. My friend was not interested in the magnificent cat at all. He was busy trying to help me to survive in America. My article on the plight of persecuted Russian Evangelicals had just been published in the terribly reactionary American monthly *National Review*. "You might be forgiven for the article," Ira worried, "but only because you're an alien and people can suppose you didn't know how staunchly conservative this publication is. However, if you do it again, no one will publish you anymore. All doors will be closed."

"What you're saying reminds me of Soviet intolerance," I was trying my best to copy his scholarly manner of speaking. "The only difference is that your unwillingness to grant equality to the diversity of opinions comes in a more democratic way, not from the government itself but from a certain opinionated stratum of society."

At exactly this point, we were rudely interrupted by the tiger. When we first came to the cage, he had been pacing back and forth, back and forth, back and forth, his heavy tail jerking. But after a while, the animal began reacting to the shrill voice of my friend. As he was changing direction, the pupils of his yellow eyes would, for a split second, fixate at my loud critic with long hairy arms endlessly dancing in the air. Soon the tiger stopped, lowered his heavy head, quickly lifted it and studied Ira at point blank range; the beast turned into a striped statue with watching, unblinking eyes. And then he found the way to put the end to our spirited discussion. The beast abruptly turned around, as if he'd grown tired of us and decided to forsake our company, but before leaving the *mise-en-scene*, he lifted his hind leg, aimed a hefty paw at the hazy sky, and sent a powerful yellow jet right into Ira's face. Ira gasped, his glasses softly dropped in the grass as he spit out the bitter yellow droplets. I almost collapsed from laughter. My friend became very angry with both of his opponents. His wife and I took him to a nearby fountain to wash his face and his shirt, no longer very white. He emanated stink and kept cursing the innocent brute.

"Ira, you're probably the only person in the world to survive such a dangerous encounter!" I said, trying to comfort him. "Immediately call the *New York Daily News*! Just imagine the front page photograph of you with the oversized headline 'New York Teacher Doesn't See Eye-to-Eye with Russian Tiger!' They love the Cold War stuff."

"Are you serious?" he asked, annoyed.

He wanted to find a drug store where he could buy some eye drops. I glanced back at the Lord of the Jungle as we left. He was outstretched on the floor, lost in deep thoughts. His serenity and confidence impressed me yet again.

"It's about time for a teacher to become a role model for youngsters," I said while helping Ira with the drops. "You teach handicapped kids. You have an unstoppable desire to learn. Your kids will tell everybody, 'Our unarmed teacher confronted Russians, armed to the teeth!'"

His Polish wife had no doubt that I was praising him.

TWENTY

Phantoms of the Past
in the Shadow of Skyscrapers

I CELEBRATED MY FIRST American New Year's Eve with my old Moscow friends Lucy and Boris Zilberstein. I had been living in their small apartment in Queens since the day of my arrival, for nearly three months.

In New York, these Russian Jews made a discovery—what had been known in Russia as the secular, atheistic "New Year's fir tree" was in fact the Christmas tree. When American synagogues found out that this tree was part and parcel of the Soviet New Year's celebrations, some rabbis got panicky. A week before Christmas, Boris showed me a New York Jewish newspaper urging Russian Jews to abandon the Christmas tree tradition. The call did not work. Soon he brought home a nostalgically fragrant tree.

Exactly at midnight, in accordance with the tradition, we emptied our glasses of champagne in one swig. Lucy had picked up a little pickle bought in a Jewish shop around the corner and said, "The whole of Russia by now is desperately looking for such a medication while we, backward Americans, are still sober."

We knew what she meant. It was already the first morning of the New Year in Moscow, and the adult and some underage population already had a terrific hangover; everybody, in accordance with the centuries-old medical tradition, was looking for a drop of booze and a pickle for his aching head. We guessed whether the Pentagon, the CIA, and American presidents knew that these first hours of January were the best time for a perfidious aggression against peace-loving Russia. At this hour the country leadership, the KGB and military brass, strategic aviation pilots, nuclear submarine crews, border and prison guards—all of them were drunk as sailors and were looking for a pickled cucumber.

At the time of my arrival, a small group of Russian dissidents already lived in New York. Almost all of them were forced into their exile. Ethnic Russians, Ukrainians, Crimean Tatars, Jews—all were given exit visas for emigration to Israel. The KGB reasoned that they should all be considered as Jews in disguise, and that was good for the propaganda machinery's health.

The man I admired, the oldest among us, general Peter Grigorievich Grigorenko "rebuked" me for not sharing with my friends the Christian money I allegedly managed to smuggle to the West. He kept asking me, "At least tell us, Arkady, was it a kilogram of rubles? Ten pounds? One shipping container?" His joke was based on an article in a Ukrainian paper that Nikolai Kunitsa managed to send to me from the city of Rovno after my arrival to Vienna. The preacher had yet once again been unmasked as a member of a deranged cult, famous for its cruelty and harm to Soviet citizens. In short, Arkady Abramovich Polishchuk—they used my patronymic, so readers wouldn't have the slightest doubt about my genetic deficiency—secretly visited an underground Baptist church in Rovno, collected from its ignorant members a bundle of money under the pretense that it would be spent on bribing important people in Moscow and then, this tricky crook emigrated with all this loot to Israel.

That was by far the best story ever written about me. When the favorite of Russian intellectuals *Literaturnaya Gazeta* exposed me as a CIA collaborator while I was already living in New York, it was quite a trivial thing. Who wasn't, in their opinion? But my money-grubbing story was unique. Since Soviet rubles were not a convertible currency, nobody in Israel would have bought the rubles—they were cheaper than the sand of the Sinai desert. Besides, I had never gone to Israel and never visited Rovno.

AT THAT TIME, Russian dissidents were popular with American politicians. The Cold War was very hot. On Capitol Hill they wanted to know our opinion on the current situation in Russia. We knew that compromises with Moscow would only strengthen its determination to expand Russia's influence in the world. In January 1980, the puppet government in Afghanistan had "invited" Soviet troops into the country. In February, when the Russian tanks were demolishing Afghan villages and killing their inhabitants, Senator Edward Kennedy criticized Jimmy Carter for trying to scare Americans with the Soviet threat. We were surprised.

Later, in August of that year, a group of Soviet dissidents was invited as guests to the Democratic Party National Convention where incumbent President Carter was nominated for president. None of us liked what Carter said about the arms race: "The Republican nominee advocates abandoning arms control policies," he said. "This radical and irresponsible course would threaten our security and could put the whole world in peril. They have now promised to launch an all-out nuclear arms race. ... There can be no winners in such a race."

It sounded ridiculous to the small group of Russian human rights activists. We knew that the entire economy of the impoverished USSR was strenuously working for the war machine and that the Soviets would consider any arms-limitation agreements to be useful tools for the further spread of their rule. At first we thought that both politicians were naive and ill informed, but soon we understood that we had to apply those epithets to

Here we are, guests of the Democratic Party Convention in New York, August 1980. At the front, the Moscow Helsinki Group's members Ludmilla Alexeeva and, on her right, a Crimean Tatar named Aishe Seytmuratova. Yuri Yarim-Agaev is poking his head up over them. On the right-hand side of the picture you can see me with some Russian and American activists (two women). This was from that time when both American political parties, Republicans and Democrats, consulted with Russian human rights activists. Photographer unknown.

ourselves. Internal political struggle was more important for them than the growing Russian threat. That is why Kennedy did not even mention the Soviet Union in his keynote speech.

Two or three days after the Convention, I was still in bed, when my telephone rang.

"I saw you there," croaked an affected hoarse voice with a ridiculous Jewish accent borrowed from Odessa jokes. "Come to your Greek neighbor promptly, and we'll show you the difference between his freshly painted and our fresh Russian pies."

It was Tom!

In three minutes, breathing heavily after my sprint, I was looking outside through a window of the Greek bakery next to my place. In seconds a big black car with tinted windows stopped in front of it. The back door opened, and I saw Tomas Kolesnichenko lying on the back seat and staring at me with anticipation in his irresistible gray eyes. With these words for him, "Are you crazy?" I plunged into the car, right into his arms.

His wife Svetlana, who was the driver, asked casually, "Alik, what do you want for breakfast, my dear?"

I blurted, "Do you want to join my friends in the hard labor camp #36 in the Perm Region's taiga?"

"Relax," said Tom, "Nobody sits on my tail. I'm the top Russian correspondent abroad. This is the most important assignment—the *Pravda* correspondent at the U.N. and in this little town."

"How do you know that your car isn't wired?"

"The KGB chief-resident would tell me. He loves me and my Party organ."

"He still loves this libidinous language," I said.

Our driver turned her head to us and smiled leniently.

"We go together to places where no Soviet citizen is allowed to tread," continued Tom. "I bring nice presents for his wife. He wouldn't want to lose me over nothing."

"So, you're as generous as ever. But there are dozens of Soviet spooks in New York—so, keep buying off all of them. Thank God the FBI guys don't need your little bribes."

"You're still not a very smart romantic," Tom said, patting my back. "The FBI would never blackmail me for contacting dissidents and immigrants. They love it. They want this affection to develop further and deeper. That's how I found you—a former Jewish refusenik told me in a Russian grocery at Brighton Beach where you live."

And he hugged me again.

We crossed the Queensboro Bridge to Midtown Manhattan and soon arrived at the gates of an underground garage. Now I was lying on the back seat, wrapped in a huge plaid blanket. Heavy Tom was sitting on me, giggling. The Russian guard waved us through with a smile when he saw Svetlana at the wheel. He couldn't make out our faces through the tinted door glass anyway. The car stopped right next to the elevator. Tom got out and pushed the button; when the elevator arrived, I stepped out of the car, covered in heavy plaid from toe to crown, and dragged myself in.

"The only neighbor on my floor is out of town," Tom said. "If someone meets us, begin shivering like hell, you have a terrible cold."

I grumbled, "Diarrhea would be more appropriate."

And we talked, and talked, and talked. About their children. About our health. About our sex life. He believed that my pre-occupation with churches kept me outside of big politics and could not understand why, with my credentials, I did not approach Radio Liberty, where my earnings would have been much bigger than in the poor Christian mission. But I wanted to talk about us.

"It was pretty unusual," I said, "that they asked you to talk me out of my rebellion. Did you tell Primakov about our rendezvous at that railroad station?"

"It looks like he knew it," he mused. "I asked him recently, 'Why didn't they kill Alik?' and he boomed, 'Because they liked him.'"

"Very funny, hah-hah-hah. So, the KGB consulted with him, too. Maybe. Four years later, in '77, they already had my sentence ready, but decided not to make another famous dissident out of me."

"Why, do you think?"

"When I was in Lefortovo, the interrogator pointed with a thumb at the prison building behind his back and said, 'You cooperated with a spy; Sharansky once lived in your apartment.'"

"Was it true?"

"Yes. You should see the belongings this super-spy left at my place after his arrest. New York beggars would look like party animals next to him."

"With your stomach you would've quickly died in a camp."

"Whenever I was in a wired place, I would say that I wouldn't leave the country. The KGB seemingly believed that, but I was sure that they would never let me escape from their clutches. ... Well, Tom, let's talk about us. I see, you two are happy. You keep gaining weight, you glutton. They won't allow me to come to your funerals."

"Just look inside this fridge full of fattening stuff from Russian groceries," Svetlana said, flinging open the huge white door.

"I don't see the Russian caviar there," I chuckled, and we recalled the cruise down the Volga River when they used me as a human shield to hide their love affair. At the river mouth we bought three jars of caviar from poachers.

Tom yelled, "Huge ones! You can't afford it anymore; that would be enough to feed both chambers of the American Congress."

"You underestimate their appetite," I said.

"I still believe that someone powerful saved you," said my pal. "Don't look for logic here. Remember how they were killing their own cadres?"

"It was quite logical," I said. "It was a part of genetic selection by means of mass killing."

"I still don't understand why they allowed Jewish emigration," he said. "Nobody in the Central Committee was able to give me a clear explanation. Prisons and *Pravda* could easily do the job."

I suggested that the KGB used this emigration to expand its espionage network. After a pause, Tom again tried to understand why I was allowed to go. "You just don't know how many sympathetic friends you had in the KGB."

"This is ridiculous." I made a face. "And so touching."

"They are humans," insisted Tom, "and they have their loyalties."

"Sure, they are humans. That's why they killed your father." I shouldn't have said it. We never talked about him. He had been executed when Tom was about five years old.

Tom paused, looked at the ceiling, and returned to Primakov. "Zhenya made a great career. He befriended many big guns, even in the Politburo. Your former sidekick is now the director of your Institute of Oriental Studies—he would have made you the editor-in-chief of your magazine."

There were still ten years before Primakov would become the First Deputy Director of the KGB, his first step on the ladder to becoming prime minister in 1998.

"Did you talk about our spooks in the West?" asked Tom.

"In public—never. Privately—with friends."

"Good," he said.

"Fear wasn't the reason. It was important for me to be treated as a human rights activist. Reporters would certainly prefer talking about spies."

"Sure," Tom said.

"After I came here, two FBI agents visited me. It was a routine visit, some formal questions for an émigré. I mentioned that I knew some Soviet agents, but they just ignored it."

"You're kidding! That's why America will lose the future war!"

"Don't bet on it," I said.

After midnight they took me back to Astoria. We did not talk. I looked at trees and thought of friendship. It takes years for trees to grow, there next to each other, seeing and touching one another in the sun and in darkness, in storms and tranquil calm, with young branches and shiny leaves, and then with the colorless leaves of your friend drifting between your dead branches. Even dying, they stay up for a while, supported by friends. When they finally crash to the ground, their friends stay wounded for quite some time.

"Calm down, crazy!" flashed through my head. "Trees live in mortal combat with each other. Stupid romantic!" But familiarity with Darwinism did not pacify me.

The next evening we met again, this time in Brooklyn Heights, at the Promenade near the Brooklyn Bridge where crowds were strolling along the East River, looking at the lights of Lower Manhattan beyond the dark river and at strange animated reflections glimmering in impermeable waters. We did not walk. We just stood there, leaning against the cast-iron railings facing the tip of Manhattan, hoping no one would recognize us. Svetlana was taking pictures of the famous skyline with the backdrop of the Twin Towers marvel a mile away. Both Tom and I were nervous and occasionally turned our heads to check out the passersby. I had the sinking feeling, and he probably did too, that we would never meet again. Tom asked, "Have you made any new friends? You can't subsist without friends, can you?"

"Yes, I have," I said. "But so far they are more like comrades in arms. You can respect and love them; maybe, you can even die for them, but it's not enough. You hide from them your moral deficiencies."

I looked at the rapid river and saw the trees appear again, now drawn by the reflections of the city lights; they were dancing, naked and crooked. I said, "When you're nearing fifty, new friendship lacks common memories of younger years, no matter how silly or shameful they may be. For me, that's the most difficult part of life in exile. But I manage."

We had picked the wrong place for this rendezvous. It was time to go. I kissed them. Then for an endless moment all three of us stood still in a silent embrace. We did not look into the eyes of each other.

My voice quavered as I walked away. "Damn them!"—they now had deprived me of even my friends. Then I just kept listening, for some subconscious reason, to the muffled sound of my own steps on the stone pavement. I was alone. They did not see my tears; I did not see theirs.

EVERYTHING THAT I write here about Tom is in flagrant contradiction with the Russian official image of Kolesnichenko. When his widow, soon after his death in 2003, asked me to write my memories of him for a book of memoirs, I refused to participate in this official undertaking. "You were always so cheerful and witty together," Svetlana said. One of the other authors was Yevgeny Primakov, the former head of Russian intelligence and now demoted from Russian prime minister to chairman of the Russian Chamber of Commerce; the rest of authors were no better.

Svetlana reminded me of one last, fleeting and unexpected meeting with Tom. I had been standing at the entrance to the American embassy in Washington with a small group of Americans and Russian immigrants, demanding to free Sakharov from exile. I was positioned right in front of the door when it suddenly opened, and Tom and I nearly collided nose to nose. Behind him stood Svetlana and some Soviet officials. We pretended that we did not know each other. Without stopping for a moment, with stone faces, the whole group passed by us. No one saw my tears. Svetlana told me that when she looked at her husband, he was holding tears in his eyes too. The wounds of true friendship and love never heal.

BUT LET'S BACK UP. Earlier, in Brooklyn on the very day I was with Tom and Svetlana walking above the pier—naturally, a meeting I told no one about—I had numerous calls from Mrs. Olga H. She was very nervous that day. Since our first meeting she had kept telling me that the city was full of Russian agents and begged me to be on guard. She asked me never make friends with random people on the street, especially with women—they could be Soviet agents or prostitutes, or both. This particular warning was given after I got acquainted with a young woman while traveling on the bus to the H.'s home. In fact, she was the very first stranger in New York with whom I overcame fear of not being understood and dared to converse; I needed to ask for directions, and she helped. It was a long trip, and we talked. She was well-read, smart and terribly lonely. We both were excited, although for different reasons. The woman could hardly move, had a tic, and her face muscles were twitching. Not too many people dared to talk with her. We called each other from time to time, but I kept it secret from Olga despite her order not to call this woman who "could've been ordered by someone else" to sit next to me.

I knew the roots of Olga's phobia and tried my best not to cause them pain.

She and her husband Reverend Blahoslav H. escaped from Czechoslovakia in 1948 after communists had established total control over the country. At their office on Riverside Drive they felt surrounded by enemies, and their past still haunted them. The small Research Center for Religion and Human Rights in Communist Dominated Areas, created by them, had an office in a sizable building of the World Council of Churches. They complained that the influential Council had cozy relations with the Russians, took part in the so-called fight for peace, and supported radical national liberation movements.

Soon they made me a member of the Center's board of directors and a member of the editorial board of their bi-monthly *Religion in Communist Dominated Areas—RCDA*. Olga translated and published my material. It was she who translated that ill-fated article for *National Review* that almost undermined my amicable relations with Ira Fybish.

Olga and Blahoslav were very good to me and continued helping me solve the everyday problems of a newcomer—she taught me where and how to buy food, how to pay bills, use a street laundry, fight immortal New York City cockroaches, and confront the other countless vagaries and demands of everyday life.

One unfortunate summer morning they invited me for a

dinner. Instead of taking a bus, I decided to continue my American education by crossing Central Park on foot. Crime was rampant in the city, and I had heard stories about violent attacks in the deteriorating park. So first, a magnifying glass in hand, I studied my route traversing the park to their home in uptown Manhattan using a Big Apple map. I planned to cross the lower part of this narrow, stretched out piece of rectangular land before dark.

Since my early childhood darkness has frightened me, especially in forests. Of course it might be obvious by now why this lion-hearted hero at night sees a tiger in every pussycat on the dark road and a psychotic killer in every innocent shrub—although if I have a companion, male or female, then I return to my senses. Almost.

When I reached the southernmost entrance of Central Park at Fifth Avenue, the afternoon was fading faster than I had anticipated. The grayish clouds were coming out of nowhere, but I still hoped that they might move away and the sun would return some daylight to the darkening park. The tops of buildings, even far away, beyond the park, raised hopes in my heart that I would be able to cross these dangerous grounds before nightfall.

Entering the park, I discovered bedrock protruding frequently from the ground. Heavy clouds were rapidly gathering over my head, and not a soul was in sight. Stones, boulders, cliffs, and even the bedrock were crawling with graffiti, this threatening art display of competing gangs' signatures.

My years-old scholarly conclusion was confirmed again: in the darkness the trees have a tendency to multiply and gather together, but until this afternoon this eagle-eyed observer was unaware that the stones and rocks tend to hide in the ground until you hit them with your foot or shin. As the sky kept darkening, I stumbled and dropped my glasses. I fumbled blindly in the dirt for a while, and was fortunate enough to find them. My vision had been poor since

I was a boy when my right eye was damaged by a knife in a street fight.

From time to time I stopped to look around in the dark, urban forest. I passed a small pond on my right dimly reflecting some city light emanating from the low, gloomy sky over a wall of obscure trees. Some fifteen minutes later I discovered a pond to my left; as if made of tar, it did not reflect any light at all, and looked like a huge bottomless black hole in the ground. I feared that it was the same pond and that I was moving in circles. Hearing suspicious sounds coming from different directions, sometimes very close to me, my shirt, sneakers and head became soaked with sweat. I was lost in the wilderness of New York City.

Yet I kept moving among hostile trees, most likely in the wrong direction and thinking about the imminent rain. I was preparing to turn back, when I saw a break ahead. The branches stopped whipping my head and shoulders, the trees parted and let me out of their vicious embrace. Behind a strip of grass I saw a street, a subway entrance and a lot of young black men, some of whom were looking at me. No white people in sight—the first time in my life. When I stepped onto the asphalt, some, while continuing to smoke marijuana, were studying this white, and I was sure, foul-smelling idiot coming from the dark park.

I decided to pick out of this gang the most dangerous looking guy. It was not difficult; he stood right in front of me, or more precisely, he towered over me, his neck thicker than my torso, and menace flared in the whites of his big dark eyes. His voice and curly beard reminded me of short-tempered Zeus, the supreme deity of the ancient Greeks. I lifted my face toward the skies and asked where I was. For a while he was laughing like thunder, loudly slapping his powerful thighs; after that he asked something that I could not grasp. Then he began stretching the words, probably, in order to help this jerk take in the English language. This time I understood "what" and "in the park?" I liked his way of talking to me and said, "I got lost."

Zeus thundered again, this time supported by lesser gods. After having a good laugh, he rumbled in a motherly tone, "D'you know where you are?"

"No," I said, "I was going to see my friends."

They laughed at me, and I joined them. The whole thing now seemed ridiculous to all present.

"Do you know where your friends live?" asked the Olympian, who couldn't have been more than twenty years old.

"Yes, I do," I said with obvious diffidence. "Maybe I should call them."

"OK, I'll take you to the phone booth, I'll tell them where we are," thundered my protector Zeus, and we went to a nearby corner.

I already admired him and admired his not very sober silent friend who did not want to miss the action and, staggering, accompanied us to the booth.

When I called Olga, she interrupted me before I could explain my predicament. "What happened?" she demanded. "Why didn't you call? Where are you?"

"I'll tell you later," I said in Russian. "Could you please pick me up? I'm probably not far away from you. Here is a gentleman, he'll tell you where we are." The word 'gentleman' I said in English.

Zeus grabbed the receiver and quickly gave Olga all the necessary information. "She'll be here in ten minutes," he said. "Now, tell me where you're from?"

"From Russia," I said.

"You all don't have blacks over there, right?"

"Well, there are some, but they're usually students selected by the Russian embassies. The government wants to educate only the future communist elite of African countries."

"I don't get it," said Zeus. "Who's paying for their education?"

"The Moscow rulers." I avoided the word "Soviets," which was by then out of fashion. Our conversation drifted for a while, and then came his surprise question.

"Are Russians—Christians?"

"Not too many," I said. "For sixty years they've been teaching that to believe in God is ridiculous, that only fools can believe in God. We learned this in kindergarten, before learning how to read."

"What do they believe, then?"

"They believe they are building paradise on Earth."

"So, this is their religion?" Zeus asked, intrigued.

"Exactly. They call this religion 'atheism'."

"But you also have Jews in Russia. Many recently came to Brooklyn. They believe in God, they were given the Old Testament. Jesus was sent to them."

"Well, Jews were brainwashed by communists just like everybody else. Never in their life back in Russia had they seen the Bible or a church."

"A synagogue," Zeus corrected me. "So, they run to America from paradise?"

"Yes."

At this moment Olga and Blahoslav arrived. I said, "Sorry, I'd love to stay here and talk with you but I have to go."

"It's OK, brother," said Zeus, "God bless you."

I shook his immense hand longer than it was required by good manners and said, "Thank you very much, brother! You're good." Then I shook the hand of his silent buddy and said, "You, too."

My friends were angry. Nonetheless I opened the car window and yelled, "What's the name of this station?" I did not hear his answer, the car was moving away too fast. So, I told them that I had this peculiarity that I call topographical cretinism: "I'm often unable to find my bearings on the ground, especially at night, and, if in a forest, at any time of the day. Sorry if I ruined your evening."

The first heavy drops of rain were making their way down the windshield. Thunder was coming from heavens; Zeus was laughing.

One hot Indian Summer day I told Lyudmila (Lucy) Thorne about my travel through Central Park. She was outraged. "The KGB is right," she said. "There are some mad dissidents in Russia."

We were walking in the New York gluey heat, and I could hardly drag my shoes along the sidewalk. Suddenly, I saw a bookstore window with a long row of red volumes—*The Complete Works of Josef Stalin.*

"Lucy! Look at this!"

"So what?" she said, lowering her voice. "And please don't yell."

"Wouldn't you yell, if it were *The Complete Works of Hitler?*"

"No, I wouldn't," she said. "Welcome to America. We have freedom of speech."

"Including the hate speech?" I asked, getting angry.

She grinned. "Now you're emanating heat."

With a faked "Hah-hah-hah," I stepped in the door of the store.

"What are you doing?" she shouted after me. "You better behave! They'll call the police!"

Lucy remained safely outside. I grinned at her through the glass door; she flashed a quick, uneasy smile. In fact, all I wanted was to understand the people who worked there: had their hatred of capitalism blinded them, or were they misinformed, or ignorant, or, speaking in plain Newyourkish, *meshuga*. At the counter stood a young woman with irresistible American white teeth.

I pointed at the red volumes. "He killed many millions of people."

"But some of them were guilty," she said after a moment.

She still had the sweet smile on her lovely face. The quiet sound of her voice turned into an unbearable bell ringing in my head. I got a lump in my throat and left the bookstore, not uttering a word.

"What happened?" Lucy asked, stroking my chest. "You've turned pale."

"She told me that *some* of them were guilty."

"Who are 'some'? Guilty of what?"

"Don't you understand?! She said that *some* of the people murdered by him were guilty. What is it? Indoctrination? Another crazy cult?"

"An incurable disease." I heard melancholy in her voice. Lucy swore in Russian, "Wait until you move to California to work for that mission. Where are they located?"

"In Glendale."

"Just don't settle in Santa Monica," she said, turning to me with a wry look.

"Why?"

"They call it the People's Republic of Santa Monica," she said. "Jane Fonda lives there, and her radical leftist husband is the town's mayor."

TWENTY-ONE

A Jew Who Spoke in Tongues

P AUL POPOV picked me up at the Los Angeles airport as the haze of smog crept over our heads. "Welcome to sunny California!" he said, and told me about his plan he had outlined to me days before over the phone. I still was unable to take it in and said, "In Europe I had an Austrian travel document."

How could I go to Canada without such a document? What border guard would take seriously this tiny rectangular scrap paper with my Social Security number, which could easily have been forged by a devilish kindergartener? Stripped of my Soviet citizenship, I had to wait for an American Green Card for one more year.

"Don't worry, Arkady," my carefree driver said. "We'll fly to Vancouver as soon as our posters with your children are ready. Nobody will ask you for any documents. We're not in Russia."

He did not know what every Russian kid knew. In the Soviet Union, an illegal border crosser would be shot dead right at the border or sent to the Gulag for fifteen years. I knew this from early childhood: my Motherland was surrounded by mortal enemies who were trying to penetrate our impregnable borders to do terrible harm to Russian children. At the age of seven I had decided to join Soviet superheroes from my favorite movie *The Border Under Lock and Key*. All three times I saw it, my heart pounded like a hammer in my chest. With my German shepherd we could find the enemy by sniffing the border air, just like Moktar and Joolbars, two highly intelligent four-legged movie stars. I was ready for patrolling our *Sacred* Borders. Yes, we called them *Sacred*. That is why Border Guard Day is still officially celebrated in Russia.

On the plane to Canada I pretended to be asleep. At Vancouver International Airport nobody asked me or anybody else for anything. Paul looked at me with certain sympathy. I was a little embarrassed and tried a recently learned reckless "okey dokey!" to show that I was no longer concerned with the consequences of my illegal arrival abroad.

In the huge Vancouver Convention Center, preparations for the upcoming Twelfth Pentecostal World Conference were nearing completion. About sixty thousand pastors and laypeople from seventy-eight countries planned to worship Jesus Christ together there. The Conference's Advisory Committee Chairman Thomas Zimmerman was informed that, in order to draw attention to the tragic plight of the Russian Pentecostals, I would spend the entire conference of the Pentecostal Fellowship fasting in front of the Convention Center. At that time Zimmerman, the General Superintendent of the US Assemblies of God, was trying to establish relations with the Soviet official All Union Council of Evangelical Christians-Baptists. His efforts were in vain. The regime viewed Evangelicals as a foreign influence, even spies. The persecuted majority of Pentecostals still belonged to unregistered underground churches.

I tried my best to be tactful. Our small group quietly stayed at a reasonable distance from the main entrance. From our cardboard posters, the Russian kids were watching with sad eyes thousands of Christians passing by. Many of them ignored us. Some would stop. A young fellow with a Southern accent stared for a couple of

'My' exposition during my hunger strike at the Twelfth Pentecostal World Congress held at the Vancouver Convention Center in 1979. The signs say:
"Zhenya Galushkin (8): 'I get beaten at school because I'm a believer'"; "Does 'Go Ye into All the World' Mean Romania" (brought by a Romanian exile who joined us); "Nikolai Pishchenko (12) Russia: 'Our teachers in school teach us that the believers sacrifice their children. Thus, they teach our schoolmates to hate us.'"

minutes at the portrait of twelve-year-old Nick Pishchenko, as if trying to look into the eyes of the boy. Then in the same manner he studied me and finally asked, "Is that true?"

"Give me your address," I said, "and I'll send you a photocopy of his letter in Russian."

"Are you familiar with the child?"

"Yes. I was his guest."

"Where does he live?"

"In the south of Russia, near the Black Sea."

"I'll talk about him in my church." With these words the fellow pulled out a pen and wrote down an excerpt from a letter we had placed on the poster under the boy's portrait: "Our teachers tell us that believers offer their children as sacrifices and thus they make all the other students hate us."

One young woman asked me angrily, "Why do you do this? We came here to worship Jesus. Do you understand what Gentiles might think of us?"

I said, "Yes, in fact, I do."

Paul and some Canadians called local media outlets, but nobody came; they were not interested. For three days it was rather quiet. We heard the worshipers, praying and singing; the solid doors stayed mainly closed, and the powerful voices of the thousands inside the Convention Center were muffled and inaudible.

We had a couple of sympathizers on the Advisory Committee of the Conference. They—Paul was asked not to mention names—had privately suggested to him that I should continue fasting, although I had no intentions to quit. They suggested to the participants of the Conference to pray for persecuted Christians of the world. I would have prefered them to be more specific and to name the USSR. But it wouldn't have done any good—the Soviets did not believe in the power of prayer—for them it would be like inaudible voices behind these solid doors.

Meanwhile, kind-hearted Doris, who visited me in New York and won my heart with her desire to help, began worrying about my health. She took me by the hand away from our group, passed me a white plastic bottle and said, "You should drink more."

With great pleasure I gulped down quite a portion. It tasted like diluted orange juice. My face clearly reflected surprise and Doris lowered her gaze, "I added a little."

I could not get angry with her.

That evening Paul saw on local television the famous Russian dissident Vladimir Bukovsky speaking at the University of British Columbia. In forty minutes we found him delivering a talk to a group of experts in political science. When they had a break, I walked over to Vladimir, who was still at the podium. We hugged and he said, "Arkady, you're on hunger strike, and, oh boy, you stink! How many days?"

"Only three days so far," I said modestly. The man who had spent twelve years in prisons, hard labor camps and psychiatric jails did not need a lengthy explanation. In two weeks, he said, I would smell like a vessel brimming with acetone. Thank God, that gathering lasted only six days.

The next evening Bukovsky mentioned my vigil on a local TV station. The following morning, on the fifth day of my fast, a television crew was already waiting for me near Convention Center. Soon I was talking with some other reporters.

A few months later, I flew from New York to Los Angeles again, and once more Paul Popov picked me up at the airport. On the way to Glendale, he said, "Why did you never ask what your position and pay in the Door of Hope would be? It's very un-American."

This more or less mature boy, I explained, was going to be paid for what he did without being paid. Paul also kept in mind my past status. "From now on you're the managing editor of our publication," he said.

"That's great!" I exclaimed. "Just don't forget to teach me to speak, read, and write in English."

When we stopped in front of the mission, Paul put his hand on my shoulder, "We have to talk. Just don't take it too seriously. Olga H. called my father from New York the other day. She said that you were a KGB officer, and we're making a serious mistake."

What would happen if Olga knew about Russian fake correspondents with whom I worked for so many years? This thought flashed through my brain.

"You think people will believe her?" I said.

"Some will," he said.

"What would you suggest I do?" I sighed.

"Just ignore it. You don't seem to be upset, that's good."

"Oh yes, I am," I said.

He changed the subject. "We have to finish the translation of your documentary. Do you like the title *Pharaoh, Let My People Go?*"

My 1977 *samizdat* report on the Christian Emigration Movement was already published by the U.S. government and served as a backbone of this documentary.

"It might help Nikolai Goretoi," I said.

Recently, before the last trial, the KGB had summoned him to say that he could go with his family at once, but on one condition—that he asked for exit visas only for his family. Goretoi refused, knowing that it would lead to his imprisonment.

"Oh, one more thing," Paul patted me on the shoulder. "Yesterday the president of a big Evangelical mission called from Pasadena to say the same spy thing. As you know, my dad served almost fourteen years for being a Western spy in Bulgaria. So we welcome another spy in our mission."

"Does this president know Olga?"

"Yes," Paul said, "he does."

Finally, we stepped into the office, and I hugged my buddy Doris. In five minutes I was telling people about an incident that she witnessed, where an anti-Semite had confronted me in a New York supermarket. They had not heard the story before. Perhaps Doris felt uncomfortable talking about this. This time, the Jew in me wanted to see the reaction of these young Christian enthusiasts.

Doris and I had been standing in line for a cashier when my shopping cart tapped a middle-aged man ahead of us. Turning around, the man shoved the innocent cart back at me and began cursing all the Jews of this world and beyond. He was becoming more and more furious, and the very presence of the Door of Hope representative concerned me; what if he hits me? I did not want to use the fighting experience of my youth. But the jerk was waving his fists, and all I could do now was to repeat, "Shut up."

With astonishment in her voice, Doris asked a strange question, "How did he find out?"

This thirty-something American was unaware that the best way to recognize a Jew was just to take a quick look at him. That was such a surprise! In my part of the world every child could recognize a Jew.

I looked at the people around us—many pretended that they did not hear a thing; some looked at me with sympathy. I breathed a sigh of relief when, after the man yelled what Jews have heard in Russia constantly, "Go to Israel where you belong!" a little woman in the line quietly asked, "Will you pay for his trip?"

My new colleagues were unaware that in Russia, just like in Nazi Germany, being a Jew was a purely ethnic category, not a religious one.

While we talked, a programmer in the back corner of the office was readjusting the position of his miniature computer. Almost effortlessly! The computers here were the size of an apple crate and even lighter to pick up. I was unaware that this paunchy paragon of beauty was just a monitor. When I said that in Moscow nobody knew the word "computer," I nearly lost the trust of my audience.

Now I could share with them one striking image I remember from the first day of my first visit here. A frivolous appeal hanging over the urinal: "Gentlemen, don't miss the point," was written by Paul's pious seventy-four-year-old mother. I concluded that nobody here, in this place devoted to spreading God's Word, would try to convert me.

My first night in my Glendale apartment was sleepless. I thought of my eighty-year-old mother, about my cruel selfishness and her refusal to go with me. She said then, "Sonny, it'll make your

Examining book proofs with staff member Arnie Derksen at the headquarters of Door of Hope International. Glendale, California, early-1980s. (Door of Hope International)

life harder. I'll stay with your sister." Her dry eyes could not hide the melancholy. I knew that she wanted to go with me. But who needed a Russian journalist in the West, much less the journalist's family?

Then I thought of my only sister and my friends whom I had left behind. Forever, what a cruel word! In the middle of the night, I mused, this stupid air-conditioner sounds like a plane engine stalled at night over the Atlantic. Why Atlantic? I thought. We're near the Pacific. Where was I flying? Only G-d knew.

After the morning began dawning behind the curtain, I thought of my first love. I still loved her. It was my fault, not hers. Still so many years after our divorce, I had stayed unmarried. Why did this fact make her nervous?

AFTER WORKING in the Glendale headquarters for a couple of months, I had to travel to British Columbia once again, this time to speak in churches. To drive for a couple of days by the ocean and in the mountains with my battered car was quite an adventure, but the memories of it were quickly overshadowed by what I went through upon my arrival in Canada.

At the doors of a huge Pentecostal Tabernacle north of Vancouver, I was welcomed by its imposing pastor. He said a couple of niceties in Ukrainian. I sprinkled my Russian with a couple of Ukrainian words. We both were satisfied with this promising beginning. Soon I found myself in the pulpit, ready to tell to two thousand Canadians about the suffering of their sisters and brothers in Christ.

The pastor said that I came to his church to call Pentecostals to organize a letter writing campaign, demanding the release Christian prisoners and to allow Christian emigration. After that we both smiled at each other, with anticipation. A gentleman in the first row also kept smiling at me as if he had been missing me for ages. He even impatiently got up from his chair and sat back again. I anticipated shaking hands with him in seconds. Only after he stopped smiling, did it dawn on me—he wasn't an interpreter, it was the minister who would undertake this job and who was nervously waiting for me to do the talking.

And I spoke. Very, very slowly. After every sentence the pastor hesitated for a stretch of time, and after that, stumbled and staggered through the sentences. Beads of sweat were shining on his forehead. We both got scared. Meanwhile, four or five people were coming to the front row, to the rescue.

"We want to help you," said an aged man in broken Russian.

"We thought that for a Ukrainian it wouldn't be difficult to interpret from Russian," said another old man in an exotic mixture of Russian, Ukrainian and English. The man of God said that he had not exercised his Ukrainian since his grandparents were called by the Lord, "But you do speak English, Arkady!" he said, his deep mellow voice returning to him. "Praise the Lord!"

A nice lady, while encouragingly shaking her shining gray hair, said in a motherly tone, "We'll help you with words, don't worry, go ahead! Speak in English! Yes," she repeated, "In English! In English!"

That was the kiss of death. My hour had struck. A very young fellow, with round metal glasses on a small nose, blushed and said in excellent Russian, "Farewell, comrade." It sounded quite appropriate, like at the conclusion of a funeral, right before the burial.

So, I began speaking in my English, in a trembling voice, wobbling over words, letting out squeaks, sending pleading looks to the ad hoc panel, and asking my advisers to interpret some Russian words into English. I felt like a perfect fool mired in impassable mud. The panel would give me a word, often after lively discussion and only more or less settling their linguistic disagreements. Every so often they would ask me for another Russian word, to replace the unknown one. It was the longest hour of my life. The logical finale to my performance came when my vocabulary was fully exhausted. My physical and mental strength had been spent as well.

But dare I say, the event nonetheless was a miraculous one. The miracle was performed by a middle-aged lady in a remote row and, to a degree, by me. The woman decided that the Holy Spirit had come upon this good man (me!) and enabled him to speak in tongues, as it is practiced in Pentecostal churches. She had logic made of steel: this good man, in order to proclaim the Gospel, has spoken in a language he never knew. And she was chosen by God to become a vessel of Grace and to interpret this unknown tongue into the language of the Christians, gathered in the tabernacle, so that all those present could understand the Holy message.

At first everybody was frozen in awkward silence, but as the sweet lady continued to perform her exciting mission, people began to smile—some, shyly, some, openly. When she completed her task, many began applauding and laughing to everybody's delight. The lady looked happy. We all sang hymns. I was happy, too. I was reading the words on a big screen and sang just like everybody else. Everybody loved me, and I loved everybody. The blushing fellow from the ad hoc panel, probably a university student, approached me again and said "thank you" in Russian. I said in English, almost sincerely, "Your Russian is excellent!"

At the end of the gathering the pastor gave a spirited sermon about the persecuted Church, and in conclusion he read, possibly for my benefit, from the Biblical narrative of the Pentecost in the second chapter of the Book of Acts: "Suddenly there was a noise from heaven like the sound of a mighty wind. It filled the house where they were meeting. Then they saw what looked like fiery tongues moving in all directions, and a tongue came and settled on each person there. The Holy Spirit took control of everyone, and they began speaking whatever languages the Spirit let them speak."

Upon my return to Glendale, both Popovs decided that my English did not need crutches anymore. My entreaties about interpreters were rejected. Cruel Paul reminded me, "Remember, you asked me to teach you to speak and write in English?"

I nodded grimly and he continued, "Now we are aware that you're capable not only to get your message across in your English, you even can chat with the Holy Spirit."

"Sure," I said. "This gift isn't given to everyone."

And we laughed like only children can laugh.

TWENTY-TWO

My Russian Habitat in California

THE JOY OF HAVING the undeserved title of managing editor for the Door of Hope publication did not last for long: the lack of donor money forced the DOH to temporarily slow down its activities. I lost my position of distinction for the second time in my life, although the only thing that the two jobs had in common was the fear of the unknown after losing them. Now came the time for some heavy thinking about boring things like food on the table and a roof over my head. On the other hand, being unemployed, I had more time for cooperating with human rights organizations, especially with the California branch of Amnesty International. Those guys did not pay a penny, but they paid for my travel to conferences and for the hotels.

Fortunately, half a year before my move to California, a family of my relatives emigrated from Ukraine to Los Angeles. Faina Shvartsman was my mother's first cousin. Once every two years, with her husband, also named Arkady, or, with their son Oscar, she stayed with my parents in Moscow. For hours they would queue in the Moscow department and grocery stores. I had more exciting things to do than to see those backward provincials whom I hardly knew and whose interests seemed foreign to me. What I was not aware of, however, was that neither of our families escaped a common destiny. I knew that my Aunt Donya, Grandma, and many other relatives were killed in Kiev soon after the Nazis captured the city in 1941. I did not know that in the same mass graves of Kiev's Babi Yar laid the bullet-riddled bodies of Faina's and Arkady's relatives.

Days after the Luftwaffe bombed Kiev on June 22, 1941, Faina and Arkady, already doctors, were drafted. Throughout the war they served in front-line hospitals and medical trains, performing operations under bombardment and fire.

We stood on their small balcony in West Hollywood, overlooking the mountainous skyline, and Faina told a story about a wounded soldier in war-ravaged Stalingrad. She was twenty-four years old then and burst into tears after that soldier—"just a little boy," she said—was killed by a shrapnel ball seconds after she tightened the last stitch on his ruptured chest. In Stalingrad, the combined casualties on both sides, including Russian civilians, were close to two million. And in that charred shed she cried over this soldier killed less than a foot away from her after a successful operation.

I thought, it could have been you, not the soldier. Faina pointed at the orange trees under the balcony and said, "The neighbors say you can pick oranges any time."

She looked absently at the enormity of the world-famous HOLLYWOOD sign on a hillside maybe a mile away and continued talking about "this snub-nosed little boy." There was something unreal about orange trees and torpid flowers under bright California sun. She felt comfortable talking about this bloody battle that lasted for almost seven months, but she refused to talk about Babi Yar. Only once did she say, "Why do you keep asking about this killing? It wasn't a war. It was just a killing of Jews, nothing new. It will always be happening."

A month later, in response to the same stubborn question she

above: Faina Shvartsman in the first days of the war.
below: Arkady Shvartsman in military uniform.
(Family archive)

said, "Did you ever ask your Papa about Babi Yar?"

"Papa didn't want to talk about it," I said.

"Your father was a wise man," Faina said. "His heart always had the final say. I felt so bad when he came from Moscow and I wasn't able…" she gave a deep sigh, "Cancer."

They didn't have enough painkillers in the richest city of Russia, and he died a painful death. I did not tell her about that.

After I lost my job at Door of Hope, they invited me without a sign of hesitation to stay in their small apartment. They lived below poverty level, receiving Supplemental Security Income, and never complained. Their son Oscar and his wife Sophie, who were studying English, worked as engineers and rented a place in Cerritos, a small but fast-growing town south of Los Angeles. They were surprised by the number of Filipinos, Chinese and Koreans in America.

Finally I found myself living with immigrants and smiled bitterly, recalling my own advice given to a young woman from Odessa—to move out of Brooklyn to America. About half of the Fuller Street inhabitants in Los Angeles were recently arrived Ukrainian Jews. My understanding of the neighborhood came at a price. Two or three days after moving in with Faina I had to meet with a teacher from a Santa Monica high school—a member of Amnesty International, she wanted to get acquainted with me before my upcoming talk at her school. I asked her to pick me up at the corner of Santa Monica Boulevard and Fuller Street and described myself: gray hair, glasses, a white short-sleeve shirt, and black shorts. Two minutes before the agreed time I was on the corner. In seconds a car of the wrong color stopped at the sidewalk, a man opened the door and waved me in. He looked kind of suspicious. I shook my head, and he immediately drove away with indifference in his face. When the next client parked at the same spot, with the same clearly expressed intentions, I was shocked and hid behind the nearest house corner and from time to time cautiously perused the sidewalk where this woman promised to stop. When she came, I ran to her car and told her the story of my success. She was surprised about my choice of the place and quoted Shakespeare: "My salad days, when I was green in judgment."

My life with two old doctors was not boring. Their son Oscar warned that I needed to be ready to help his mother in her many endeavors and to obey her orders. Faina proudly showed me several heavy cheese blocks in her refrigerator, about eight or ten pounds each, and guaranteed me a steady supply of such cheese as soon as I decided to move out to my future place. That evening Oscar dropped by to see how his parents accommodated me. He immediately was forced to take "just a couple" of those blocks to Cerritos. His shaky argument that the children and his wife disliked this particular kind of cheese did not impress his mother. When she was in the kitchen, Oscar explained in a low voice that the cheese was coming from some military depot, tasted like raw brick, and no hungry Russian soldier would eat it. Needless to say, I also would not have dared.

Faina was a very busy lady taking good care of two Arkadys and her grandchildren; almost every day she cooked and delivered meals to her ill and ungrateful older brother, five houses down the street.

One bright September morning she woke me up and commanded, "Hurry up! We should go immediately, too many people will try to do this." Angelinos in need could go to nearby flower shops and pick up a watermelon for free that day. Faina, her husband and I sat in my old Chevy and she said, to my dismay, "It's so good, Alik, that it has this spacious trunk."

In five minutes I parked the car on the corner of La Brea Avenue and Sunset Boulevard, next to a florist. "No—no," commanded Faina, "go to the backyard."

"Yes, Ma'am," I said timidly, praying nobody would be there. "Maybe we aren't allowed to enter here." I already had a foreboding.

"Don't you see that the gate is wide open?" she said. "Look at these huge watermelons. They're like fat pigs."

So I backed up my Chevy close to the 'pigs,' hundreds of which lay on the ground. We were alone in the backyard.

"Look," Faina said, "nobody's in the yard, nobody guards them, and nobody will count the watermelons we are going to load."

Her overweight husband and I, groaning, lifted one and put it in the trunk. After putting in the second watermelon I asked, "*Fanechka*, maybe it's enough, one 'pig' for us and one for Oscar?"

"Are you making fun of me?" she said. "We need three for us, three for my son, and three for my ungrateful brother."

"They will rot," I said. "You see, passersby are already giving us dirty looks."

"I don't understand how you could be a dissident in Moscow," Faina said. "You're afraid of your own shadow. Look, nobody wants these watermelons."

After we loaded six huge 'pigs' she said, "We should go. A woman is looking at us from the shop," and we promptly moved out. The survival operation was over. Sitting next to me, Faina looked happy. Then I blurted out the next nonsense, "Your son might refuse to take more than one."

She looked at me with compassion, "Alik, you're such an impractical man. We have to find a nice, down-to-earth, sane Jewish wife for you; otherwise, you won't survive in capitalist America."

At home she immediately called Oscar, "Sonny, I have something very good for my grandchildren. Don't forget to empty the trunk before coming here, and stop moaning like a wounded hare."

Thanks to her son's connections, I got a cheap efficiency in a nice, subsidized, twenty-story building near the famous Santa Monica Pier. Not far from there was a bookstore. Those guys were sane, did not promote Stalin's books, despised the Soviet rulers, and believed in the benevolence of a big democratic government.

I told them that the very word "socialism" has been used by mortal enemies for their political ends, by dictators and European democracies, by atheists and Catholic priests, by slave owners and freedom fighters, by Zionists and anti-Semites, by Hitler and Stalin.

It was not long after that when Paul Popov and Swedish Slaviska Mission managed to arrange my second visit to Sweden. In Stockholm some radicals asked me for an interview for their little Trotskyite paper. My Christian hosts and I believed that any publicity for the cause of persecuted Russian Evangelicals would be helpful. At a nice apartment, for two hours I answered all kind of questions from a dozen young men and women. As usual, they asked about Soviet free education, free healthcare, and free housing. The slave owners of the distant past, I said, did exactly the same—they fed their slaves, gave them shelter, and tried to keep them healthy, so the slaves could perform their tasks.

My decent friends from the Santa Monica bookstore believed that Sweden was successfully moving toward true socialism. The Swedes believed that Swedish capitalists hijacked the very word "socialism." Yet this apartment was of a subsidized kind. Then I caught them in a trap. "How many families live in this apartment?"

"Of course, one," they said. "We have a boy and a girl."

"In Moscow, such a dwelling would house four families—one room for each family," I said.

Upon returning home and sitting again in the Santa Monica bookstore, I thought of similarities between two incompatible socialist movements. They both, Californian socialists and Swedish Trotskyites, wanted to make the world a better place, and they knew how to do this. The thunderous Zeus from Manhattan would ask them, "So, is this your religion?"

I FOUND TIME when I could do some ice dancing in Burbank but soon hit the road again; this time I was invited to be a keynote speaker at a regional conference of Amnesty International in Dallas, Texas. In Dallas, someone handed me a letter received at Amnesty's headquarters in New York. My name was written on the envelope in Russian and dubious English, and it had an American postage stamp but no return address. The letter was short:

"My dearest friend Alik, you were right. You know that I don't read Soviet publications, but Fred brought me the *Literary Gazette* with an article that delighted me. It said that you were working for the CIA, which indicated to us that you were fine and had friends. What a relief! Ask the CIA to assign you and me on reconnaissance to that sequoia forest in California and to British Columbia to spy on bears hunting salmon. The jeans that you sent me were probably stolen upon their arrival in Russia. Do you remember how you got fed up with your writing? Now, I have almost ceased writing. Gena."

It was Gennady Snegiryov. His letter was a sweet reminder of our lasting friendship that had continued even after I was no longer able to see my friends. They knew that I did not want to endanger their lives. This letter returned me back to Russia, and I did not like it. My brave Gena was afraid to show his address to unfriendly eyes, even in an American post office.

"You were right" maybe meant that almost thirty years ago, after a boxing workout at the University, I had been right to reject his offer to acquire a fake certificate of my mental illness. Gena had close relationship with his psychiatrist. Walking between palms surmounted by large crowns, I remembered how after my graduation he applied to me his version of Buddhism. "You still have this stupid Soviet soul," he said, "but I solemnly predict that soon it will be pushed out of your heart by a healthy anti-Soviet soul and it will torment you for the rest of your life."

It did not happen soon, but at the time I asked, "So you think that a soul wears out as the sole of a shoe?"

"Exactly. Not exactly," he said almost in the same breath.

After that infallible prognosis, he washed down a huge portion of pills from my medicine cabinet and fell asleep on my floor. At daybreak I put a pillow under his head and covered him with a plaid blanket. We never used the word addict.

"You were right" could also mean that years later, after the publication of my scandalous lampoon in Moscow, Kostroma authorities, armed with such a diagnosis, could have tried to put me in a madhouse. Or, who knows, maybe he meant something else.

Looking out from the steep Santa Monica Coast, across the Pacific and onto the distant, impeccably rounded skyline, I thought, you'll never see your soulmates again. It's unhealthy to be an expert on human suffering, so it's time to stop looking at the past.

The ocean was getting darker with every minute, the distant waves turning into hardened lava. Where moments ago had shone the crown of the sun, a long red stripe now rapidly faded. It was absolutely clear to me that the sun had disappeared exactly behind that far-flung part of the Pacific where the sixteen-year-old Gena Snegiryov once sailed along the Russian coast with university biologists. Now I was loudly explaining to my buddy that I would try to get his address through my ex-wife or just send her his jeans.

The gloomy boulevard was already empty as I continued talking to Gena, when he and my favorite bard and stagehand, Fred Solyanov, appeared to me, emerging out of pungently odorous black bushes behind dark palm trees. My dear friends—here, next to me. Gena inhaled deeply the fragrant air and said, "Exotics!"

"Snegiryov," I mumbled, embarrassed, "I did not send you the jeans."

"The devil with them," Gena said and suggested, "Let's race to that line."

"The horizon line?" I asked readily.

"Yes, where else," he said.

"If Tom Kolesnichenko were here, he'd say you guys were crazy," Fred said and gently touched a palm tree.

"And our Marxist Nahl," Gena said, "would've implied that it's impossible to even reach the horizon, no matter how fast we are."

Fred tried to defend our Marxist. "He was the fastest runner at Moscow University."

They were gone as suddenly as they had appeared—into the same, now jet-black, sharply smelling bushes. I turned and trudged back to America, muttering, "Tom would never say such a thing."

Five minutes later, I looked at the horizon again, now from the height of my twentieth floor. However, the horizon had almost disappeared, and somewhere far away the dark sky merged with the dark ocean.

Images and Documents

Russian Christian signatories of a petition for emigration from the USSR.

WHY DO RUSSIAN CHRISTIANS WANT
TO LEAVE THEIR MOTHERLAND

INTRODUCTION

BY: ARKADY POLISHCHUK
*The Western Representative of Christian Emigration
Movement and Council of Churches of Evangelical
Christians – Pentecostals [CCECP].*

The mass Christian Emigration Movement was born in the USSR after President L. Brezhnev, President G. Ford and 33 other leaders signed the Helsinki Accords on August 1, 1975. This movement was initiated under the influence of the Helsinki Final Act. Soviet Christians took seriously the signatures of the most influential European and American politicians.

In signing the Helsinki Final Act the Soviet Union committed itself to: "....recognize and respect the freedom of the individual to profess and practice, alone or in the community with others, religion or beliefs acting in accordance with the dictates of his own conscience." Despite all evidence to the contrary, Soviet authorities persist in maintaining that there is total freedom of religion in our country.

But why do so many Christians, particularly Baptists and Pentecostals, want to leave the Soviet Union? The answer is very simple, because of incessant persecution. The Helsinki Final Act has encouraged emigration requests in that its signatories promised to promote "free movement... among persons... the participating states" and to abide by their commitments in other international agreements.

The problem of the seven Pentecostal refugees, members of the Chmykhalov and Vashchenko families, sealed inside the Moscow U.S. Embassy since June 27, 1978, remains unresolved. The Soviet authorities are persistent in their refusal to permit them to emigrate and in their continuous harassments of the other members of these families in Chernogorsk and Aleksandr Vashchenko in a concentration camp.

The seven in the embassy are permitted no mail through diplomatic channels, cannot meet with reporters in the embassy building, and live in relative isolation.

The problem of Christian emigration from the Soviet Union, symbolized by the seven courageous Pentecostals living in the embassy basement room, remains an

1

Select pages from *Pharaoh, Let My People Go!* edited by Arkady Polishchuk and published by Door of Hope International. Glendale, California, 1980.
The marks and notes are by various people who used the book to make presentations about human rights in Russia.

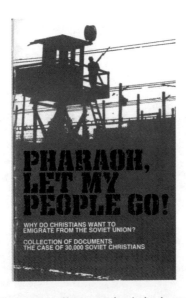

PHARAOH, LET MY PEOPLE GO!

WHY DO CHRISTIANS WANT TO
EMIGRATE FROM THE SOVIET UNION?

COLLECTION OF DOCUMENTS
THE CASE OF 30,000 SOVIET CHRISTIANS

This is a digest of letters, appeals and other documents sent to Soviet officials and leaders of countries—— signatories of Helsinki Agreements by Soviet Christians. The purpose of this small collection is to present the case of the Christian Emigration Movement from the 1975 Helsinki Conference up to the 1980 Review Conference in Madrid, Spain.
All materials are abridged without sacrificing of sense.

******

The compiler of this book and the author of introduction is a Soviet dissident, Arkady Polishchuk, a participant of USSR Helsinki Movement, now the Western Representative of Christian Emigration Movement and the newly formed Council of Churches of Evangelical Christians - Pentecostals.

******

I would like to thank the staff of Evangelism to Communist Lands (ECL, the founder Rev. Haralan Popov, the President Paul Popov. The International Headquarters in Glendale, California, USA) for helping me prepare and publish this work.
Without their support and cooperation this work would not have been possible.

Arkady Polishchuk
November 1980

convicted for their religious beliefs and sentenced to various periods (from three to ten years) of incarceration in prison and camps, or exile. Some believers were convicted more than once, and some are still incarcerated. The same thing is happening to believers in numerous other towns; e.g., in Korosten, Vinnitsa, and Nikolayev in the Ukrainian SSR. Many believers of various denominations are confined in camps in the Mordovian SSR in the town of Novo-Troitskoye, Dzhambul Oblast. In many towns the authorities employed fines and threats to force the discontinuation of religious services, so that believers have been compelled to congregate only at night, hiding from the authorities' repressions and persecutions. And in many areas services have been discontinued entirely. As for fines, in recent years there have been such a great number of them that they are difficult to count.

In 1974, in the town of Chernogorsk, several persons were fined (including a widow with four dependents); and the same thing happened in Simferpol, Nakhodka, and many other towns. During these years children, property, and homes were taken away from many believers. Many were deprived of work and their means of subsistence in the towns of Kansk, Chernogorsk, Barnaul, and many others. Believers were beaten in apartments where services were being held. Tear-gas cannisters were thrown in, and fire hoses were turned on both adults and children in order to break up the services.

We do not have the right or the opportunity to be true believers in our country, to impress religious convictions in our children, or to preach the Gospel to others. We do not have religious literature available, since almost everywhere in recent years it has been confiscated from us: the Bible, the New Testament, and hymn books. And believers have a great need for such things. If everyone succeeds in obtaining a Bible in a foreign edition, he is harassed and it is confiscated in the course of a search.

VaRU. Nik.

All these actions by the Soviet authorities have compelled many congregations in various town to decide to follow the instructions given in the New Testament: "But when the persecute you in this city, flee ye into another...." (Matt. 10.23.) And the commandment: "....Come out of her, my people, that ye be not partakers of her sins, and that ye receive not of her plagues. For her sins have reached unto heaven, and God hath remembered her iniquities." (Rev. 18:4, 5.)

Owing to such circumstances in many cities and towns of the USSR, believers have decided it is necessary to emigrate from the USSR. But the attempts of many to leave the USSR have met with refusals on the part of the Government, which cites as its grounds the fact that the believers desirous of emigrating from the USSR do not have an invitation, either from relatives or governments, to come

12

to another country. The majority of believers do not have relatives abroad. We therefore appeal to you, as Christians, to petition the governments of your countries to permit us to come there for permanent residence, and to send invitations and the necessary documents to all those desirous of emigrating from the USSR. We also beg you, Christians of all denominations, to protest the situation of believers in the USSR, and to entreat the Soviet Government not to obstruct the emigration of believers.

On behalf of believers:
Grigory Vashchenko,
Primorsky krai, g. Nakhodka, ul. Veselaya
Evgeny Bresenden,
Primorsky krai, g. Nakhodka, ul. Lineinaya

Clandestine photo by Paul Popov of the Vushchenko-Chmykhalov families seeking asylum at the U.S. Embassy. Moscow, 1978.

YEAR OF 1976

WE WERE DISPERSED IN FIELDS

I attended a worship service when a KGB officer came and dispersed the people at the prayer meeting. The captain dragged me out from behind a table, grabbed me by the shoulder and began to choke me. My wife, with a child in her arms, wanted to intercede for me but the captain struck the baby who fell. I said: "How can I be a Soviet citizen with a Soviet passport when they choke me and almost kill my children and do not let us fulfill God's commandments?" I took my military registration card to the military headquarters and we sent our passports to the ministry in Moscow with the information about the repressions, fines and the kind of persecution we have been subjected to. We had been poisoned with teargas, dispersed in the fields, sprayed with water.

I was released in 1970 and imprisoned again in 1972 for one year of strict regime. At the end of my term in 1973 I was not permitted to get a job. The repressions became even worse, with the difference that official Terskikh at the administrative commission said that whoever would employ me would be fined. They would not give me a job and then they demanded a tax for being unemployed. Since I would not pay the tax, the authorities came to inventory my property. They inventoried a sewing machine but could not find anything else.

Peter Chmykhalov   *1976*

13

17 DAYS IN AN AIRLESS CELL

I was imprisoned and held 17 days in an airless cell where I had to sit on the ground. My five children came to the basement and shouted through the opening. The guards heard them and threatened to shoot them. My children cried: "Shoot, we don't care, just give us our mother!" After 17 days they took me, half-dead, to the prison. I thought my life was over. From the prison they took me by taxi and again placed me in that airless basement cell for another 17 days. [.....] When finally I was brought into light, I could not stand up against the wall and fell down. [.....]

Maria Chmykhalov   *1976*
(Since June 27, 1978 in USA Embassy, Moscow, USSR)

WE DRINK BAD WATER

My father was tried according to Article 58, point 10 and was sentenced to 10 years in the camps. The prosecutor stated: "For raising his children in a religious spirit." Only God Himself knows what torments we have experienced, seven children with their mother. We were deprived of our home and we suffered the Far Eastern cold and hunger.

At the present time I have 12 children. My salary in 82 kopecks per hour. They refused to award my wife the golden medal of motherhood which she deserved. We were not allowed to lay on the water supply from the central water works and we drink bad water from the well. We wrote to Moscow about this matter, but everything remains the same.

Vladimir Arbuzov   *1976*
Krasnodar region, Kavkazskiy district, village of Karyer, Lermontov Street.

YEAR OF 1977

YOU WILL DIE IN THIS CELL

My wife, Mariya, and I have 15 children aged 22 years to 1 year and 4 months. We are Evangelical Christian-Baptists. Because of our faith we have encountered cruel repression in our country. I have appealed to the Soviet government, the

14

heads of 35 countries, pointing out all the insidious schemes and actions of the atheists. And the more I appealed, the crueler were the repressions they brought down on my family. As early as 1970 the local authorities informed me that the paths to study and work would be closed to my children. Right then, I immediately appealed to Soviet bodies and described these threats, but I didn't find any investigation of my statements nor a just defense, only that further persecutions were brought down on my household. What is the reason for all this? When the persecution of the Church began in 1960, in every city the children of God rose up, opposing the persecution; they stood in the breach to defend God's Church, and the Council of Evangelical Christians and Baptist Churches was formed. At this time, like the others, I stood in the breach of the church wall.

When my eldest son Anatoli, my helper in the family, turned 18 years old and became an adult, they put him in prison; they had fabricated a false case against him and they sentenced him to 8 years. And now he is already serving his fifth year. I appealed with protests against the judgment. Witnesses to his innocence also appealed, but it was all in vain. Cruel atheism, would only repeat, "Guilty." And even in the labor camp they cruelly persecute him: they threw him in the punishment cell, where he spent six months. KGB agents came into his cell and suggested that he write lies and slander about his parents to gain his freedom, or else, they informed him, "You'll die in this cell." And in fact he cought a lung disease in that cell.

Besides my eldest son Anatoli they also took away two other sons. For three years they didn't certify them for school, and then without our permission took them away and put them in a special institution. This is in fact a children's prison, where the criminal world reigns. When we went to visit our children, my son Misha told me, "If you hadn't taught us religion, if I didn't know that there is eternal life, I'd commit suicide here. I'm treated like a football here, they beat me first on the back, then on the stomach, until I'm choking. One time the director came in when they were doing this and I said to him, 'Look what they're doing to me,' and he said, 'Well, give it right back to them'. What kind of advice is that?" Misha will be 18 years old and they will have to let him out of the special institution, and if he did respond to the beatings and defend himself, they would put him in jail as they did my eldest son Anatoli; he'd be found guilty of fighting. Similar beatings were repeated again and again. We, his parents, saw him bruised and swollen when we visited him.

I sent a telegram to Brezhnev about our son's beatings and nothing came of it. For the rest of our children school has become a place of torment and persecution, so that the children themselves wrote a letter to all who could help them, asking people to defend them. In that letter they described the bad conditions

15

SELECTION OF TESTIMONIES

Marina Bobarykina (12 years): I wish we could have children's meetings like in your country. People get sent to prison for that.

Mikhail Bobarykin (15 years): The kids in school stuck pins in my sister. They yell at us in the street: You believers ought to be killed!

Tatyana Bobarykina (17 years): The doors of educational institutions are closed to us believers. We have to make a choice: either learning, or God.

Alla and Nellie Galushkin (10 and 11 years): Our schoolmates throw stones at us.

Valery Goretoi, the cherry picker (Starotitarovskaya) (11 years): Our teachers tell us that there is no God, but I say that there is God.

Victor Goretoi (14 years): From the time of our childhood, we believers have to go through many hardships!

Daniel Matyash (17 years): If the government won't let us emigrate, many of us will be sent to prison.

Elena Matyash (11 years): The officials are taunting us... My Mother was sent to jail... We do not want to live in this country.

Olga Matyash (14 years): When we grow up, they will also send us to prison for our faith.

Anatoly Pishchenko from Krasnodarsky region (12 years): Many believers are being sent to prison now.

Valya Pishchenko (15 years): Children from atheistic families got so incited against us by our teachers that they beat me so that I have suffered from poor health for six years.

Vladimir Pishchenko (15 years): I beg you: help us emigrate so we won't have to look at the tears of our parents anymore.

Nadezhda (Nadia) Shchukina (17 years): I cannot accept the Soviet government's criminal deceitful allegations about freedom of religion in the USSR.

left to right: Alla and Nellie Galushkin, Vladimir Pishchenko, Elena Matyash, Victor Goretoi, Valery Goretoi, Tatyana Bobarykina

left to right: Valya Pishchenko, Marina Bobarykina, Mikhail Bobarykin, Nadezhda Shchukina, Olga Matyash, a Pentecostal family from Ukraine: Nikolai Nikolaevich Gordievsky, his wife Anna Andreevna, and their children. 1975.

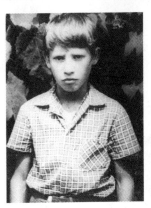

left to right: Anatoly Pishchenko, Daniel Matyash, a Pentacostal family from Ukraine: Petr Alexeevich Melnechuk, his wife Sofia Petrovna, and their children. 1975.

Ахтёров Павел Алексеевич, 1930 год рождения, проживает по адресу
Донецкая область, город Славянск, ул. Крымская 17. Он и его семья
верующие-пятидесятники. В течение 5 лет он добивается выезда из
СССР в США на постоянное жительство , имеет вызов из США для
всей семьи. Но в выезде ему устно отказали. 7 июля 1981 года
Ахтёров П.А. арестован и обвиняется по статье 62 УК УССР /со
слов следователя Емельницкого/. Ему ставят в вину написанную им
книгу "На пути к бессмертию". В ней он правдиво описал свою жизнь,
все преследования и гонения за веру в Бога, за его мировоззрение.
В 1961 году Ахтёров П.А. был сужден на 5 лет по ст.209 часть I
УК УССР, срок отбыл полностью. 14 января 1980 года его сын Ахтёров Ф.П. сужден по статье 72 УК УССР на 2,5 года за отказ от
службы в армии в знак протеста против незаконного удержания в
СССР.

свежие судимости

ПОДПИСИ.
Булаха Эдуарда Петровича 17 июля сего года
в г.Вильнюсе состоялся суд, судим на 1 год
обвинном, что он с своей семьей уплатив
госпошлину, 1000руб,отказались от гражданин
СССР.
18.9.1928г. в г.Днепропетровеке УССР в много-
детной семьи Рыбакова Михаила 8 детей "пятидесятника" без
уважительной причины был раскидан дом
местными властями, которого построили
сами дети. Семья на этот день без покрова
находится в сарае. прилагаем фото.

9 мая 1980г. в г.Донецке УССР был арестован
на 15 суток Голенков Пётр Михайлович
за бракосочетание молодых
фото прилагается
подписали 838 человек
желающих покинуть страну

A sample of numerous appeals made by Russian Christians to Soviet authorities
asking for permission to emigrate. To sign was dangerous. Signatures could be
used in courts.

Birthday celebration of former Soviet general turned one of the leading human rights activists, Pyotr Grigorievich Grigorenko (*center left on the couch*), in his Moscow apartment. October 16, 1977. The photograph was taken when I was already in Vienna. Next to him is his fearless wife Zinaida Mikhailovna.

Both Grigorenkos are in the chapter "The Assault on the American Embassy" and "Russian Jews, Russian Tigers, and Some Other Russians." Nine years after this photograph was taken, we celebrated Grigorenko's 80th birthday in New York, and four months later we buried him.

From left to right, on the floor: G.O. Altunyan, member of the Initiative Group for the Protection of Human Rights. In 1969, he was sentenced to three years in prison; in 1981, to seven years of camps for especially dangerous state criminals, followed by five years of exile. Next to him is Alexander P. Podrabinek, just released from 15 days imprisonment, who famously fought against the use of psychiatry for the persecution of dissidents.

From left to right, on the couch, members of the Moscow Helsinki Group (MHG): The well-known physicist N.N. Meiman. He contributed to the mathematical aspect of the development of nuclear weapons, and in 1953, became a laureate of the Stalin Prize in Theoretical Physics. Lawyer S.V. Kallistratova, who defended various Soviet dissidents and from 1977 was a member of the MHG. Grigorenko and his wife Zinaida. N.A. Velikanova, the mother of well-known human rights activist Tatyana Velikanova (who, before my departure, gave me the Viennese phone number of former political prisoner L. Kwachevsky). Priest S.A. Zheludkov. Andrei D. Sakharov. His human rights activism began in the 1960s with a speech in defense of Pyotr Grigorenko, who had been placed in a psychiatric prison.

Alexander Podrabinek told me that this picture was taken by Yuri Grimm, a former political prisoner. (Sakharov Archive)

A.D. Sakharov (*left*) participated in the International symposium on magnetic resonance imaging. Winnipeg, Canada. February 16, 1989. Photographer unknown. (Sakharov Archive)

I flew to Winnipeg from Washington as a correspondent for Radio Liberty to interview Sakharov at this symposium. He and Lusia (as we called his wife Elena Bonner) told me that it would be better to do without an interview. In the Russian parliament there was an ongoing slanderous attack on Sakharov because of his open opposition against Soviet aggression in Afghanistan. Most of the deputies were growling and spewing curses. They would have used this "anti-Soviet interview" to continue their slanderous attacks against him. I was the only exiled Russian dissident who met with them abroad not long before his premature death. (In the past, he had not been allowed to travel; for example, to receive his Nobel Peace Prize in 1975.) I returned from Winnipeg without having fulfilled the assignment. Ten months later, on December 14, 1989, he died from a sudden cardiac arrest in his apartment on Chkalov Street. Sakharov was sixty-eight years old.

opposite: Attending the McWhirter Human Rights Foundation Award ceremony in London, 1981. Next to me is the widow of the publisher Ross McWhirter, killed by terrorists. On my right is Ross McWhirter's twin brother, Norris. In 1980, Vladimir Bukovsky was the first Russian who received this award. In 1982 it was given to Alexander Ginsburg.

ЧЕРНАЯ МЕТКА АПАРТЕИДА

My last article in Soviet media, "The Black Mark of Apartheid," *Journalist*, circa 1970. It was a professional's dream to appear in this magazine. It had an unusual feature for Russia—some of the authors were pictured, and even more that that, they were given a short introduction. But I made a mistake. When then editor-in-chief Yegor Yakovlev asked me to write several lines under my picture, I wrote something very short; however, when my article was published and my career in the USSR was over, I wished I had written a longer "goodbye" about my accomplishments. Interestingly, it was this very Yegor who was ordered years earlier to fire me from the newspaper *Lenin's Banner* (*Leninskoye Znamya*) and who advised Tom Kolesnichenko after that to avoid contact with me.

Index

Arkady Polishchuk is designated as AP. Photographs are indicated by page numbers in *italics*.

Correspondent for Radio Free Europe/Radio Liberty. Prague, 2002.

Arkady Polishchuk (b. 1930) is a Russian Jewish dissident and former journalist who has authored articles, essays, and satires for leading Russian periodicals, as well as two books about Africa. For many years in the USSR and later in the West, he was heavily involved in human rights, including as a testimonial speaker for Amnesty International and working on behalf of 30,000 Russian Evangelicals trying to escape decades of persecution under communist rule.

In 1981, Polishchuk was awarded the British McWhirter Human Rights Foundation Award. His activities were covered by *Life*, the *New York Times*, *Los Angeles Times*, *Christian Science Monitor*, *Nightline* with Ted Koppel, the 700 Club, and many international publications. From 1985–2008, Polishchuk was a broadcaster and correspondent for Radio Free Europe/Radio Liberty based in Washington, D.C.; Munich; and Prague. His writings have appeared in the *National Review*, *Chicago Tribune*, and *Witness*, as well as several international publications.

Polishchuk holds an advanced degree in Philosophy from Moscow University.